PLAYFAIR
OLYMPICS 1984
LOS ANGELES

D0416123

Queen Anne Press
Macdonald & Co
London and Sydney

A QUEEN ANNE PRESS BOOK

© Queen Anne Press 1984

Cover photograph: Straub leads in the 1980
Olympic 1500m final, with Coe and Ovett in hot
pursuit. Coe later overtook Straub to win in
3min 38.4secs/Allsport

First published in Great Britain in 1984 by
Queen Anne Press, a division of
Macdonald & Co (Publishers) Ltd
London and Sydney
A BPCC plc Company

ISBN 0 356 10336 6

Typeset in Helvetica by Wyvern Typesetting
Limited & Acorn Origination.
Printed and bound in Great Britain by
The Pitman Press, Bath.
Edited, designed and produced by First
Editions, Chancery House, 319 City Road,
London EC1V 1LS

Macdonald & Co (Publishers) Ltd
Maxwell House
74 Worship Street
London
EC2A 2EN

CONTENTS

INTRODUCTION

The Games of the XXIIIrd Olympiad in Los Angeles from 28 July to 12 August, 1984, promise to be among the most spectacular ever staged. Yet they will not cost the Californian tax payers a penny.

Unlike the Montreal Games of 1976 which bankrupted the city, or the Moscow Games of 1980 which mortgaged the State, the Los Angeles Games are totally self-financing.

In the best traditions of Capitalism, everything that matters has been sold on franchise, or sponsored. Big Mac hamburgers, for instance, are providing the new Olympic pool as part of their deal for the fast food franchise. General Motors are supplying the trucks and cars, Coca Cola the official soft drink, Levi Strauss the official outfits, American Express the official charge card . . . and so it goes on.

Even the once sacred Olympic flame is up for grabs with a payment of 3000 dollars securing the right to carry it for one kilometre of its journey across the United States.

All in all the Los Angeles Olympic Organising Committee expect to raise comfortably the 500 million dollars it is costing them to stage the Games – not surprisingly as the American Broadcasting Company (ABC) alone have paid a record 225 million dollars for exclusive live transmissions.

Twenty one sports

The 21 sports represented are: archery, athletics, basketball, boxing, canoeing, cycling, equestrianism, fencing, football, gymnastics, handball, hockey, judo, modern pentathlon, rowing, shooting, swimming (including diving and water polo), volleyball, weightlifting, wrestling and yachting, plus two demonstration sports, baseball and tennis.

Apart from the return of China after 32 years, there are several innovations, with women in particular benefiting. For the first time in Olympic athletics, women will be running over 3000 metres, 400 metres hurdles and the marathon. The marathon, especially, will have an enormous following in jogging-mad California and it is interesting to note that the current women's world best of 2h 22:43 secs by America's Joan Benoit in 1983 would have been good enough to win the men's gold medal up to 1956 – beating even the great Emil Zatopek in 1952.

In addition the women's pentathlon competition, comprising five events, has been expanded to the seven-event heptathlon.

Synchronised swimming, or water ballet as it is sometimes called, appears for the first time. It is a competition between duets of swimmers who choreograph artistic movement to music of their choice. Many of the routines require them to keep their heads under water for exhausting periods.

The other Olympic discipline exclusively for women is rhythmic gymnastics. No acrobatic movements are allowed, only balletic interpretation in four routines using hoop, ball, ribbon and club.

Cycling introduces an individual road race for women and shooting also includes the first women-only competitions: standard rifle, air rifle and pistol match. Canoeing adds a 500 metre event for kayak fours for women.

There will be a total of 75 events for women at the Los Angeles Olympics – at the inaugural Games in 1896 there were none!

At the turn of the century sport was still perceived as an exclusively male domain, but the original Olympics in Ancient Greece were even more chauvinist. Then women, along with slaves, were forbidden from watching, let alone competing. Some defied the rules and, according to legend, were hurled to their deaths.

The ancient Games

The Olympic Games, begun in Greece some 1000 years before Christ, proceeded continuously until 393 AD when the Roman Emperor Theodosius, under whose aegis Greece fell, decreed they must end. By then corruption had tainted the lofty ideals of the Olympic movement. Contestants, who had originally competed for laurel wreaths, chased more and more valuable prizes, and cheating and bribery were rife.

The Olympic torch was thus extinguished for 1500 summers apart from the occasional attempt at revival – such as the Cotswolds Olympics in Britain during the seventeenth century.

It was not until the emergence of a young French nobleman, Pierre de Fredi, Baron de Coubertin, that the idea of a modern Olympics began to take true shape. The Baron had been commissioned by the French government to study physical culture programmes throughout Europe. As he travelled, he became more and more fascinated by the possibility of restoring the ancient Greek ideal. On 25 November, 1892, he made his dream public at the Sorbonne and two years later the International Olympic Committee was formed under the presidency of Demetrius Vikelas of Greece, with de Coubertin as secretary general. Athens, they decided, would host the first modern Olympic Games in 1896.

The Los Angeles Games

The ancient Olympic Games had always been linked with cultural activites and this association will be re-established by Los Angeles in 1984, when a ten-week Olympic Arts Festival from 1 June to 12 August will feature leading figures in dance, music, art, film and theatre.

Filmland, in fact, is already represented in the Los Angeles Games as their official mascot 'Sam the Olympic Eagle' is a Walt Disney creation. Sam, say the organisers, expresses the cheerful optimism of the Olympic spirit and, as an eagle, embodies the ideals *Citius, Altius, Fortius* – Swifter, Higher, Stronger.

The official Olympic symbol of the 'Star in Motion' was chosen because *'The star is a universal symbol of the highest aspirations of mankind. The horizontal bars portray the speed of the competitors as they pursue excellence, while the repetition of the star shape connotes the spirit of competition between equally outstanding physical forms. The 13 horizontal bars not only portray movement, but also symbolise the emergence of the United States from 13 individual colonies. The symbol colours – red, white and blue – were chosen for their traditional significance in the awarding of prizes for first, second and third. They are also the national colours of the USA.'*

Seven million tickets have been issued for the 1984 Games and the City of Los Angeles, with a population of 3 million, is expecting up to 1 million guests. They should not go short of information. Los Angeles has 16 television stations, 80 radio stations and 45 newspapers. Whatever happens in Los Angeles, 1984 one thing is certain: everyone will get to hear about it. –

THE PREVIOUS OLYMPICS FROM 1896-1980

1896 ATHENS

Baron Pierre de Coubertin's heroic idea of resurrecting the ancient Olympic Games became a reality on 6 April, 1896 – the 75th anniversary of Greek Independence.

A crowd of 80,000 heard King George I officially open the Games to athletes from 13 nations, whose arrival was announced by a fanfare of trumpets. Of the 311 competitors, 230 came from Greece, 19 from both France and Germany, 14 from the United States and eight from both Great Britain and Hungary. Some had entered privately, in keeping with the relaxed, non-nationalistic ambiance of the Games . . . Irishman James Boland, on holiday in Athens, decided he fancied a crack at the tennis and entered there and then, while one Italian hitch-hiked from Milan.

Only the first and second in each event were rewarded: the first received a diploma, a crown of olive branches and a silver medal; the second a diploma, a crown of laurel and a bronze medal. American James Connolly, in the triple jump, became the first modern Olympic champion, setting the trend for his team who won nine of the 12 track and field events. The last race – the inaugural Olympic marathon – brought the wildest scenes as a local farmer, Spyridon Louis, headed those of the 16 starters who managed to finish into the stadium.

Prince George and Prince Nicholas joined in to run alongside him through the tape and King George I promised him a horse and cart as a special gift. Louis, who never ran competitively again, also gained free meals and free shaves for life from his delighted countrymen.

1900 Paris

The Paris Games, which should have provided a crowning tribute to Baron Pierre de Coubertin, founder of the modern Olympics, teetered on the edge of disaster. *"We have made a hash of it,"* said de Coubertin prophetically before the Games opened . . . and so it proved. The organising committee made two fundamental errors – first, the Games were part of the World Exhibition being held in the French capital and were, therefore, totally overshadowed; second, they were spread from 20 May to 28 October, five increasingly muddled months when events suddenly started and ended with hardly anyone knowing quite what was going on. Official records are vague, but it is certain 1330 competitors took part from 22 countries. Cricket, croquet and tennis were included as official events and, with women allowed to compete for the first time, Britain's Charlotte Cooper became the first female champion by winning the tennis singles. Hardly surprising as she had been three times a Wimbledon champion by then.

American Ray Ewry, a polio victim as a child, began his outstanding collection of ten gold medals in the standing jumps and an unknown, ten-year-old French boy became the youngest ever gold medallist when he coxed the Dutch rowing pair.

American Alvin Kraenzlein gained four individual track and field victories – 60m, 110m hurdles, 200m hurdles and long jump – a record for a single Games which still stands.

1904 St Louis

Failing to learn from their blunders in Paris four years earlier, the Olympic organisers again scheduled the Games as part of a World Fair. Nor was the venue, in the centre of North America, attractive to European countries because of travelling expenses. Only 13 nations took part, contributing a paltry 625 (including eight women) athletes of whom 533 were Americans. All round the world sports administrators shook their heads . . . the Olympic movement seemed doomed. It was saved, in part, by the excellence of the competition. Several world records were set, including the 400m where American Harry Hillman clocked 49.2 despite having to contest the final with 12 others. Hillman also won the 400m hurdles in which third placed George Poage became the first black Olympic medallist. The greatest medal haul went to American gymnast Anton Heida with five golds and a silver.

The Games continued as they had begun – in controversy. The first man home in the Marathon, Fred Lorz, looked remarkably fresh and sweat-free as he posed for pictures with Alice Roosevelt, daughter of the US President. It turned out he had taken a ten mile lift in a car and was disqualified in favour of rightful champion Tommy Hicks. Lorz protested it had all been a joke. So, very nearly, had the Games.

1908 London

The Olympic movement really took off in London with capacity crowds packing the new White City stadium and an estimated quarter of a million lining the streets to watch the Marathon. Nationalism also reared its head with the Finns refusing to march behind the Russian flag and the Americans furious that their flag had accidentally been left off the stadium masts. The bad feeling persisted when one American was disqualified from the 400m for obstruction. His team mates scratched in protest and Britain's William Halswelle won his gold in a walkover.

On a happier historical note, the length of the Marathon was extended to 26 miles 385 yards to comply with Princess Mary's request that the start at Windsor be under the windows of the Royal nursery. That distance is now statutory. In the race itself Italian Dorando Pietri, stimulated by draughts of alcohol, arrived in the stadium on the edge of exhaustion. He fell five times and sympathetic officials helped him over the line. He was disqualified for receiving aid – but was presented with a gold cup by Queen Alexandra.

1912 Stockholm

From 21 sports in London, the agenda was cut to just 14 for Stockholm and the standard of competition improved dramatically. Hero of the Games was American Indian Jim Thorpe who won both the pentathlon and decathlon golds. He was later disqualified on charges of professionalism when it was discovered he had accepted payment for playing baseball. Thorpe became a *cause célèbre* and in 1982, some 30 years after his death, he was reinstated by the International Olympic Committee and his medals presented to his family.

Thorpe's magnificent athleticism overshadowed the other outstanding competitor of the Games – Hannes Kolehmainen, first of the flying Finns, who won the 5000m, 10,000m and 12,000m cross country. He also set a world record in the 3000m team race but the Finns failed to qualify for the final. In swimming, the majestic Duke Kahanamoku, son of Hawaiian royalty, won the 100m freestyle as a prelude to his Hollywood career.

1920 Antwerp

With the Games of 1916 being cancelled because of the First World War, the Olympics resumed in Belgium after a gap of eight years. None of the recent enemies – Germany, Austria, Hungary and Turkey – were invited. The Russians also declined to participate and would remain absent until 1952. On the credit side, New Zealand appeared for the first time, having previously been part of the Australasia team.

The Olympic oath and Olympic flag were both introduced. The Finns, made independent three years earlier, celebrated with some outstanding successes in athletics led by their rising young star, Paavo Nurmi, who was to go on to win 12 Olympic medals and set 29 world records.

1924 Paris

Paris was given a second chance to stage the Olympics – and this time got it right with a record number of 44 countries including Romania and Poland for the first time.

Johnny Weissmuller, later to become Hollywood's most famous Tarzan, won three golds for sprint swimming and a bronze in water polo. Finland's Paavo Nurmi continued his outstanding Olympic career with five golds – 1500m, 5000m, 10,000m cross country (team and individual) and 3000m team event. In rowing a certain Benjamin Spock, who would later colour the thinking of generations of parents as Dr Spock, won a gold. *Chariots of Fire* men, Harold Abrahams and Eric Liddell struck gold for Britain in the 100m and 400m.

1928 Amsterdam

Women's events were introduced in track and field for the first time. The Germans were back. And the Olympic flame made its debut. All five women's track events produced world records but the 800m was attended by such disturbing scenes of exhaustion that this longer event was left out of the women's programme until 1964.

Lord Burghley took time off from the House of Lords to win the 400m hurdles gold for Britain, Nurmi a relative failure with only one gold (10,000m) and two silvers, and Weissmuller collected two final golds before devoting his energies to his career on the silver screen.

1932 Los Angeles

The Wall Street Crash was still sending shock waves throughout America and the Western world, but nothing could unsettle the Olympic juggernaut now. It was set well and truly on its course and by the end of these Games, watched by more than 1½ million people, the Los Angeles Organising Committee had made a profit of one million dollars. Part of their cost-effectiveness came from the introduction of the Olympic Village, where the male competitors were housed together (the 127 women stayed in a nearby hotel).

The Californian sunshine brought a plethora of records – 16 world marks were set and every Olympic track and field record was improved, with the exception of the long jump, high jump and hammer. Nurmi was found guilty of professionalism and banished to the stands, from where he watched the demise of Finland's great middle distance era.

Outstanding athlete was Mildred 'Babe' Didrikson, who set two world records and collected two golds and a silver in the javelin, 80m hurdles and high jump.

1936 Berlin

Hitler's Nazi flag flew over his now 100,000 capacity stadium and the politics of *Mein Kampf* were in full, ugly flow. But the Third Reich's attempt to turn the Games into a grotesque propaganda exercise was gloriously upstaged by black American Jesse Owens.

Called Jesse because of his initials J.C., Owens proved himself one of athletics' immortals by claiming four gold medals in the 100m, 200m, 4 × 100m relay and long jump. Altogether, the ten black members of America's track and field team – reviled and abused by Nazi newspapers – claimed seven gold, three silver and three bronze medals.

The best race of the Games, though, was the 1500m, where New Zealander Jack Lovelock began his country's great middle distance tradition by holding off the challenge of American Glenn Cunningham in world record time. The Dutch women dominated the swimming, led by Hendrika Mastenbroek who won three golds and a silver.

1948 Wembley

After the ravages of the Second World War, a record 59 countries and more than 4000 competitors celebrated the new peace. Fanny Blankers-Koen, a 30-year-old Dutch mother of two, followed the outstanding examples of Nurmi and Owens by capturing four gold medals in the 100m, 200m, 80m hurdles, and the 4 × 100m relay. American Bob Mathias won the decathlon at the age of 17 and a young Czech called Emil Zatopek caught the eye as he swept to victory in the 10,000m.

The biggest success story of all, however, was the organisation of the Games under the leadership of Lord Burghley. Cleverly improvising existing facilities – rowing at Henley, yachting at Torbay – the British Olympic Association managed to stage the whole affair for just £600,000 – and made a tidy profit.

1952 Helsinki

The Russians were back after an absence of 40 years to swell the number of participating nations to 69. And in a break from Olympic ideals they were allowed to set up their own Olympic Village together with other Eastern European neighbours Hungary, Bulgaria, Czechoslovakia, Poland and Romania. From that 'Eastern' camp emerged the Man of the Games – Emil Zatopek, who scored a unique treble in the 5000m, 10,000m and marathon. Each was an Olympic record and on the day he was winning the 5000m title, his wife, Dana, was taking the javelin gold medal, again with an Olympic record.

Bob Mathias became the only man to retain the decathlon title, with a world record 7,887 points, and Britain's Roger Bannister was beaten into fourth place in the 1500m by the almost unknown Josef Barthel, who thus claimed Luxembourg's first and only gold medal.

In the boxing ring future world heavyweight champions Floyd Patterson and Ingemar Johansson met with mixed fortunes – Patterson claiming the middleweight crown and Johansson being disqualified in the heavyweight final for lack of effort.

1956 Melbourne

Australia's strict quarantine laws meant that the Games were split for the first, and only time, with the equestrian sports being held in Stockholm.

Russia's invasion of Hungary and the Suez Canal fracas had the world trembling on the edge of war, but far away in the Melbourne sunshine Soviet sailor Vladimir Kuts provided a thrilling diversion by claiming the 5000-10,000m double. American sprinter Bobby-Joe Morrow took three golds in the 100m, 200m and 4 × 100m relay and Australia's Betty Cuthbert set the crowd wild by repeating the same treble in the women's events.

Britain's Chris Brasher won the steeplechase, lost it on disqualification and then regained it on appeal, and Alain Mimoun, the Frenchman who had three times finished runner-up to Zatopek, at last struck gold in the Marathon. This time Zatopek signed off his Olympic career by finishing sixth. Australia overpowered all else in the swimming pool, taking eight of the 13 titles.

1960 Rome

Italy provided a magnificent setting for the XVIIth Games with scorching conditions in Rome, a marathon finish on the Appian way and yachting in the Bay of Naples. The jewel in this silver setting was undoubtedly Australian Herb Elliott who majestically took the 1500m in world record time, some 20 yards ahead of the rest. Barefooted Ethiopian Abebe Bikila, a member of Emperor Haile Selassie's personal guard, won the marathon in a world best time of 2h 15m 16.2s.

Black American Wilma Rudolph completed a sprint treble and in the boxing ring another young negro called Cassius Clay was making them all sit up and take notice as he powered to the light heavyweight title.

1964 Tokyo

The 'Happy Games' as they were dubbed were the last Olympics to be free from the shadow of politics. Ninety-three nations and more than 5000 athletes competed in a joyous atmosphere that truly represented the Olympic spirit. Australian swimmer Dawn Fraser was the heroine, winning the 100m sprint blue riband for the third successive Olympics and becoming the first woman to dip below 60 seconds in the process. Also in the pool, American Don Scholiander took four golds, having shaved every hair off his body and head to streamline his action.

Future world heavyweight champion Joe Frazier dominated that division, New Zealander Peter Snell claimed a track 800-1500m double and American Al Oerter won his third successive discus title. But as far as almost everybody was concerned the athlete of the Games was Ethiopian Abebe Bikila, who arrived five weeks after an appendix operation and proceeded to win his second marathon championship unchallenged and in record time.

1968 Mexico City

Student riots in Mexico, Russia's invasion of Czechoslovakia and the black power salute of American athletes Tommie Smith and John Carlos gave the first Latin American Games a sour political taste. There were problems, too, over the altitude of 2240m, which left distance athletes like Ron Clarke gasping in the thin air.

Competitors in the explosive events, however, produced some startling performances and none more so than American Bob Beaman whose long jump of 29ft 2½in (8.90m) increased the world record by 1ft 9¾in. That record still stands, as do the marks set in the men's 400m and 4×400m relay.

American sprint queen Wyomia Tyus became the only woman to successfully defend the 100m title, Al Oerter won his fourth consecutive discus championship and Dick Fosbury 'flopped' to the high jump gold. David Hemery of Great Britain won the 400m hurdles in world record time and Lillian Board, who was to die so tragically two years later, was just caught on the line in a thrilling women's 400m.

1972 Munich

The massacre of the 11 Israeli competitors and officials by Palestinian terrorists cast an appalling shadow over a Games which attracted the current record of 122 countries and more than 7000 competitors. Until the tragedy unfolded, the world had been captivated by the smile of Russia's elfin gymnast Olga Korbut and the style of American swimmer Mark Spitz. Miss Korbut finished with three golds and a silver, Spitz with an Olympic record seven golds.

Russia's blond bombshell Valery Borzov became the first European to gain the sprint double – helped by two top Americans who misread their timetable and missed their heats. Finland's Lasse Viren followed the example of Kolehmainen, Zatopek and Kuts by landing the 5000 and 10,000m. The Games also heralded the emergence of East Germany (GDR) as an awesome force in world athletics.

1976 Montreal

A last minute boycott by 22 African nations in protest of New Zealand's rugby tour of South Africa caused organisational chaos and robbed the Games of several spectacular clashes, such as Filbert Bayi versus John Walker in the 1500m.

It was left to Lasse Viren and Alberto Juantorena to electrify the crowds in the giant 200 million pound stadium. Viren, treading where no athlete had ventured before, successfully defended both the 5000 and 10,000m titles he had claimed in Munich while Juantorena, the giant Cuban nicknamed 'White Lightning' streaked to a 400-800m double with irresistible strength.

Russia's Viktor Saneev won his third consecutive triple jump title and the 400m victory by Poland's 30-year-old Irena Szewinska made her the first woman to win medals at four Games. In gymnastics, diminutive Romanian Nadia Comaneci scored the first perfect ten in Games history.

1980 Moscow

Russia's invasion of Afghanistan led to a boycott by America, West Germany, Japan, and some other countries, which again crippled the Games as a meaningful world championship. Britain took four track and field gold medals through Daley Thompson (decathlon), Allan Wells (100m), Steve Ovett (800m) and Sebastian Coe (1500m) to equal their best ever haul of 1964. Miruts Yifter, the 'Shifter' from Ethiopia, showed what might have been in Montreal four years earlier but for the African boycott, by completing a consumate 5000-10,000m double in the Lenin Stadium.

Waldemar Cierpinski of East Germany emulated Yifter's late countryman Abebe Bikila by successfully defending the marathon title. Hero of the Games, though, was Russian gymnast Aleksandr Ditiatin who won three golds, four silvers and a bronze – the record number of medals won in a single Games. The East German women continued their domination of swimming with 11 of the 13 titles. And in the ring explosive Cuban Teofilo Stevenson claimed the heavyweight title again to become the first boxer to win the same division in three consecutive Games.

OFFICIAL OLYMPIC ABBREVIATIONS FOR NAMES OF COUNTRIES

AFG	Afghanistan	GER	German Federal Republic (Germany until 1968)
AHO	Netherlands Antilles		
ALB	Albania	GHA	Ghana
ALG	Algeria	GRE	Greece
ARG	Argentina	GUA	Guatemala
ARS	Saudi Arabia	GUI	Guinea
AUS	Australia	GUY	Guyana
AUT	Austria	HAI	Haiti
BAH	Bahamas	HBR	British Honduras
BAR	Barbados	HKG	Hong Kong
BEL	Belgium	HOL	Netherlands
BER	Bermuda	HON	Honduras
BIR	Burma	HUN	Hungary
BOL	Bolivia	INA	Indonesia
BRA	Brazil	IND	India
BUL	Bulgaria	IRL	Ireland
CAF	Central Africa	IRN	Iran
CAN	Canada	IRQ	Iraq
CEY	Ceylon (up to 1972)	ISL	Iceland
		ISR	Israel
CGO	Congo Republic	ISV	Virgin Islands
CHA	Chad	ITA	Italy
CHI	Chile	JAM	Jamaica
CIV	Ivory Coast	JOR	Jordan
CMR	Cameroon Republic	JPN	Japan
COK	Congo Kinshasa	KEN	Kenya
COL	Colombia	KHM	Cambodia
CRC	Costa Rica	KOR	South Korea
CUB	Cuba	KUW	Kuwait
DAH	Dahomey	LBA	Libya
DEN	Denmark	LBR	Liberia
DOM	Dominican Republic	LES	Lesotho
ECU	Ecuador	LIB	Lebanon
EGY	Egypt (or United Arab Republic)	LIE	Liechtenstein
		LUX	Luxembourg
ESP	Spain	MAD	Madagascar
ETH	Ethiopia	MAL	Malaysia
FIJ	Fiji	MAR	Morocco
FIN	Finland	MAW	Malawi
FRA	France	MEX	Mexico
FRG	Federal Republic of Germany (after 1968)	MGL	Mongolia
		MLI	Mali
GAB	Gabon	MLT	Malta
GBR	Great Britain	MON	Monaco
GDR	German Democratic Republic (1968 on)	MRI	Mauritius
		NCA	Nicaragua

12

OFFICIAL OLYMPIC ABBREVIATIONS FOR NAMES OF COUNTRIES

NEP	Nepal	SUI	Switzerland
NGR	Nigeria	SUR	Surinam
NIG	Niger	SWE	Sweden
NOR	Norway	SWZ	Swaziland
NZL	New Zealand	SYR	Syria
PAK	Pakistan	TAN	Tanzania
PAN	Panama	TCH	Czechoslovakia
PAR	Paraguay	THA	Thailand
PER	Peru	TOG	Togoland
PHI	Philippines	TRI	Trinidad and Tobago
POL	Poland	TUN	Tunisia
POR	Portugal	TUR	Turkey
PRK	North Korea	UAR	United Arab Republic
PUR	Puerto Rico	UGA	Uganda
RHO	Rhodesia	URS	USSR
ROC	Republic of China	URU	Uruguay
ROM	Romania	USA	United States of America
RUS	Russia (until 1917)	VEN	Venezuela
SAF	South Africa	VNM	Vietnam
SAL	El Salvador	YOL	Upper Volta
SEN	Senegal	YUG	Yugoslavia
SIN	Singapore	ZAI	Zaire
SLE	Sierra Leone	ZAM	Zambia
SMR	San Marino	ZIM	Zimbabwe
SOM	Somali Republic		
SRI	Sri Lanka (formerly Ceylon)		
SUD	Sudan		

OPENING AND CLOSING CEREMONIES

Opening and Closing Ceremonies
Los Angeles Memorial Coliseum

28 July Saturday	Opening ceremony	4.00pm
12 August Sunday	Closing ceremony (Men's marathon finish included)	6.30pm

TIMETABLE FOR XXIIIrd OLYMPIAD, LOS ANGELES 28 JULY TO 12 AUGUST 1984

This is the timetable for the Los Angeles Olympics. Some events may be subect to alteration.

Archery
El Dorado Park, Long Beach

8 August Wednesday	70m women, 90m men	10.00am-12.45pm
	60m women, 70m men	2.30pm-5.00pm
9 August Thursday	50m women, 50m men	10.00am-1.00pm
	30m women, 30m men	2.30pm-5.15pm
10 August Friday	70m women, 90m men	10.00am-12.45pm
	60m women, 70m men	2.30pm-5.00pm
11 August Saturday	50m women, 50m men	10.00am-1.00pm
	30m women, 30m men	2.30pm-5.15.pm

Athletics (men and women)
Los Angeles Memorial Coliseum

3 August Friday	Heptathlon 100m hurdles and high jump, Triple jump qualifying 400m hurdles 1st round, men 400m 1st round, women Shot put qualifying, women 100m 1st & 2nd rounds, men	9.30am-1.00pm
	800m 1st round, women Heptathlon shot put, 220m 800m 1st round, men 20km walk final (start & finish) Shot put final, women 10000m 1st round	4.00pm-8.15pm
4 August Saturday	Heptathlon long jump 400m 1st round, men 400m 2nd round, women Javelin throw qualifying, men 100m 1st round, women	9.30am-1.00pm
	100m 2nd round, women Heptathlon javelin throw, 800m (final event) 100m semi–final, men 800m semi–final, women	4.00pm-8.15pm

	800m 2nd round, men	
	Triple jump final	
	400m hurdles semi–final, men	
	100m final, men	
5 August Sunday	Marathon, women (final)	8.00am-12.30pm
	Javelin throw qualifying, women	
	400m hurdles, 1st round, women	
	110m hurdles 1st round	
	Hammer throw qualifying	
	100m semi–final & final, women	4.00pm-7.30pm
	Long jump qualifying, men	
	110m hurdles 2nd round	
	400m 2nd round, men	
	400m semi–final, women	
	Javelin throw final, men	
	800m semi–final, men	
	400m hurdles final, men	
6 August Monday	Pole vault qualifying	9.30am-12.30pm
	200m 1st & 2nd rounds, men	
	3000m 1st round	
	110m hurdles semi–final & final	4.00pm-8.15pm
	Hammer throw final	
	400m hurdles semi–final, women	
	400m semi–final, men	
	400m final, women	
	800m final, women	
	Long jump final, men	
	800m final, men	
	Javelin throw final, women	
	3000m steeplechase 1st round	
	10,000m final	
8 August Wednesday	Decathlon 100m, long jump, Shot put, discus throw qualifying, men	9.30am-1.00pm
	200m 1st & 2nd rounds, women	
	1500m 1st round, women	
	200m semi–final & final, men	4.00pm-8.30pm
	Decathlon, high jump, 400m	
	Pole vault final	
	400m hurdles final, women	
	400m final, men	
	5000m 1st round	
	Long jump qualifying, women	
	3000m semi–final	
	3000m steeplechase semi–final	
9 August Thursday	Decathlon discus throw, 110m hurdles, pole vault	9.30am-8.00pm
	100m hurdles 1st round	

	High jump qualifying, women	
	200m semi–final & final, women	
	Decathlon javelin throw, 1500m (final event)	
	1500m 1st round, men	
	1500m semi–final, women	
	Long jump final, women	
	5000m semi–final	

10 August Friday	High jump qualifying, men	9.30am-12.30pm
	4×400m relay 1st round, women	
	4×400 relay 1st round, men	
	Discus throw qualifying, women	
	4×100m relay 1st round, women	
	4×100m relay 1st round, men	
	High jump final, women	4.00pm-7.45pm
	100m hurdles, semi–final	
	4×400m relay semi–final, men	
	4×400 relay semi–final, women	
	Discus throw final, men	
	1500m semi–final, men	
	100m hurdles final	
	3000m final	
	3000 steeplechase final	

11 August Saturday	50km walk final (start & finish)	8.00am-12.30pm
	Shot put qualifying, men	
	4×100m relay semi–final, women	
	4×100m relay semi–final, men	
	Discus throw final, women	4.00pm-8.00pm
	4×100m relay final, women	
	High jump final, men	
	4×100m relay final, men	
	4×400m relay final, women	
	4×400m relay final, men	
	Shot put final, men	
	1500m final, women	
	1500m final, men	
	5000m final	

| 12 August
Sunday | Marathon men (final) | |

Baseball
Dodger Stadium

| 31 July
Tuesday | 2 games – preliminaries | 4.00pm-11.00pm |
| 1 August
Wednesday | 2 games – preliminaries | 4.00pm-11.00pm |

2 August Thursday	2 games – preliminaries	4.00pm-11.00pm
3 August Friday	2 games – preliminaries	1.00pm-8.00pm
4 August Saturday	2 games – preliminaries	10.00am-5.00pm
5 August Sunday	2 games – preliminaries	1.00pm-8.00pm
6 August Monday	2 games – semi–finals	1.00pm-8.00pm
7 August Tuesday	2 games – finals	4.00pm-11.00pm

Basketball
The Forum, Inglewood

29 July Sunday	2 games – preliminaries, men	9.00am-12.30pm
	2 games – preliminaries, men	2.30pm-6.00pm
	2 games – preliminaries, men	8.00pm-11.30pm
30 July Monday	1 game – round robin, women 1 game – preliminary, men	9.00am-12.30pm
	1 game – round robin, women 1 game – preliminary, men	2.30pm-6.00pm
	1 game – round robin, women 1 game – preliminary, men	8.00pm-11.30pm
31 July Tuesday	1 game – round robin, women 1 game – preliminary, men	9.00am-12.30pm
	1 game – round robin, women 1 game – preliminary, men	2.30pm-6.00pm
	1 game – round robin, women 1 game – preliminary, men	8.00pm-11.30pm
1 August Wednesday	2 games – preliminaries, men	9.00am-12.30pm
	2 games – preliminaries, men	2.30pm-6.00pm
	2 games – preliminaries, men	8.00pm-11.30pm
2 August Thursday	1 game – round robin, women 1 game – preliminary, men	9.00am-12.30pm
	1 game – round robin, women 1 game – preliminary, men	2.30pm-6.00pm
	1 game – round robin, women 1 game – preliminary, men	8.00pm-11.30pm

3 August Friday	1 game – round robin, women 1 game – preliminary, men	9.00am-12.30pm
	1 game – round robin, women 1 game – preliminary, men	2.30pm-6.00pm
	1 game, round robin, women 1 game – preliminary, men	8.00pm-11.30pm
4 August Saturday	2 games – preliminaries, men	9.00am-12.30pm
	2 games – preliminaries, men	2.30pm-6.00pm
	2 games – preliminaries, men	8.00pm-11.30pm
5 August Sunday	2 games – round robin, women	9.00am-12.30pm
	1 game – semi–final, men consolation	2.30pm-4.15pm
	1 game – round robin, women 1 game – semi–final, men consolation	6.30pm-10.00pm
6 August Monday	2 games – quarter–finals, men	10.00am-1.30pm
	2 games – quarter–finals, men	5.00pm-8.30pm
7 August Tuesday	2 games – finals (1-4 places), women	5.00pm-8.30pm
8 August Wednesday	2 games – semi–finals, men	10.00am-1.30pm
	2 games – semi–finals, men	5.00pm-8.30pm
9 August Thursday	2 games – finals (9-12 places), men	10.00am-1.30pm
	1 game – final (3-4 places), men	7.00pm-8.45pm
10 August Friday	2 games – finals (5-8 places), men	10.00am-1.30pm
	1 game – final (1-2 places), men	7.00pm-8.45pm

Boxing
Los Angeles Sports Arena

29 July Sunday	Preliminary bouts	11.00am-2.00pm
	Preliminary bouts	6.00pm-9.30pm
30 July Monday	Preliminary bouts	11.00am-2.00pm
	Preliminary bouts	6.00pm-9.30pm

31 July Tuesday	Preliminary bouts	11.00am-2.00pm
	Preliminary bouts	6.00pm-9.30pm
1 August Wednesday	Preliminary bouts	11.00am-2.00pm
	Preliminary bouts	6.00pm-9.30pm
2 August Thursday	Preliminary bouts	11.00am-7.00pm
	Preliminary bouts	6.00pm-9.30pm
3 August Friday	Preliminary bouts	11.00am-2.00pm
	Preliminary bouts	6.00pm-9.30pm
4 August Saturday	Preliminary bouts	11.00am-2.00pm
	Preliminary bouts	6.00pm-9.30pm
5 August Sunday	Preliminary bouts	11.00am-2.00pm
	Preliminary bouts	6.00pm-9.30pm
6 August Monday	Preliminary bouts	11.00am-2.00pm
	Preliminary bouts	6.00pm-9.30pm
7 August Tuesday	Quarter–final bouts	11.00am-2.00pm
	Quarter–final bouts	6.00pm-9.00pm
8 August Wednesday	Quarter–final bouts	11.00am-2.00pm
	Quarter–final bouts	6.00pm-9.00pm
9 August Thursday	Semi–final bouts	11.00am-2.00pm
	Semi–final bouts	6.00pm-9.00pm
11 August Saturday	Final bouts	11.00am-2.00pm
	Final bouts	6.00pm-9.00pm

Canoeing
Lake Casitas, Ventura County

6 August Monday	500m heats, men & women	7.30am-10.45am
	500m repechage, men & women	4.30pm-6.45pm

7 August Tuesday	1000m heat, men 500m heats, women	7.30am-10.45am
	1000m repechage, men 500m repechage, women	4.30pm-6.45pm
8 August Wednesday	500m semi–finals, men & women	7.30am-10.30am
9 August Thursday	1000m semi–finals, men 500m semi–finals, women	7.30am-10.30am
10 August Friday	500m finals, men & women	8.00am-10.30am
11 August Saturday	1000m finals, men	8.00am-10.30am

Cycling
California State University, Dominguez Hills
7-Eleven Velodrome

29 July Sunday	190km individual road race, men	9.00am-2.00pm
	70km individual road race, women (Held in Mission Viejo, Orange County)	3.00pm-5.30pm
30 July Monday	Individual pursuit– qualification 1km time trial – final	10.00am-1.00pm
31 July Tuesday	Individual pursuit – quarter–finals Sprint repechage Points race – qualification	10.00am-3.00pm
1 August Wednesday	Individual pursuit – semi–finals & finals Sprint – quarter–finals Points race – qualification	10.00am-3.00pm
2 August Thursday	Sprint – semi–finals Team pursuit – qualification & quarter–finals	10.00am-3.00pm
3 August Friday	Sprint – finals Team pursuit – semi–finals & finals Points race – final	10.00am-3.00pm
5 August Sunday	100km road race team time trial (Held on Artesia Freeway, Route 91)	8.00am-1.00pm

Diving
University of Southern California
McDonald's Swim Stadium

5 August Sunday	Springboard preliminaries, women	10.00am-12.30pm
	Springboard preliminaries, women	3.00pm-5.30pm
6 August Monday	Springboard finals, women	4.30pm-6.00pm
7 August Tuesday	Springboard preliminaries, men	10.00am-1.00pm
	Springboard preliminaries, men	4.00pm-6.30pm
8 August Wednesday	Springboard finals, men	4.30pm-6.30pm
9 August Thursday	Platform preliminaries, women	10.00am-12 noon
	Platform preliminaries, women	4.30pm-6.30pm
10 August Friday	Platform finals, women	4.30pm-6.30pm
11 August Saturday	Platform preliminaries, men	10.00am-12 noon
	Platform preliminaries, men	3.00pm-5.00pm
12 August Sunday	Platform finals, men	11.00am-1.00pm

Equestrian events
Santa Anita Park, Arcadia

29 July Sunday	Three day event – dressage test	8.00am-6.00pm
30 July Monday	Three day event – dressage test	8.00am-6.00pm
1 August Wednesday	Three day event – endurance test (Held at Fairbanks Country Club, San Diego)	10.00am-6.00pm
3 August Friday	Three day event – jumping test	11.30am-2.30pm
4 August Saturday	Jumping training competition	2.00pm-6.00pm
7 August Tuesday	Team jumping competition	10.00am-2.00pm

8 August Wednesday	Team dressage competition	2.00pm-6.00pm
9 August Thursday	Team dressage competition	2.00pm-6.00pm
10 August Friday	Individual dressage competition	2.00pm-5.00pm
12 August Sunday	Individual jumping competition	7.00am-2.00pm

Fencing
Long Beach Convention Centre

1 August Wednesday	Foil – individual preliminaries, men	9.00am-6.00pm
2 August Thursday	Foil – individual preliminaries, men & women	9.00am-5.00pm
	Foil – individual finals, men	8.00pm-11.00pm
3 August Friday	Foil – individual preliminaries, women Sabre – individual preliminaries, men	9.00am-5.00pm
	Foil – individual finals, women	8.00pm-11.00pm
4 August Saturday	Foil – team preliminaries, men Sabre – individual preliminaries, men	9.00am-5.00pm
	Sabre – individual finals, men	8.00pm-11.00pm
5 August Sunday	Foil – team preliminaries, men & women	9.00am-6.00pm
	Foil – team finals, men	8.00pm-11.00pm
7 August Tuesday	Foil – team preliminaries, women Epee – individual preliminaries, men	9.00am-6.00pm
	Foil – team finals, women	8.00pm-11.00pm
8 August Wednesday	Sabre – team preliminaries, men Epee – individual preliminaries, men	9.00am-5.00pm
	Epee – individual finals, men	8.00pm-11.00pm
9 August	Sabre – team preliminaries, men	12 noon-6.00pm
Thursday	Sabre – team finals, men	8.00pm-11.00pm
10 August Friday	Epee – team preliminaries, men	10.00am-4.00pm

| 11 August | Epee – team preliminaries, men | 10.00am-6.00pm |
| Saturday | Epee – team finals, men | 8.00pm-11.00pm |

Gymnastics
University of California, Los Angeles

29 July Sunday	Compulsory exercises, men	9.30am-11.30am
	Compulsory exercises, men	2.00pm-4.00pm
	Compulsory exercises, men	6.30pm-8.30pm
30 July Monday	Compulsory exercises, women	10.00am-12.45pm
	Compulsory exercises, women	5.30pm-8.15pm
31 July Tuesday	Optional exercises, men	9.30am-11.30am
	Optional exercises, men	2.00pm-4.00pm
	Optional exercises – team finals, men	6.30pm-8.30pm
1 August Wednesday	Optional exercises, women	10.00am-12.45pm
	Optional exercises – team women	5.30pm-8.15pm
3 August Friday	All-around finals, women	5.30pm-8.00pm
4 August Saturday	Apparatus finals, men	5.30pm-8.30pm
5 August Sunday	Apparatus finals, women	5.30pm-7.30pm
9 August Thursday	Rhythmic preliminaries, women	6.30pm-10.30pm
10 August Friday	Rhythmic preliminaries, women	6.30pm-10.30pm
11 August	Rhythmic finals, women	6.30pm-10.30pm

Handball (Team)
California State University, Fullerton

31 July Tuesday	3 games – preliminaries, men	11.00am-3.30pm
	3 games – preliminaries, men	6.30pm-11.00pm
1 August Wednesday	3 games – round robin, women	6.30pm-11.00pm

2 August	3 games – preliminaries, men	11.00am-3.30pm
	3 games – preliminaries, men	6.30pm-11.00pm
3 August Friday	3 games – round robin, women	6.30pm-11.00pm
4 August Saturday	3 games – preliminaries, men	11.00am-3.30pm
	3 games – preliminaries, men	6.30pm-11.00pm
5 August Sunday	3 games – round robin, women	6.30pm-11.00pm
6 August Monday	3 games – preliminaries, men	11.00am-3.30pm
	3 games – preliminaries, men	6.30pm-11.00pm
7 August Tuesday	3 games – round robin, women	6.30pm-11.00pm
8 August Wednesday	3 games – preliminaries, men	11.00am-3.30pm
	3 games – preliminaries, men	6.30pm-11.00pm
9 August Thursday	3 games – round robin, women	6.30pm-11.00pm
10 August Friday	2 games – finals (9-12 places), men	11.00am-2.00pm
	2 games – finals (5-8 places), men	6.30pm-9.30pm

The Forum, Inglewood

11 August Saturday	2 games – finals (1-4 places), men	2.00pm-5.00pm

Hockey (Field)
East Los Angeles College, Monterey Park

29 July Sunday	3 games – preliminaries, men	1.45pm-6.45pm
30 July Monday	3 games – preliminaries, men	1.45pm-6.45pm
31 July Tuesday	2 games – preliminaries, men	8.30am-11.45am
	1 game – round robin, women 1 game – preliminary, men	2.30pm-5.45pm
1 August Wednesday	1 game – preliminary, men 1 game – round robin, women	8.00am-11.15am
	2 games – preliminaries, men 1 game – round robin, women	1.45pm-6.45pm

2 August Thursday	2 games – preliminaries, men	8.30am-11.45am
	1 game – round robin, women 1 game – preliminary, men	2.30pm-5.45pm
3 August Friday	1 game – round robin, women 1 game – preliminary, men	8.00am-11.15am
	2 games – preliminaries, men 1 game – round robin, women	1.45pm-6.45pm
4 August Saturday	2 games – preliminaries, men	8.30am-11.45am
	1 game – preliminary, men 1 game – round robin, women	2.30pm-5.45pm
5 August Sunday	1 game preliminary, men 1 game – round robin, women	8.00am-11.15am
	2 games – preliminaries, men 1 game – round robin, women	1.45pm-6.45pm
6 August Monday	2 games – preliminary, men 1 game – preliminary, men 1 game – round robin, women	8.30pm-11.45am 2.30pm-5.45pm
7 August Tuesday	1 game – preliminary, men 1 game – round robin, women	8.00am-11.15am
	1 game – round robin, women 2 games – preliminaries, men	1.45pm-6.45pm
8 August Wednesday	2 games – semi–finals, men	7.00pm-10.30pm
9 August Thursday	2 games – semi–finals, men	8.00am-11.15am
	1 game – round robin, women 2 games – semi–finals, men	1.15pm-6.15pm
10 August Friday	1 game – final (11-12 places), men 1 game – round robin, women	8.00am-11.15am
	2 games – finals (7-10 places), men 1 game – round robin, women	1.15pm-6.15pm
11 August Saturday	3 games – finals (1-6 places), men	9.15am-2.45pm

Judo
California State University

| 4 August Saturday | Extra lightweight | 4.00pm-8.00pm |

25

5 August Sunday	Half lightweight	4.00pm-8.00pm
6 August Monday	Lightweight	4.00pm-8.00pm
7 August Tuesday	Half middleweight	4.00pm-8.00pm
8 August Wednesday	Middleweight	4.00pm-8.00pm
9 August Thursday	Half heavyweight	4.00pm-8.00pm
10 August Friday	Heavyweight	4.00pm-8.00pm
11 August Saturday	Open category	4.00pm-8.00pm

Modern Pentathlon
Coto de Caza, Orange County

29 July Sunday	Riding Riding	9.00am-11.00am 4.00pm-6.00pm
30 July Monday	Fencing	8.00am-8.30pm
31 July Tuesday	Swimming	2.00pm-4.00pm
1 August Wednesday	Shooting Running	9.00am-12 noon 5.00pm-6.00pm

Rowing
Lake Casitas, Ventura County

30 July Monday	Elimination heats, women	7.30am-10.00am
31 July Tuesday	Elimination heats, men	7.30am-10.30am
1 August Wednesday	Repechage, men & women	7.30am-10.30am
2 August Thursday	Semi–finals, men & women	7.30am-10.30am
3 August Friday	Finals (7-12 places) men & women	8.00am-10.30am
4 August Saturday	Finals (1-6 places), women	8.00am-10.00am
5 August Sunday	Finals (1-6 places), men	8.00am-10.30am

Shooting
Prado

29 July Sunday	Free pistol Sport pistol Clay target-trap	9.00am-4.00pm
30 July Monday	Small-bore rifle English match Clay target-trap Running game target	9.00am-4.00pm
31 July Tuesday	Clay target-trap Running game target Air rifle	9.00am-4.00pm
1 August Wednesday	Small-bore rifle 3 positions Rapid-fire pistol	9.00am-4.00pm
2 August Thursday	Small bore rifle 3 positions Rapid-fire pistol Clay target-skeet	9.00am-4.00pm
3 August Friday	Air rifle Clay target-skeet	9.00am-4.00pm
4 August Saturday	Clay target-skeet	9.00am-3.00pm

Soccer
Rose Bowl, Pasadena, California

29 July Sunday	Preliminary match	7.00pm-9.00pm
30 July Monday	Preliminary match	7.00pm-9.00pm
31 July Tuesday	Preliminary match	7.00pm-9.00pm
1 August Wednesday	Preliminary match	7.00pm-9.00pm
2 August Thursday	Preliminary match	7.00pm-9.00pm
3 August Friday	Preliminary match	7.00pm-9.00pm
5 August Sunday	Quarter–final match	7.00pm-9.00pm
6 August Monday	Quarter–final match	7.00pm-9.00pm
8 August Wednesday	Semi–final match	6.00pm-8.00pm
10 August Friday	Final match (3-4 places)	7.00pm-9.00pm

| 11 August
Saturday | Final match (1-2 places) | 7.00pm-9.00pm |

Soccer
Harvard University, Cambridge, Massachusetts

29 July Sunday	Opening ceremonies and preliminary match	7.00pm-9.00pm
30 July Monday	Preliminary match	7.00pm-9.00pm
31 July Tuesday	Preliminary match	7.00pm-9.00pm
1 August Wednesday	Preliminary match	7.00pm-9.00pm
2 August Thursday	Preliminary match	7.00pm-9.00pm
3 August Friday	Preliminary match	7.00pm-9.00pm

Soccer
U.S. Naval Academy, Annapolis, Maryland

29 July Sunday	Opening ceremonies and preliminary match	7.00pm-9.00pm
30 July Monday	Preliminary match	7.00pm-9.00pm
31 July Tuesday	Preliminary match	7.00pm-9.00pm
1 August Wednesday	Preliminary match	7.00pm-9.00pm
2 August Thursday	Preliminary match	7.00pm-9.00pm
3 August Friday	Preliminary match	7.00pm-9.00pm

Soccer
Stanford University, Palo Alto, California

29 July Sunday	Opening ceremonies and preliminary match	7.00pm-9.00pm
30 July Monday	Preliminary match	7.00pm-9.00pm
31 July Tuesday	Preliminary match	7.00pm-9.00pm

1 August Wednesday	Preliminary match	7.00pm-9.00pm
2 August Thursday	Preliminary match	7.00pm-9.00pm
3 August Friday	Preliminary match	7.00pm-9.00pm
5 August Sunday	Quarter–final match	3.00pm-5.00pm
6 August Monday	Quarter–final match	5.00pm-7.00pm
8 August Wednesday	Semi–final match	8.30pm-10.30pm

Swimming
University of Southern California
McDonald's Swim Stadium

29 July Sunday	Heats – 100m freestyle, women	8.30am-11.30am
	Heats – 100m breaststroke, men	
	Heats – 400m medley, women	
	Heats – 200m freestyle, men	
	Finals – 100m freestyle, women	4.15pm-6.00pm
	Finals – 100m breaststroke, men	
	Finals – 400m medley, women	
	Finals – 200m freestyle, men	
30 July Monday	Heats – 100m butterfly, men	8.30am-11.30am
	Heats – 200m freestyle, women	
	Heats – 400m medley, men	
	Heats – 200m breaststroke, women	
	Heats – 4×200m freestyle relay, men	
	Finals – 100m butterfly, men	4.15pm-6.00pm
	Finals – 200m freestyle, women	
	Finals – 400m medley, men	
	Finals – 200m breaststroke, women	
	Finals – 4×200m freestyle relay, men	
31 July Tuesday	Heats – 400m freestyle, women	8.30am-11.30am
	Heats – 100m freestyle, men	
	Heats – 100m backstroke, women	
	Heats – 200m backstroke, men	
	Heats – 4×100m freestyle relay, women	
	Finals – 400m freestyle, women	4.15pm-6.00pm
	Finals – 100m freestyle, men	
	Finals – 100m backstroke, women	
	Finals – 200m backstroke, men	
	Finals – 4×100m freestyle relay, women	

2 August Thursday	Heats – 400m freestyle, men 8.30am-11.30am
	Heats – 100m butterfly, women
	Heats – 200m breaststroke, men
	Heats – 100m breaststroke, women
	Heats – 4×100m freestyle relay, men
	Heats – 800m freestyle, women
	Finals – 400m freestyle, men 4.15pm-6.00pm
	Finals – 100m butterfly, women
	Finals – 200m breaststroke, men
	Finals – 100m breaststroke, women
	Finals – 4×100m freestyle relay, men
3 August Friday	Heats – 200m medley, women 8.30am-11.30am
	Heats – 200m butterfly, men
	Heats – 100m backstroke, men
	Heats – 4×100m medley relay, women
	Heats – 1500m freestyle, men
	Finals – 200m medley, women 5.00pm-7.00pm
	Finals – 200m butterfly, men
	Finals – 800m freestyle, women
	Finals – 100m backstroke, men
	Finals – 4×100m medley relay, women
4 August Saturday	Heats – 200m medley, men 8.30am-11.30am
	Heats – 200m butterfly, women
	Heats – 200m backstroke, women
	Heats – 4×100m medley relay, men
	Finals – 200m medley, men 5.00pm-7.00pm
	Finals – 200m butterfly, women
	Finals – 1500m freestyle, men
	Finals – 200m backstroke, women
	Finals – 4×100m medley relay, men

Synchronized Swimming
University of Southern California
McDonald's Swim Stadium

6 August Monday	Duet routines preliminary	10.00am-2.00pm
9 August Thursday	Duet routines final	1.30pm-2.30pm

Tennis
University of California, Los Angeles

6 August Monday	16 matches	9.00am-5.30pm
7 August Tuesday	16 matches	9.00am-5.30pm

8 August Wednesday	16 matches	9.00am-5.30pm
9 August Thursday	8 matches, quarter–finals	9.00am-5.30pm
10 August Friday	4 matches, semi–finals	9.00am-5.30pm
11 August Saturday	2 matches, finals	10.00am-2.00pm

Volleyball
Long Beach Sports Arena

29 July Sunday	2 matches – preliminaries, men	10.00am-2.00pm
	2 matches – preliminaries, men	6.30pm-10.30pm
30 July Monday	2 matches – preliminaries, women	10.00am-7.00pm
	2 matches – preliminaries, women	6.30pm-10.30pm
31 July Tuesday	2 matches – preliminaries, men	10.00am-2.00pm
	2 matches – preliminaries, men	6.30pm-10.30pm
1 August Wednesday	2 matches – preliminaries, women	10.00am-2.00pm
	2 matches – preliminaries, women	6.30pm-10.30pm
2 August Thursday	2 matches – preliminaries, men	10.00am-2.00pm
	2 matches – preliminaries, men	6.30pm-10.30pm
3 August Friday	2 matches – preliminaries, women	10.00am-2.00pm
	2 matches – preliminaries, women	6.30pm-10.30pm
4 August Saturday	2 matches – preliminaries, men	10.00am-2.00pm
	2 matches – preliminaries, men	6.30pm-10.30pm
5 August Sunday	2 matches – semi–finals (5-8 places) women	10.00am-2.00pm
	2 matches – semi–finals (1-4 places) women	6.30pm-10.30pm

6 August Monday	2 matches – preliminaries, men	10.00am-2.00pm
	2 matches – preliminaries, men	6.30pm-10.30pm
7 August Tuesday	2 matches – finals (5-8 places), women	10.00am-2.00pm
	1 match – final (3-4 places), women	4.00pm-6.00pm
	1 match – final (1-2 places), women	8.30pm-10.30pm
8 August Wednesday	2 matches – semi–finals, men 1 match – final (9-10 places), men	9.00am-3.00pm
	2 matches – semi–finals, men	6.30pm-10.30pm
10 August Friday	2 matches – finals (5-8 places), men	6.30pm-10.30pm
11 August Saturday	1 match – final (3-4 places), men	12 noon-2.00pm
	1 match – final (1-2 places), men	6.30pm-8.30pm

Water Polo
Pepperdine University, Malibu

1 August Wednesday	2 games – preliminaries	8.30am-11.00am
	2 games – preliminaries	1.30pm-4.00pm
	2 games – preliminaries	7.30pm-10.00pm
2 August Thursday	2 games – preliminaries	8.30am-11.00am
	2 games – preliminaries	1.30pm-4.00pm
	2 games – preliminaries	7.30pm-10.00pm
3 August Friday	2 games – preliminaries	8.30am-11.00am
	2 games – preliminaries	1.30pm-4.00pm
	2 games – preliminaries	7.30pm-10.00pm
6 August Monday	2 games – preliminaries	8.30am-11.00am
	2 games – preliminaries	1.30pm-4.00pm
	2 games – preliminaries	7.30pm-10.00pm
7 August Tuesday	2 games – preliminaries	8.30am-11.00am
	2 games – preliminaries	1.30pm-4.00pm
	2 games – preliminaries	7.30pm-10.00pm

9 August Thursday	2 games – preliminaries	8.30am-11.00am
	2 games – preliminaries	1.30pm-4.00pm
	2 games – preliminaries	7.30pm-10.00pm
10 August Friday	2 games – preliminaries	8.30am-11.00am
	2 games – preliminaries	1.30pm-4.00pm
	2 games – preliminaries	7.30pm-10.00pm

Weightlifting
Loyola Marymount University

29 July Sunday	Flyweight (up to 52kg) group B	2.00pm-4.00pm
	Flyweight, group A	6.00pm-9.00pm
30 July Monday	Bantamweight (up to 56kg), group B	2.00pm-4.00pm
	Bantamweight, group A	6.00pm-9.00pm
31 July Tuesday	Featherweight (up to 60kg), group B	2.00pm-4.00pm
	Featherweight, group A	6.00pm-9.00pm
1 August Wednesday	Lightweight (up to 67.5kg), group C	11.00am-1.00pm
	Lightweight, group B	2.00pm-4.00pm
	Lightweight, group A	6.00pm-8.00pm
2 August Thursday	Middleweight (up to 75kg), group C	11.00am-1.00pm
	Middleweight, group B	2.00pm-4.00pm
	Middleweight, group A	6.00pm-8.00pm
4 August Saturday	Light heavyweight (up to 82.5kg), group C	11.00am-1.00pm
	Light heavyweight, group B	2.00pm-4.00pm
	Light heavyweight, group A	6.00pm-8.00pm
5 August Sunday	Middle heavyweight (up to 90kg), group C	11.00am-1.00pm
	Middle heavyweight, group B	2.00pm-4.00pm
	Middle heavyweight, group A	6.00pm-8.00pm
6 August Monday	First heavyweight (up to 100kg), group B	2.00pm-4.00pm
	First heavyweight, group A	6.00pm-9.00pm

7 August Tuesday	Second heavyweight (up to 110kg), group B	2.00pm-4.00pm
	Second heavyweight, group A	6.00pm-9.00pm
8 August Wednesday	Super heavyweight (over 110kg), group B	2.00pm-4.00pm
	Super heavyweight, group A	6.00pm-9.00pm

Wrestling
Anaheim Convention Center

Greco-Roman Style

30 July Monday	Preliminaries – 48, 62, 90kg	12 noon-3.00pm
	Preliminaries – 48, 62, 90kg	6.00pm-8.30pm
31 July Tuesday	Preliminaries – 48, 52, 62, 74, 90, over 100kg	12 noon-3.00pm
	Preliminaries – 48, 52, 62, 74, 90, over 100kg	6.00pm-8.30pm
1 August Wednesday	Preliminaries – 52, 57, 68, 74, 82, 100, over 100kg Semi–finals – 48, 62, 90kg	12 noon-3.00pm
	Preliminaries – 52, 57, 68, 74, 82, 100, over 100kg Finals – 48, 62, 90kg	6.00pm-8.30pm
2 August Thursday	Preliminaries – 57, 68, 82, 100kg Semi–finals – 52, 74, over 100kg	12 noon-3.00pm
	Preliminaries – 57, 68, 82, 100kg Finals – 52, 74, over 100kg	6.00pm-8.30pm
3 August Friday	Preliminaries – 57, 68, 82, 100kg	12 noon-3.00pm
	Semi–finals/finals – 57, 68, 82, 100kg	6.00pm-8.30pm

Freestyle

7 August Tuesday	Preliminaries – 48, 62, 90kg	12 noon-3.00pm
	Preliminaries – 48, 62, 90kg	6.00pm-8.30pm
8 August Wednesday	Preliminaries – 48, 52, 62, 74, 90, over 100kg	12 noon-3.00pm
	Preliminaries – 48, 52, 62, 74, 90, over 100kg	6.00pm-8.30pm

9 August Thursday	Preliminaries – 52, 57, 68, 74, 82, 100, over 100kg Semi–finals – 48, 62, 90kg	12 noon-3.00pm
	Preliminaries – 52, 57, 68, 74, 82, 100, over 100kg Finals – 48, 62, 90kg	6.00pm-8.30pm
10 August Friday	Preliminaries – 57, 68, 82, 100kg Semi–finals – 52, 74, over 100kg	12 noon-3.00pm
	Preliminaries – 57, 68, 82, 100kg Finals – 52, 74, over 100kg	6.00pm-8.30pm
11 August Saturday	Preliminaries – 57, 68, 82, 100kg	12 noon-3.00pm
	Semi–finals – 57, 68, 82, 100kg	6.00pm-8.30pm

Yachting
Olympic Yachting Center, Long Beach
All races held at sea

31 July Tuesday	First race	1.30pm-6.30pm
1 August Wednesday	Second race	1.30pm-6.30pm
2 August Thursday	Third race	1.30pm-6.30pm
3 August Friday	Fourth race	1.30pm-6.30pm
6 August Monday	Fifth race	1.30pm-6.30pm
7 August Tuesday	Sixth race	1.30pm-6.30pm
8 August Wednesday	Seventh race	1.30pm-6.30pm

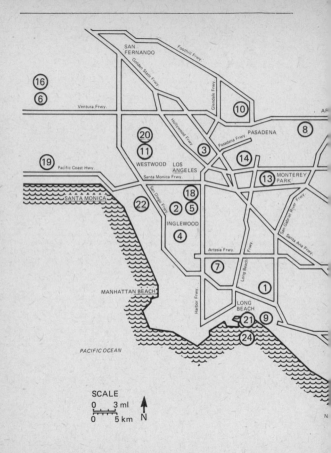

SCALE

0 ——— 3 ml

0 ——— 5 km

N

XXIIIrd OLYMPIAD, LOS ANGELES 1984, MAP OF VENUES

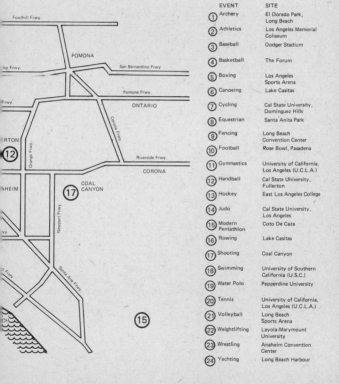

	EVENT	SITE
①	Archery	El Dorado Park, Long Beach
②	Athletics	Los Angeles Memorial Coliseum
③	Baseball	Dodger Stadium
④	Basketball	The Forum
⑤	Boxing	Los Angeles Sports Arena
⑥	Canoeing	Lake Casitas
⑦	Cycling	Cal State University, Dominguez Hills
⑧	Equestrian	Santa Anita Park
⑨	Fencing	Long Beach Convention Center
⑩	Football	Rose Bowl, Pasadena
⑪	Gymnastics	University of California, Los Angeles (U.C.L.A.)
⑫	Handball	Cal State University, Fullerton
⑬	Hockey	East Los Angeles College
⑭	Judo	Cal State University, Los Angeles
⑮	Modern Pentathlon	Coto De Caza
⑯	Rowing	Lake Casitas
⑰	Shooting	Coal Canyon
⑱	Swimming	University of Southern California (U.S.C.)
⑲	Water Polo	Pepperdine University
⑳	Tennis	University of California, Los Angeles (U.C.L.A.)
㉑	Volleyball	Long Beach Sports Arena
㉒	Weightlifting	Loyola-Marymount University
㉓	Wrestling	Anaheim Convention Center
㉔	Yachting	Long Beach Harbour

37

XXIIIrd OLYMPIAD, LOS ANGELES 1984
VENUES

El Dorado Park (archery)

The archers will need to face due north to avoid aiming into a sun which will beat down at anything up to 90 degrees Fahrenheit. But if they do allow themselves to look around they will realise they are in one of the most beautiful archery centres in the world. Situated in Long Beach, El Dorado Park was built as a range in 1972 and is the only one of its kind in Southern California. The range is about 275m wide and can accommodate 50 targets. Temporary grandstands are being erected to seat 4000.

The Los Angeles Memorial Coliseum (athletics)

The Coliseum, home of the 1932 Games, has rarely been used for track and field meetings since 1974. Atlantic Richfield Company, one of the ten largest US industrial concerns, are spending 5 million dollars refurbishing the facilities and laying a new synthetic Rekortan track made by the West German firm of Voigt. Lasers were used to ensure the precise measurements of the track, which will last for 25 years and is guaranteed to stay firm even if temperatures hit the nineties as predicted.

The Coliseum was finished on 1 May 1923 at a cost of 954,872 dollars. Seating capacity was 75,000. In 1931, at the cost of another 950,000 dollars, it was enlarged to house 101,574, but the introduction of theatre-type seats later reduced the capacity to its present 92,604.

A giant Olympic torch stands 150ft above ground level on the east side above a 1.6 million dollar electronic scoreboard. The Coliseum has 90 entrances and 74 turnstiles.

The Forum (basketball)

The Forum at Inglewood is home to the Los Angeles Lakers professional basketball team. Built in 1966, the Forum has six times hosted the National Basketball Association Professional Championships. Seating capacity is 17,505.

The Los Angeles Memorial Sports Arena (boxing)

Used as location for the films *Rocky* and *Rocky II*, the Sports Arena was opened on Independence Day, 4 July 1959 by then Vice President Richard Nixon. It cost 7,407,664 dollars to build and seats 16,353. It has housed 17 championship bouts and its record attendance of 16,230 was set on 15 November 1962 when Cassius Clay knocked out Archie Moore in four rounds.

Lake Casitas (canoeing and rowing)

The 1984 Olympic competitions will be the first to be held on a natural lake since 1960 when events were contested on Italy's Lake Albano. New facilities have been provided to add modern efficiency to the Lake's natural beauty, including seating for 10,000. The Lake is some 80 miles from the main Los Angeles Memorial Coliseum.

California State University Velodrome, Dominguez Hills (cycling)

Built especially for the 1984 Games at a cost of 4 million dollars, the impressive Velodrome is the only world-class cycling track in the western United States. The oval track measures 333.33m long and 7m wide. Turns are banked at 33 degrees, allowing cyclists to attain speeds of up to 47 miles per hour. Permanent seating exists for 2000 spectators but an additional 6000 temporary seats will be erected for the Games.

Santa Anita Park (equestrian events)

Santa Anita Park, in the shadow of the San Gabriel Valley mountains, has installed temporary seating to increase its capacity to 50,000. Parking is available for some 22,000 cars and there is ample stable accommodation for the estimated 350 horses.

Long Beach Convention Centre Exhibition Hall (fencing)

The 100,000 square foot hall was opened in 1977 and seats 6000. It is situated in the Long Beach Convention Centre complex.

University of California, Los Angeles (gymnastics)

UCLA's Pauley Pavilion, built in 1965, will be the site of all gymnastics events. With a seating capacity of more than 12,000, this first-class facility annually hosts many of the nation's outstanding college competitions, including the UCLA Gymnastic Classic. The attractively landscaped 411-acre campus with more than 85 buildings will also be the site of one of the two main Olympic Villages.

The Pavilion is named after Edwin Pauley, University of California Regent, who was the principal individual donor to the Pavilion's building fund of 5 million dollars.

California State Polytechnic and California State University, Fullerton (handball)

Handball will be at two sites: California State Polytechnic University, Pomona, and at California State University, Fullerton. Each venue seats 4000 in the gymnasium. Both are about 30 miles from the Coliseum.

East Los Angeles College (hockey)

An artificial turf 'SuperTurf 84' will be installed in the College's 15-year-old stadium. The 22,000-seater arena is used each year for the Los Angeles City Track and Field Championships and has hosted numerous other athletics meetings as well as soccer and grid iron.

California State University, Los Angeles (judo)

The 4200-seat gymnasium at Cal State Los Angeles has already hosted the United States National Judo Championships. The university is seven miles east of Los Angeles.

Coto de Caza, Orange County (modern pentathlon)

For the first time all five disciplines of the modern pentathlon will be held at a single venue. In the past the five days of competition – riding, swimming, shooting, fencing and cross country running – have been split with the competitors travelling daily. Coto de Caza, a popular resort, is owned by the Florida-based Arvida Corporation and the 5000 acre residential community sits at the base of the Saddleback Mountains.

Coal Canyon (shooting)

Coal Canyon, situated near the intersection of Orange, Riverside and San Bernadino counties, comprises 1600 acres of untamed terrain. Some 600 acres will be developed for the new shooting site. It will be the first world class shooting complex in the United States and will be kept as a permanent site.

The Rose Bowl (soccer)

The beautiful Rose Bowl in Pasadena will host the Olympic soccer finals. More than 3000 rose bushes of 100 different varieties surround the stadium which has a seating capacity of 104,696. The vast Bowl is used annually for the inter-collegiate grid iron competition and was once the home of the North American Soccer League's Los Angeles Aztecs.

First round matches will be played at Stanford University Stadium, Palo Alto, California; Harvard University Stadium, Cambridge, Massachusetts; and the Navy-Marine Corps Memorial Stadium, United States Naval Academy, Annapolis, Maryland. Quarter–finals will be held in the Rose Bowl and Stanford Stadium.

University of Southern California (swimming and diving)

Mcdonald's, makers of Big Mac hamburgers, have plunged into sponsorship in a big way, underwriting the 4 million dollar cost of building a new world-class pool and diving well at the University. Temporary seating will be provided for 11,000 spectators, 3500 more than were housed in Moscow's Olympiiski Swimming Pool four years ago.

Long Beach Arena (volleyball)

Long Beach Arena, built in 1962 as part of the Long Beach Convention Centre Complex, will provide seating for 11,300.

Pepperdine University (water polo)

The Runnels Memorial Pool at Pepperdine University in Malibu will host the water polo. There will be seating for 4500, compared to the massive 9000 capacity of the Lenin Stadium Pool in 1980. Pepperdine University is 30 miles from the Coliseum, and the Pacific Ocean provides a magnificent backdrop.

Loyola Marymount University (weightlifting)

This small private college — the first to be founded in Los Angeles – houses the Albert Gersten Pavilion where the Olympic weightlifting will take place. The 63,800-square-foot building was completed in 1981.

During the Games, competitors will be able to warm up and train in the Loyola Marymount Gymnasium next door to the Pavilion.

Anaheim Convention Centre (wrestling)

The Centre, opened in July 1967, will have seating for 8900 and parking for more than 3500 vehicles.

Long Beach Marina and Harbour (yachting)

For the first time in 28 years Olympic yachtsman will not feel isolated from the rest of the Games. The Long Beach area is also hosting archery, fencing and volleyball. The Southern California Yachting Association was the first body to sign an agreement with the Los Angeles Olympic Organising Committee for rent of sites. Olympic class regattas have been held at Long Beach for 20 years.

In addition two exhibition sports are being held:
Baseball at the Dodger Stadium and tennis at the University of California.

RULES AND REGULATIONS

This event-by-event guide outlines some of the most important and interesting rules and regulations relating to track and field athletics.

Hurdle races

The total weight of the hurdle should not be less than 10kg. The extreme width is 1.20m and the extreme length of the base 70cm. The top bar should be 70mm wide, between 10mm and 25mm thick and striped in black and white. The hurdle, made of wood or metal, is designed so that a force of at least 3.6kg applied to the centre of the top of the crossbar is required to overturn it.

A competitor who trails his foot or leg on any hurdle not in his own lane, or jumps any hurdle not in his own lane, or deliberately knocks down any hurdle by hand or foot will be disqualified.

Specifications:

Distance of race (m)	Height of hurdle (cm)	Number of flights	Distance from start to first hurdle (m)	Distance between flights (m)	Distance from last hurdle to finish (m)
Men					
110	106.7	10	13.72	9.14	14.02
400	91.4	10	45	35	40
Women					
100	84.0	10	13	8.5	10.5
400	76.2	10	45	35	40

Steeplechase

In the standard Olympic distance of 3000m there are 28 hurdles and seven water jumps. The hurdles are 91.4cm in height and at least 3.66m in total width. The width of the top bar of all hurdles should be 12.7cm. The water jump is 3.66m in width and length and the water 70cm deep at the hurdle end, remaining at this depth for a distance of about 30cm before sloping to the level of the track at the farther end.

Heptathlon

The heptathlon (women) consists of seven events held on two consecutive days in the following order:
First day: 100 metres hurdles, high jump, shot, 200 metres.
Second day: long jump, javelin, 800 metres.

Decathlon

The decathlon (men) consists of ten events held on two consecutive days in a fixed order.
First day: 100 metres, long jump, shot, high jump, 400 metres.
Second day: 110 metres hurdles, discus, pole vault, javelin, 1500 metres.

In both heptathlon and decathlon these rules apply: Three attempts only are allowed in the long jump and throwing events.

Disqualification will follow three false starts in the running and hurdles events.

Any athlete failing to take part in any of the events is not allowed to take part in a subsequent event but is considered to have abandoned the competition.

In the event of a tie, the winner is the competitor who has scored the higher points in a majority of events.

Relay races

The baton should be a smooth, hollow tube between 28cm and 30cm in length. The circumference is 12cm and 13cm and the weight not less than 50g.

No competitor may run two sections.

The takeover zone is an area 10m before and after the scratch line. In the 4 × 100m relays the last three runners can start their run up to 10m outside the takeover zone. In 4 × 400m relays the outgoing runner must start his run within the takeover zone.

The baton must be carried by hand throughout the race. If it is dropped it must be recovered by the athlete who dropped it. Within the takeover zone it is the position of the baton which is decisive, NOT the position of the body or limbs of the competitors.

Assistance such as pushing-off is not allowed.

Once a team has competed in the preliminary round it cannot be altered except for illness or injury – although the running order of the team can be changed.

High jump

A competitor can start jumping at any height above the agreed starting height and may miss out subsequent heights at his own discretion. Three consecutive failures, regardless of the height at which they occur, disqualify from further jumping – except in the case of a jump-off after a first place tie.

The use of weights or grips is forbidden.

A competitor can place marks to assist his run-up and take-off and a handkerchief or similar object on the crossbar for sighting purposes. The distance of the run-up is unlimited.

The jump does not count if a competitor takes off with both feet.

The distance between the uprights of the high jump is not less than 3.66m or more than 4.04m.

In the event of a tie, the competitor with the fewest jumps at the height at which the tie occurred is the winner; if the tie still remains the competitor with the lowest total of failures throughout the competition is the winner.

Pole vault

A competitor can start vaulting at any height above the agreed starting height and can vault at his discretion at subsequent heights. Three consecutive failures, regardless of the heights at which they occur, disqualify from further vaulting.

Marks can be placed alongside – not on – the runway and a handkerchief, or similar object, can be placed on the crossbar for sighting purposes. The distance of the run-up is unlimited.

Competitors can have the uprights moved in any direction, but not more than 60cm from the prolongation of the inside edge of the top of the stopboard.

A vault fails if, after leaving the ground, a competitor places his lower hand above the upper one or moves the upper hand higher up on the pole.

The pole can be made of any material and measure any length or diameter, but the basic surface must be smooth. The pole may have a binding of not more than two layers of adhesive tape of uniform thickness.

The use of tape on the hands or fingers is not allowed unless to cover an open wound. But adhesive substances on the hands or pole are allowed to gain a better grip.

If, while making an attempt, the competitor's pole breaks, it is not counted as a failure.

The width between the uprights is not less than 3.66m or more than 4.37m. The box in which the pole is planted is 1m long, 60cm wide at the front end, tapering to 15cm at the stopboard where it is 20cm in depth.

Long jump

Each competitor in the final has three jumps and then the leading eight go on for three extra jumps.

The run-up is unlimited and competitors can place markers alongside – not on – the runway.

If a competitor, after jumping, walks back through the landing area, that is a failure.

The measurement of the jump is made at right angles from the nearest break in the ground in the landing area made by any part of the body to the take-off board. If a competitor touches the ground outside the landing area and nearer to the take-off board than his mark in the landing area, that is a failure.

No form of somersault is permitted.

The take-off board, fixed flush with the ground, is made of wood and is 1.21m and 1.23m long, 19.8cm and 20.2cm wide and maximum 10cm deep.

The landing area is at least 2.75m wide and at least 10m long. The surface of the sand in the landing area should be level with the top of the take-off board.

Triple jump

Rules as for long jump except that the hop must be made so that the competitor lands on the same foot he took off with; in the step he must land on the other foot, from which he subsequently makes the jump. If the coing' leg while jumping, that is a failure. The landing area should be at least 5.5m long.

Shot

The men's shot weighs 7.265kg; the women's 4kg.

Each competitor in the final has three throws and the best eight go on for three extra attempts.

Competitors can use only those implements which are provided.

Gloves may not be worn.

Belts may be worn to protect the spine.

Adhesive substances are allowed on the hands, but not on the shoes.

A throw is a foul if a competitor touches the ground outside the circle, the top of the stopboard or the top of the circle. He may touch the inside of the stopboard. He must not leave the circle until the shot has touched the ground and he must leave through the rear of the circle.

The shot must be put from the shoulder with one hand only. From the moment he takes his stance inside the ring, the competitor must hold the shot against or close to his chin and the hand must not be dropped from this position during the action of putting. The shot must not be brought back behind the line of the shoulders.

Hammer

The hammer weighs 7.265kg with a solid metal head between 110mm and 130mm in diameter attached to a single straight length of spring steel wire not less than No. 11 Standard Wire Gauge in diameter. The overall length of the hammer must be between 117.5cm and 121.5cm.

Each competitor in the final is allowed three throws with the eight best going on for three extra attempts.

Competitors may use only those implements provided for general use.

Gloves may be worn but they must be smooth back and front with finger holes.

Belts may be worn to protect the spine.

Adhesive substances are allowed on the hands but not on shoes.

It is a foul throw if the competitor touches the ground outside the circle or the top of the circle. He must not leave the circle until the hammer has hit the ground and then he must leave by the rear of the circle.

In his starting position prior to preliminary swings, the competitor is allowed to put the head of the hammer on the ground inside or outside the circle.

If the head of the hammer touches the ground when the competitor makes his preliminary swings it is not a foul – unless he stops and attempts to start again.

If the hammer breaks on a throw, that is not counted against the competitor.

Discus

The men's discus weight 2kg and the women's 1kg. Made of wood with a smooth metal rim, the discus is 220mm in diameter for men and 180mm for women.

In the final, competitors are given three throws with the best eight going on for three extra attempts.

Competitors may use only those implements provided for general use.

Gloves may not be worn.

Belts may be worn to protect the spine.

Adhesive substances are allowed on the hands but not the shoes.

It is a foul throw if the competitor touches the ground outside the circle or the top of the circle. He must not leave the circle until the discus has touched the ground and then he must leave by the rear of the circle.

If a discus breaks during a throw it will not be counted against the competitor.

Javelin

The javelin consists of three parts – a metal head, a shaft and a cord grip. For men it measures between 260cm and 270cm in length and weighs 800g. For women it measures between 220cm and 230cm and weighs 600g.

In the final, each competitor will be given three throws with the eight best going on for three extra attempts.

Competitors shall use only those implements provided for general use.

Gloves may not be worn.

Belts may be worn to protect the spine.

Adhesive substances are allowed on the hands but not the shoes.

For a valid throw the javelin must be held with one hand only, and at the grip, so that the little finger is nearest to the point. It must be thrown over the shoulder and not slung or hurled. The metal head must strike the ground first.

THE DECATHLON AND HEPTATHLON EVENTS

The Ancient Greeks included a pentathlon for men in their Olympic Games, but it was not until the Stockholm Olympics of 1912 that the ten event decathlon was introduced into international competition. The same format has existed ever since: 100 metres, long jump, shot, high jump, 400 metres, 110 metres hurdles, discus, pole vault, javelin and 1500 metres.

Winner of that inaugural competition in Sweden was the great Jim Thorpe, part Crow Indian. His score of 6756 points stood as a world record for 15 years and when the King of Sweden congratulated him – *'Mr Thorpe you are the greatest athlete in the world'*, Thorpe is supposed to have replied, *'Thanks, King'*.

In more recent years the event has been dominated by Britain's Daley Thompson, whose six year unbeaten run has brought Olympic, European, Commonwealth and World titles. The all-time list at the end of last season read:

(Points)

8779	Jurgen Hingsen (FRG)	1983
8743	Daley Thompson (GBR)	1982
8723	Hingsen (FRG)	1982
8718	Sigfried Wentz (FRG)	1983
8704	Thompson (GBR)	1982
8666	Thompson (GBR)	1983
8649	Guido Kratschmer (FRG)	1980
8622	Thompson (GBR)	1980
8618	Bruce Jenner (USA)	1976

The massive Hingsen (6ft 6¾in and 15st 10lb) was beaten by Thompson in both the European Games and the World Championships but had the satisfaction of taking away the Briton's world record at Bernhausen, West Germany, on 4/5 June 1983.

His performances over those two days were:

		(Points)
100 metres	10.92m	824
Long jump	7.74m	969
Shot	15.94m	844
High jump	2.15m	983
400 metres	47.89	904
110 metres hurdles	14.10	950
Discus	46.80	815
Pole vault	4.70	981
Javelin	67.26	848
1500 metres	4:19.74	661

On the following pages is a scoring chart which will give an idea of the number of points scored in each discipline during the decathlon in Los Angeles:

100 metres

Seconds	Points
10.00	1073
10.10	1044
10.20	1015
10.30	987
10.40	959
10.45	946
10.50	932
10.55	919
10.60	906
10.70	880
10.80	854
10.85	841
10.90	829
10.95	817
11.00	804
11.15	768
11.25	745
11.30	733
11.45	699
11.50	687
11.60	665
11.70	644
11.80	622
11.90	601
11.95	591
12.00	580
12.20	540
12.30	520
12.60	463
12.80	426
13.00	390

Long jump

Metres	Points
8.35	1087
8.30	1077
8.25	1068
8.20	1058
8.15	1049
8.10	1039
8.05	1030
8.00	1020
7.95	1010
7.90	1000
7.85	990
7.80	980
7.75	971
7.70	961
7.65	951
7.60	941
7.55	931
7.50	921
7.45	911
7.40	901
7.35	891
7.30	881
7.25	871
7.20	861
7.15	850
7.10	840
7.05	830

Shot

Metres	Points
22.68	1200
22.57	1195
22.47	1190
22.37	1185
22.27	1180
22.17	1175
22.06	1170
21.96	1165
21.86	1160
21.76	1155
21.66	1150
21.56	1145
21.46	1140
21.36	1135
21.26	1130
21.16	1125
21.06	1120
20.96	1115
20.86	1110
20.76	1105
20.66	1100
20.57	1095
20.47	1090
20.37	1085
20.27	1080
20.18	1075
20.08	1070
19.99	1065
19.89	1060
19.79	1055
19.69	1050
19.60	1045
19.50	1040
19.41	1035
19.31	1030
19.22	1025
19.12	1020
19.03	1015
18.93	1010
18.84	1005
18.75	1000
18.66	995
18.56	990
18.47	985
18.37	980
18.28	975
18.19	970
18.10	965
18.00	960
17.91	955
17.82	950
17.41	927
17.37	925
17.28	920
17.19	915
17.10	910
17.01	905
16.80	893
16.55	879
16.38	869
16.01	848
15.85	839
15.65	827
15.39	812
15.20	801
15.05	792
14.90	783
14.70	771
14.55	762
14.40	753
14.21	741
14.09	734
14.00	728

High jump

Metres	Points
2.40	1186
2.35	1146
2.30	1106
2.25	1066
2.20	1025
2.17	1000
2.14	975
2.11	950
2.08	925
2.05	900
2.02	874
1.99	849
1.96	822
1.93	796
1.90	769
1.87	743
1.84	716
1.80	680

400 metres

Seconds	Points
45.00	1054
45.31	1037
45.70	1016
45.98	1001
46.09	995
46.30	984
46.50	974
46.81	958
47.00	948
47.26	935
47.50	923
47.79	909
47.99	899
48.20	889
48.60	870
48.98	852
49.15	844
49.48	829
49.70	819
49.99	806
50.23	795
50.50	783
50.80	770
51.01	761

110 metres hurdles

Seconds	Points
12.20	1214
12.30	1199
12.40	1183
12.50	1168
12.80	1123
13.00	1094
13.30	1053
13.60	1013
13.90	975
14.10	950
14.30	927
14.60	892
14.90	859
15.00	848
15.15	833
15.40	807
15.60	787
15.90	758
16.00	749
16.20	730
16.40	712
16.50	703

Discus

Metres	Points
56.89	990
56.59	985
56.29	980
55.99	975
55.69	970
55.39	965
55.09	960
54.80	955
53.91	940
53.03	925
52.16	910
51.01	890
50.50	881
50.04	873
49.48	863
49.03	855
48.64	848
48.02	837
47.46	827
47.02	819
46.47	809
46.04	801
45.50	791
45.02	782
44.53	773
44.00	763
43.52	754
43.00	744
42.53	735
42.01	725

Pole Vault

Metres	Points
5.30	1121
5.25	1111
5.20	1098
5.15	1860
5.10	1075
5.05	1064
5.00	1052
4.95	1040
4.90	1028
4.85	1017
4.80	1005
4.75	993
4.70	981
4.65	969
4.60	957
4.55	945
4.50	932
4.45	920
4.40	909
4.35	896

Metres	Points
4.30	884
4.25	871
4.20	859
4.15	845
4.10	832
4.05	820
4.00	807
3.95	794
3.90	780
3.80	754
3.70	728
3.60	700
3.50	672

Javelin

Metres	Points
79.58	985
79.11	980
78.64	975
78.18	970
77.71	965
77.25	960
76.79	955
76.33	950
71.81	900
71.28	894
70.65	887
70.04	880
69.60	875
69.16	870
68.55	863
68.03	857
67.51	851
67.08	846
66.56	840
66.04	834
65.53	826
65.02	822
64.51	816
64.01	810
63.50	804
63.00	798
62.51	792
62.01	786
61.51	780
61.02	774
60.53	768
60.03	762
59.55	756

1500 metres

Minutes	Points
3:59.0	825
3:59.6	820
4:00.1	815
4:00.7	810
4:01.3	805
4:08.2	750
4:08.8	745
4:09.4	740
4:10.0	735
4:10.7	730
4:11.3	725
4:11.9	720
4:12.5	715
4:13.3	710
4:13.9	705
4:14.5	700
4:15.2	695
4:15.9	690
4:16.5	685
4:17.2	680
4:17.9	675
4:18.6	670
4:19.3	665
4:20.0	660
4:20.6	655
4:21.3	650
4:22.0	645
4:22.7	640
4:23.4	635
4:24.2	630
4:24.9	625
4:25.6	620
4:26.2	615
4:27.0	610
4:27.7	605
4:28.4	600
4:29.2	595
4:29.9	590
4:30.7	585
4:31.4	580
4:32.2	575
4:32.9	570
4:33.7	565
4:34.5	560
4:35.2	555
4:36.0	550
4:36.8	545
4:37.6	540
4:38.3	535
4:39.1	530
4:40.0	525

The women's heptathlon will be seen in the Olympic Games for the first time in Los Angeles. It is a tougher offspring of the five event pentathlon which was introduced in the 1964 Tokyo Olympics.

The heptathlon comprises seven events – the pentathlon's original five of 100 metres hurdles, shot, high jump, long jump and 800 metres plus the 200 metres and javelin.

The following are simplified examples of the scoring charts used in each of the seven disciplines:

100 metres hurdles

Seconds	Points
11.80	1195
11.85	1186
11.90	1177
11.95	1169
12.00	1160
12.05	1152
12.10	1143
12.15	1135
12.20	1126
12.25	1118
12.30	1110
12.35	1102
12.40	1094
12.45	1086
12.50	1078
12.55	1070
12.60	1062
12.65	1054
12.70	1047
12.75	1039
12.80	1031
12.85	1024
12.90	1016
12.95	1009
13.00	1002
13.05	994
13.10	987
14.38	860
14.29	855
14.20	850
14.11	845
14.02	840
13.94	835
13.85	830
13.76	825
13.68	820
13.59	815
13.51	810
13.42	805
13.34	800
13.25	795
13.17	790
13.08	785
13.00	780
12.92	775
12.83	770
12.75	765
12.67	760
12.58	755
12.50	750
12.42	745
12.34	740
12.26	735
12.17	730
12.09	725
12.01	720
12.00	719

1.62	854
1.59	823
1.56	791
1.53	759
1.50	726
1.47	693
1.44	650
1.41	624

200 metres

Seconds	Points
21.60	1191
21.65	1185
21.70	1179
21.75	1173
21.80	1168
21.85	1162
21.90	1156
21.95	1150
22.00	1145
22.05	1139
22.10	1134
22.15	1125
22.20	1122
22.25	1117
22.30	1111
22.35	1106
22.40	1100
22.45	1095
22.50	1090
22.55	1084
22.60	1079
22.65	1073
22.70	1068
22.75	1063

Shot

Metres	Points
16.38	970
16.29	965
16.19	960
16.10	955
15.09	900
15.00	895
14.91	890
14.82	885
14.73	880
14.64	875
14.55	870
14.46	865

High Jump

Metres	Points
1.98	1193
1.95	1166
1.92	1140
1.89	1113
1.86	1086
1.83	1059
1.80	1031
1.77	1002
1.74	974
1.71	945
1.68	915
1.65	885

2:05.0	1002
2:05.5	994
2:06.0	986
2:06.5	978
2:07.0	971
2:07.5	963
2:08.0	955
2:08.5	948
2:09.0	941
2:09.5	933
2:10.0	926
2:10.5	918
2:11.0	911
2:11.5	904
2:12.0	897
2:12.5	890
2:13.0	883
2:13.5	876
2:14.0	869
2:14.5	862
2:15.0	855
2:16.0	842
2:17.0	829
2:18.0	815
2:19.0	803
2:20.0	790
2:20.5	784
2:21.0	778
2:21.5	777
2:22.0	765
2:22.5	759
2:23.0	753
2:23.5	747
2:24.0	741
2:24.5	735
2:25.0	729

800 metres

Minutes	Points
2:02.0	1051
2:02.5	1042
2:03.0	1834
2:03.5	1026
2:04.0	1018
2:04.5	1010

Javelin

Metres	Points
55.22	985
54.84	980
54.46	975
54.08	970
53.72	965
53.34	960

52.98	953	6.30	971
52.62	950	6.25	960
52.24	945	6.20	950
51.88	940	6.15	939
51.52	935	6.10	928
51.56	930	6.05	917
50.80	925	6.00	906
50.44	920	5.95	895
50.08	915	5.90	884
49.00	900	5.85	873
48.16	888	5.80	862
47.24	875	5.75	851
46.28	861	5.70	839
46.00	857	5.65	828
45.32	847	5.60	817
45.04	843	5.55	805
44.30	832	5.50	794
43.16	815	5.00	677
42.50	805		
41.84	795		
41.20	785		
40.22	770		
39.58	760		
39.26	755		
38.64	745		
38.32	740		
38.02	735		
37.08	720		
36.46	710		
35.86	700		
35.26	690		
34.66	680		
34.06	670		
33.48	660		
32.90	650		
32.60	645		
32.20	638		
32.02	635		

Long jump

Metres	Points
7.00	1117
6.95	1107
6.90	1097
6.85	1087
6.80	1076
6.75	1066
6.70	1056
6.65	1045
6.60	1035
6.55	1024
6.50	1014
6.45	1003
6.40	992
6.35	982

MEDAL TOTALS AND POSITIONS SINCE SECOND WORLD WAR

1948 London

Country	Gold	Silver	Bronze
USA	38	27	19
SWE	16	11	17
FRA	10	6	13
HUN	10	5	12
ITA	8	12	9
FIN	8	7	6
TUR	6	4	2
TCH	6	2	3
SUI	5	10	5
DEN	5	7	8
HOL	5	2	9
GBR	3	14	6
ARG	3	3	1
AUS	2	6	5
BEL	2	2	3
EGY	2	2	1
MEX	2	1	2
SAF	2	1	1
NOR	1	3	3
JAM	1	2	0
AUT	1	1	3
IND	1	0	0
PER	1	0	0
CAN	0	1	2
YUG	0	2	0
POR	0	1	1
URU	0	1	1
CEY	0	1	0
CUB	0	1	0
ESP	0	1	0
TRI	0	1	0
KOR	0	0	2
PAN	0	0	2
BRA	0	0	1
IRN	0	0	1
PUR	0	0	1
POL	0	0	1

1952 Helsinki

Country	Gold	Silver	Bronze
USA	40	19	17
URS	22	30	19
HUN	16	11	16
SWE	12	12	10
ITA	8	9	4
TCH	7	3	3
FRA	6	6	6
FIN	6	3	13
AUS	6	2	3
NOR	3	2	0
SUI	2	6	6
SAF	2	4	4
JAM	2	3	0
BEL	2	2	0
DEN	2	1	2
TUR	2	0	1
JAP	1	6	2
GBR	1	2	8
ARG	1	2	2
POL	1	2	1
CAN	1	2	0
YUG	1	2	0
ROM	1	1	2
BRA	1	0	2
NZL	1	0	2
IND	1	0	1
LUX	1	0	0
GER	0	7	17
HOL	0	5	0
IRN	0	3	4
CHI	0	2	0
AUT	0	1	1
LIB	0	1	1
IRL	0	1	0
MEX	0	1	0
ESP	0	1	0
KOR	0	0	2
TRI	0	0	2
URU	0	0	2
BUL	0	0	1
EGY	0	0	1
POR	0	0	1
VEN	0	0	1

1956 Melbourne

Country	Gold	Silver	Bronze
URS	37	29	32
USA	32	25	17
AUS	13	8	13
HUN	9	10	7
ITA	8	8	9
SWE	8	5	6
GER	6	13	7
GBR	6	7	11
ROM	5	3	5
JAP	4	10	5
FRA	4	4	6
TUR	3	2	2
FIN	3	1	11
IRN	2	2	1
CAN	2	1	3
NZL	2	0	0
POL	1	4	4
TCH	1	4	1
BUL	1	3	1
DEN	1	2	1
IRL	1	1	3
NOR	1	0	2
MEX	1	0	1
BRA	1	0	0
IND	1	0	0
YUG	0	3	0
CHI	0	2	2
BEL	0	2	0
ARG	0	1	1
KOR	0	1	1
ISL	0	1	0
PAK	0	1	0
SAF	0	0	4
AUT	0	0	2
BAH	0	0	1
GRE	0	0	1
SUI	0	0	1
URU	0	0	1

1960 Rome

Country	Gold	Silver	Bronze
URS	43	29	31
USA	34	21	16
ITA	13	10	13
GER	12	19	11
AUS	8	8	6
TUR	7	2	0
HUN	6	8	7
JAP	4	7	7
POL	4	6	11
TCH	3	2	3
ROM	3	1	6
GBR	2	6	12
DEN	2	3	1
NZL	2	0	1
BUL	1	3	3
SWE	1	2	3
FIN	1	1	3
AUT	1	1	0
YUG	1	1	0
PAK	1	0	1
ETH	1	0	0
GRE	1	0	0
NOR	1	0	0
SUI	0	3	3
FRA	0	2	3
BEL	0	2	2
IRN	0	1	3
SAF	0	1	2
HOL	0	1	2
ARG	0	1	1
EGY	0	1	1
CAN	0	1	0
GHA	0	1	0
IND	0	1	0
MAR	0	1	0
POR	0	1	0
SIN	0	1	0
BRA	0	0	2
JAM	0	0	2
IRQ	0	0	1
MEX	0	0	1
ESP	0	0	1
VEN	0	0	1

1964 Tokyo

Country	Gold	Silver	Bronze
USA	36	26	28
URS	30	31	35
JAP	16	5	8
GER	10	22	18
ITA	10	10	7
HUN	10	7	5
POL	7	6	10
AUS	6	2	10
TCH	5	6	3
GBR	4	12	2
BUL	3	5	2
FIN	3	0	2
NZL	3	0	2
ROM	2	4	6
HOL	2	4	4
TUR	2	3	1
SWE	2	2	4
DEN	2	1	3
YUG	2	1	2
BEL	2	0	1
FRA	1	8	6
CAN	1	2	1
SUI	1	2	1
BAH	1	0	0
ETH	1	0	0
IND	1	0	0
KOR	0	2	1
TRI	0	1	2
TUN	0	1	1
ARG	0	1	0
CUB	0	1	0
PAK	0	1	0
PHI	0	1	0
IRN	0	0	2
BRA	0	0	1
GHA	0	0	1
IRL	0	0	1
KEN	0	0	1
MEX	0	0	1
NGR	0	0	1
URU	0	0	1

1968 Mexico City

Country	Gold	Silver	Bronze
USA	45	28	34
URS	29	32	30
JAP	11	7	7
HUN	10	10	12
GDR	9	9	7
FRA	7	3	5
TCH	7	2	4
FRG	5	11	10
AUS	5	7	5
GBR	5	5	3
POL	5	2	11
ROM	4	6	5
ITA	3	4	9
KEN	3	4	2
MEX	3	3	3
YUG	3	3	2
HOL	3	3	1
BUL	2	4	3
IRN	2	1	2
SWE	2	1	1
TUR	2	0	0
DEN	1	4	3
CAN	1	3	1
FIN	1	2	1
ETH	1	1	0
NOR	1	1	0
NZL	1	0	2
TUN	1	0	1
PAK	1	0	0
VEN	1	0	0
CUB	0	4	0
AUT	0	2	2
SUI	0	1	4
MGL	0	1	3
BRA	0	1	2
BEL	0	1	1
PRK	0	1	1
UGA	0	1	1
CMR	0	1	0
JAM	0	1	0
ARG	0	0	2
GRE	0	0	1
IND	0	0	1
TAI	0	0	1

1972 Munich

Country	Gold	Silver	Bronze
URS	50	27	22
USA	33	31	30
GDR	20	23	23
FRG	13	11	16
JAP	13	8	8
AUS	8	7	2
POL	7	5	9
HUN	6	13	16
BUL	6	10	5
ITA	5	3	10
SWE	4	6	6
GBR	4	5	9
ROM	3	6	7
CUB	3	1	4
FIN	3	1	4
HOL	3	1	1
FRA	2	4	7
TCH	2	4	2
KEN	2	3	4
YUG	2	1	2
NOR	2	1	1
PRK	1	1	3
NZL	1	1	1
UGA	1	1	0
DEN	1	0	0
SUI	0	3	0
CAN	0	2	3
IRN	0	2	1
BEL	0	2	0
GRE	0	2	0
AUT	0	1	2
COL	0	1	2
ARG	0	1	0
LIB	0	1	0
MEX	0	1	0
MGL	0	1	0
PAK	0	1	0
KOR	0	1	0
TUN	0	1	0
TUR	0	1	0
BRA	0	0	2
ETH	0	0	2
ESP	0	0	1
GHA	0	0	1
IND	0	0	1
JAM	0	0	1
NIG	0	0	1
NGR	0	0	1

1976 Montreal

Country	Gold	Silver	Bronze
URS	49	41	35
GDR	40	25	25
USA	34	35	25
FRG	10	12	17
JAP	9	6	10
POL	7	6	13
BUL	6	9	7
CUB	6	4	3
ROM	4	9	14
HUN	4	5	13
FIN	4	2	0
SWE	4	1	0
GBR	3	5	5
ITA	2	7	4
FRA	2	3	4
YUG	2	3	3
TCH	2	2	4
NZL	2	1	1
KOR	1	1	4
SUI	1	1	2
JAM	1	1	0
PRK	1	1	0
NOR	1	1	0
DEN	1	0	2
MEX	1	0	1
TRI	1	0	0
CAN	0	5	6
BEL	0	3	3
HOL	0	2	3
POR	0	2	0
ESP	0	2	0
AUS	0	1	4
IRN	0	1	1
MGL	0	1	0
VEN	0	1	0
BRA	0	0	2
AUT	0	0	1
BER	0	0	1
PAK	0	0	1
PUR	0	0	1
THA	0	0	1

1980 Moscow

Country	Gold	Silver	Bronze
URS	80	69	46
GDR	47	37	42
BUL	8	16	17
CUB	8	7	5
ITA	0	3	4
HUN	7	10	15
ROM	6	6	13
FRA	6	5	3
GBR	5	7	9
POL	3	14	15
SWE	3	3	6
FIN	3	1	4
TCH	2	3	9
YUG	2	3	4
AUS	2	2	5
DEN	2	1	2
BRA	2	0	2
ETH	2	0	2
SUI	2	0	0
ESP	1	3	2
AUT	1	2	1
GRE	1	0	2
BEL	1	0	0
IND	1	0	0
ZIM	1	0	0
PRK	0	3	2
MGL	0	2	2
TAN	0	2	0
MEX	0	1	3
HOL	0	1	2
IRL	0	1	1
UGA	0	1	0
VEN	0	1	0
JAM	0	0	3
GUY	0	0	1
LIB	0	0	1

MEDALLISTS SINCE SECOND WORLD WAR

Archery (men)

Double Men's International Round — 36 arrows each at 90m, 70m, 50m and 30m.

			Points
1972	1	J. Williams (USA)	2528
	2	G. Jarvil (SWE)	2481
	3	K. Laasonen (FIN)	2467
1976	1	D. Pace (USA)	2571
	2	H. Michinaga (JPN)	2502
	3	G.C. Ferrari (ITA)	2495
1980	1	T. Poikoliainen (FIN)	2455
	2	B. Isachenko (URS)	2452
	3	A. Gazov (URS)	2449

Archery (women)

Double Women's International Round — 36 arrows each at 70m, 60m, 50m and 30m.

			Points
1972	1	D. Wilber (USA)	2424
	2	I. Szdlowska (POL)	2407
	3	E. Gapchenko (URS)	2403
1976	1	L. Ryon (USA)	2499
	2	V. Kovpan (URS)	2460
	3	Z. Rustamova (URS)	2407
1980	1	K. Losaberidze (URS)	2491
	2	N. Butuzova (URS)	2477
	3	P. Meriluoto (FIN)	2449

Association Football

	Gold	Silver	Bronze
1948	SWE	YUG	DEN
1952	HUN	YUG	SWE
1956	URS	YUG	BUL
1960	YUG	DEN	HUN
1964	HUN	TCH	GER
1968	HUN	BUL	JPN
1972	POL	HUN	GDR & URS*
1976	GDR	POL	URS
1980	TCH	GDR	URS

* Still drawing after extra time

Athletics (men)
100 metres

			Time
1948	1	H. Dillard (USA)	10.3
	2	H.N. Ewell (USA)	10.4
	3	L. La Beach (PAN)	10.4
1952	1	L. Remigino (USA)	10.4
	2	H. McKenley (JAM)	10.4
	3	E.McD. Bailey (GBR)	10.4
1956	1	B. Morrow (USA)	10.5
	2	T. Baker (USA)	10.5
	3	H. Hogan (AUS)	10.6
1960	1	A Hary (GFR)	10.2
	2	D. Sime (USA)	10.2
	3	P. Radford (GBR)	10.3
1964	1	R. Hayes (USA)	10.0
	2	E. Figuerola (CUB)	10.2
	3	H. Jerome (CAN)	10.2
1968	1	J. Hines (USA)	9.9
	2	L. Miller (JAM)	10.0
	3	C. Greene (USA)	10.0
1972	1	V. Borzov (URS)	10.14
	2	R. Taylor (USA)	10.24
	3	L. Miller (JAM)	10.33
1976	1	H. Crawford (TRI)	10.06
	2	D. Quarrie (JAM)	10.08
	3	V. Borzov (URS)	10.14
1980	1	A. Wells (GBR)	10.25
	2	S. Leonard (CUB)	10.25
	3	P. Petrov (BUL)	10.39

200 metres

			Time
1948	1	M. Patton (USA)	21.2
	2	H.N. Ewell (USA)	21.1
	3	L. La Beach (PAN)	21.2
1952	1	A. Stanfield (USA)	20.7
	2	T. Baker (USA)	20.8
	3	J. Gathers (USA)	20.8
1956	1	B. Morrow (USA)	20.6
	2	A. Stanfield (USA)	20.7
	3	T. Baker (USA)	20.9

1960	1	L. Berutti (ITA)	20.5
	2	L. Carney (USA)	20.6
	3	A. Seye (FRA)	20.7
1964	1	H. Carr (USA)	20.3
	2	P. Drayton (USA)	20.5
	3	E. Roberts (TRI)	20.6
1968	1	T. Smith (USA)	19.8
	2	P. Norman (AUS)	20.0
	3	J. Carlos (USA)	20.0
1972	1	V. Borzov (URS)	20.0
	2	L. Black (USA)	20.19
	3	P. Mennea (ITA)	20.30
1976	1	D. Quarrie (JAM)	20.23
	2	M. Hampton (USA)	20.29
	3	D. Evans (USA)	20.43
1980	1	P. Mennea (ITA)	20.19
	2	A. Wells (GBR)	20.21
	3	D. Quarrie (JAM)	20.29

400 metres

			Time
1948	1	A. Wint (JAM)	46.2
	2	H. McKenley (JAM)	46.4
	3	M. Whitfield (USA)	46.9
1952	1	G. Rhoden (JAM)	45.9
	2	H. McKenley (JAM)	45.9
	3	O. Matson (USA)	46.8
1956	1	C. Jenkins (USA)	46.7
	2	K.F. Haas (GER)	46.8
	V	Hellsten (FIN)	
	A.	Ignatiev (URS)	47.0
1960	1	O. Davis (USA)	44.9
	2	C. Kaufmann (GER)	44.9
	3	M. Spence (SAF)	45.5
1964	1	M. Larrabee (USA)	45.1
	2	W. Mottley (TRI)	45.2
	3	A. Badenski (POL)	45.6
1968	1	L. Evans (USA)	43.8
	2	L. James (USA)	43.9
	3	R. Freeman (USA)	44.4

1972	1 V. Matthews (USA)	44.66
	2 W. Collett (USA)	44.80
	3 J. Sang (KEN)	44.92
1976	1 A. Juantorena (CUB)	44.26
	2 F. Newhouse (USA)	44.40
	3 H. Frazier (USA)	44.95
1980	1 V. Markin (URS)	44.60
	2 R. Mitchell (AUS)	44.84
	3 F. Schaffer (GDR)	44.87

800 metres

		Time
1948	1 M. Whitfield (USA)	1:49.2
	2 A. Wint (JAM)	1:49.5
	3 M. Hansenne (FRA)	1:49.8
1952	1 M. Whitfield (USA)	1:49.2
	2 A. Wint (JAM)	1:49.4
	3 H. Ulzheimer (GER)	1:49.7
1956	1 T. Courtney (USA)	1:47.7
	2 D. Johnson (GBR)	1:47.8
	3 A. Boysen (NOR)	1:48.1
1960	1 P. Snell (NZL)	1:46.3
	2 R. Moens (BEL)	1:46.5
	3 G. Kerr (JAM)	1:47.1
1964	1 P. Snell (NZL)	1:45.1
	2 W. Crothers (CAN)	1:45.6
	3 W. Kiprugut (KEN)	1:45.9
1968	1 R. Doubell (AUS)	1:44.3
	2 W. Kiprugut (KEN)	1:44.5
	3 T. Farrell (USA)	1:45.4
1972	1 D. Wottle (USA)	1:45.9
	2 Y. Arzhanov (URS)	1:45.9
	3 M. Boit (KEN)	1:46.01
1976	1 A. Juantorena (CUB)	1:43.50
	2 I. Van Damme (BEL)	1:43.86
	3 R. Wohlhuter (USA)	1:44.12
1980	1 S. Ovett (GBR)	1:45.4
	2 S. Coe (GBR)	1:45.9
	3 N. Kirov (URS)	1:46.0

1500 metres

		Time
1948	1 H. Eriksson (SWE)	3:49.8
	2 L. Strand (SWE)	3:50.4
	3 W. Slijkhuis (HOL)	3:50.4
1952	1 J. Barthel (LUX)	3:45.1
	2 R. McMillen (USA)	3:45.2
	3 W. Lueg (GER)	3:45.4
1956	1 R. Delany (IRL)	3:41.2
	2 K. Richtzenhain (GER)	3:42.0
	3 J. Landy (AUS)	3:42.0
1960	1 H. Elliott (AUS)	3:35.6
	2 M. Jazy (FRA)	3:38.4
	3 I. Rózsavölgyi (HUN)	3:39.2
1964	1 P. Snell (NZL)	3:38.1
	2 J. Odlózil (TCH)	3:39.6
	3 J. Davies (NZL)	3:39.6
1968	1 K. Keino (KEN)	3:34.9
	2 J. Ryun (USA)	3:37.8
	3 B. Tümmler (FRA)	3:39.0
1972	1 P. Vasala (FIN)	3:36.3
	2 K. Keino (KEN)	3:36.8
	3 R. Dixon (NZL)	3:37.5
1976	1 J. Walker (NZL)	3:39.17
	2 I. Van Damme (BEL)	3:39.27
	3 P.H. Wellmann (GER)	3:39.33
1980	1 S. Coe (GBR)	3:38.4
	2 J. Straub (GDR)	3:38.8
	3 S. Ovett (GBR)	3:39.0

5000 metres

		Time
1948	1 G. Rieff (BEL)	14:17.6
	2 E. Zátopek (TCH)	14:17.8
	3 W. Slijkhuis (HOL)	14:26.8
1952	1 E. Zátopek (TCH)	14:06.6
	2 A. Mimoun (FRA)	14:07.4
	3 H. Schade (GER)	14:08.6
1956	1 V. Kuts (URS)	13:39.6
	2 G. Pirie (GBR)	13:50.6
	3 D. Ibbotson (GBR)	13:54.4

1960	1	M. Halberg (NZL)	13:43.4
	2	H. Grodotzki (GER)	13:44.6
	3	K. Zimny (POL)	13:44.8
1964	1	R. Schul (USA)	13:48.8
	2	H. Norpoth (GER)	13:49.6
	3	W. Dellinger (USA)	13:49.8
1968	1	M. Gammoudi (TUN)	13:05.0
	2	K. Keino (KEN)	14:05.2
	3	N. Temu (KEN)	14:06.4
1972	1	L. Virén (FIN)	13:26.4
	2	M. Gammoudi (TUN)	13:27.4
	3	I. Stewart (GBR)	13:27.6
1976	1	L. Virén (FIN)	13:24.76
	2	D. Quax (NZL)	13:25.16
	3	K.P. Hildenbrand (FRG)	13:25.38
1980	1	M. Yifter (ETH)	13:21.0
	2	S. Nyambui (TAN)	13:21.6
	3	K. Maaninka (FIN)	13:22.0

10000 metres

			Time
1948	1	E. Zátopek (TCH)	29:59.6
	2	A. Mimoun (FRA)	30:47.4
	3	B. Albertsson (SWE)	30:53.0
1952	1	E. Zátopek (TCH)	29:17.0
	2	A. Mimoun (FRA)	29:32.8
	3	A. Anufriev (URS)	29:48.2
1956	1	V. Kuts (URS)	28:45.6
	2	J. Kovács (HUN)	28:52.4
	3	A. Lawrence (AUS)	28:53.6
1960	1	P. Bolotnikov (URS)	28:32.2
	2	H. Grodotzki (GER)	28:37.0
	3	D. Power (AUS)	28:38.2
1964	1	B. Mills (USA)	28:24.4
	2	M. Gammoudi (TUN)	28:24.8
	3	R. Clarke (AUS)	28:25.8
1968	1	N. Temu (KEN)	29:27.4
	2	M. Wolde (ETH)	29:28.0
	3	M. Gammoudi (TUN)	29:34.2

1972	1	L. Virén (FIN)	27:38.4
	2	E. Puttemans (BEL)	27:39.6
	3	M. Yifter (ETH)	27:41.0
1976	1	L. Virén (FIN)	27:40.38
	2	C. Sousa Lopes (POR)	27:45.17
	3	B. Foster (GBR)	27:54.92
1980	1	M. Yifter (ETH)	27:42.7
	2	K. Maaninka (FIN)	27:44.3
	3	M. Kedir (ETH)	27:44.7

Marathon

			Time
1948	1	D. Cabrera (ARG)	2h 34:51.6
	2	T. Richards (GBR)	2h 35:07.6
	3	E. Gailly (BEL)	2h 35:33.6
1952	1	E. Zátopek (TCH)	2h 23:03.2
	2	R. Gorno (ARG)	2h 25:35.0
	3	G. Jansson (SWE)	2h 26:07.0
1956	1	A. Mimoun (FRA)	2h 25:00.0
	2	F. Mihalic (YUG)	2h 26:32.0
	3	V. Karvonen (FIN)	2h 27:47.0
1960	1	A. Bikila (ETH)	2h 15:16.2
	2	R. Ben Abdesselam (MAR)	2h 15:41.6
	2	B. Magee (NZL)	2h 17:18.2
1964	1	A. Bikila (ETH)	2h 12:11.2
	2	B. Heatley (GBR)	2h 16:19.2
	3	K. Tsuburaya (JPN)	2h 16:22.8
1968	1	M. Wolde (ETH)	2h 20:26.4
	2	K. Kimihara (JPN)	2h 23:31.0
	3	M. Ryan (NZL)	2h 23:45.0
1972	1	F. Shorter (USA)	2h 12:19.8
	2	K. Lismont (BEL)	2h 14:31.8
	3	M. Wolde (ETH)	2h 15:08.4
1976	1	W. Cierpinski (GDR)	2h 09:55.0
	2	F. Shorter (USA)	2h 10:45.8
	3	K. Lismont (BEL)	2h 11:12.6
1980	1	W. Cierpinski (GDR)	2h 11:03
	2	G. Nijboer (HOL)	2h 11:20
	3	S. Dzhumanazarov (URS)	2h 11:35

110 metre hurdles

		Time
1948	1 W. Porter (USA)	13.9
	2 C. Scott (USA)	14.1
	3 C. Dixon (USA)	14.1
1952	1 H. Dillard (USA)	13.7
	2 J. Davis (USA)	13.7
	3 A. Barnard (USA)	14.1
1956	1 L. Calhoun (USA)	13.5
	2 J. Davis (USA)	13.5
	3 J. Shankle (USA)	14.1
1960	1 L. Calhoun (USA)	13.8
	2 W. May (USA)	13.8
	3 H. Jones (USA)	14.0
1964	1 H. Jones (USA)	13.6
	2 B. Lindgren (USA)	13.7
	3 A. Mikhailov (URS)	13.7
1968	1 W. Davenport (USA)	13.3
	2 E. Hall (USA)	13.4
	3 E. Ottoz (ITA)	13.4
1972	1 R. Milburn (USA)	13.24
	2 G. Drut (FRA)	13.34
	3 T. Hill (USA)	13.48
1976	1 G. Drut (FRA)	13.30
	2 A. Casanas (CUB)	13.33
	3 W. Davenport (USA)	13.38
1980	1 T. Munkelt (GDR)	13.39
	2 A. Casanas (CUB)	13.40
	3 A. Puchkov (URS)	13.44

400 metre hurdles

		Time
1948	1 R. Cochran (USA)	51.1
	2 D. White (CEY)	51.8
	3 R. Larsson (SWE)	52.2
1952	1 C. Moore (USA)	50.8
	2 Y. Lituyev (URS)	51.3
	3 J. Holland (NZL)	52.2
1956	1 G. Davis (USA)	50.1
	2 E. Southern (USA)	50.8
	3 J. Culbreath (USA)	51.6

1960	1 G. Davis (USA)	49.3
	2 C. Cushman (USA)	49.6
	3 R. Howard (USA)	49.7
1964	1 R. Cawley (USA)	49.6
	2 J. Cooper (GBR)	50.1
	3 S. Morale (ITA)	50.1
1968	1 D. Hemery (GBR)	48.1
	2 G. Hennige (FRG)	49.0
	3 J. Sherwood (GBR)	49.0
1972	1 J. Akii-Bua (UGA)	47.82
	2 R. Mann (USA)	48.51
	3 D. Hemery (GBR)	48.52
1976	1 E. Moses (USA)	47.64
	2 M. Shine (USA)	48.69
	3 E. Gavrilenko (URS)	49.45
1980	1 V. Beck (GDR)	48.70
	2 V. Arkhipenko (URS)	48.86
	3 G. Oakes (GBR)	49.11

3000 metres steeplechase

		Time
1948	1 T. Sjöstrand (SWE)	9:04.6
	2 E. Elmsäter (SWE)	9:08.2
	3 G. Hagström (SWE)	9:11.8
1952	1 H. Ashenfelter (USA)	8:45.4
	2 V. Kazantsev (URS)	8:51.6
	3 J. Disley (GBR)	8:51.8
1956	1 C. Brasher (GBR)	8:41.2
	2 S. Rozsnyói (HUN)	8:43.6
	3 E. Larsen (NOR)	8:44.0
1960	1 Z. Krzyszkowiak (POL)	8:34.2
	2 N. Sokolov (URS)	8:36.4
	3 S. Rzhishchin (URS)	8:42.2
1964	1 G. Roelants (BEL)	8:30.8
	2 M. Herriott (GBR)	8:32.4
	3 I. Belyaiev (URS)	8:33.8
1968	1 A. Biwott (KEN)	8:51.0
	2 B. Kogo (KEN)	8:51.6
	3 G. Young (USA)	8:51.8

1972	1	K. Keino (KEN)	8:23.6
	2	B. Jipcho (KEN)	8:24.6
	3	T. Kantanen (FIN)	8:24.8
1976	1	A. Garderud (SWE)	8:08.02
	2	B. Malinowski (POL)	8:09.11
	3	F. Baumgartl (GDR)	8:10.36
1980	1	B. Malinowski (POL)	8:09.7
	2	F. Bayi (TAN)	8:12.5
	3	E. Tura (ETH)	8:13.6

20 kilometres walk

			Time
1956	1	L. Spirin (URS)	1h 31:27.4
	2	A. Mikenas (URS)	1h 32:03.0
	3	B. Junk (URS)	1h 32:12.0
1960	1	V. Golubnichiy (URS)	1h 34:07.2
	2	N. Freeman (AUS)	1h 34:16.4
	3	S. Vickers (GBR)	1h 34:56.4
1964	1	K. Matthews (GBR)	1h 29:34.0
	2	D. Lindner (GER)	1h 31:13.2
	3	V. Golubnichiy (URS)	1h 31:59.4
1968	1	V. Golubnichiy (URS)	1h 33:58.4
	2	J. Pedraza (MEX)	1h 34:00.0
	3	N. Smaga (URS)	1h 34:03.4
1972	1	P. Frenkel (GDR)	1h 26:42.4
	2	V. Golubnichiy (URS)	1h 26:55.2
	3	H. Reimann (GDR)	1h 27:16.6
1976	1	D. Bautista (MEX)	1h 24:40.6
	2	H. Reimann (GDR)	1h 25:13.8
	3	P. Frenkel (GDR)	1h 25:29.4
1980	1	M. Damilano (ITA)	1h 23:35.5
	2	P. Pochenchuk (URS)	1h 24:45.4
	3	R. Wieser (GDR)	1h 25:58.2

50 kilometres walk

			Time
1948	1	J. Ljunggren (SWE)	4h 41:52.0
	2	G. Godel (SUI)	4h 48:17.0
	3	T. Johnson (GBR)	4h 48:31.0
1952	1	G. Dordoni (ITA)	4h 28:07.8
	2	J. Dolezal (TCH)	4h 30:17.8
	3	A. Róka (HUN)	4h 31:27.2
1956	1	N. Read (NZL)	4h 30:42.8
	2	Y. Maskinskov (URS)	4h 32:57.0
	3	J. Ljunggren (SWE)	4h 35:02.0
1960	1	D. Thompson (GBR)	4h 25:30.0
	2	J. Ljunggren (SWE)	4h 25:47.0
	3	A. Pamich (ITA)	4h 27:55.4
1964	1	A. Pamich (ITA)	4h 11:12.4
	2	P. Nihill (GBR)	4h 11:31.2
	3	I. Pettersson (SWE)	4h 14:17.4
1968	1	C. Höhne (GDR)	4h 20:13.6
	2	A. Kiss (HUN)	4h 30:17.0
	3	L. Young (USA)	4h 31:55.4
1972	1	B. Kannenberg (FRA)	3h 56:11.6
	2	V. Soldatenko (URS)	3h 58:24.0
	3	L. Young (USA)	4h 00:46.0

1976 Not held

1980	1	H. Gauder (GDR)	3h 49:24
	2	J. Llopart (ESP)	3h 51:25
	3	Y. Ivchenko (URS)	3h 56:32

4 x 100 metres relay

	Gold	Silver	Bronze
1948	USA 40.6	GBR 41.3	ITA 41.5
1952	USA 40.1	URS 40.3	HUN 40.5
1956	USA 39.5	URS 39.8	GER 40.3
1960	GER 39.5	URS 40.1	GBR 40.2
1964	USA 39.0	POL 39.3	FRA 39.3
1968	USA 38.2	CUB 38.3	FRA 38.4
1972	USA 38.19	URS 38.50	FRG 38.79
1976	USA 38.33	GDR 38.66	URS 38.78
1980	URS 38.26	POL 38.33	FRA 38.53

4 x 400 metres relay

	Gold	Silver	Bronze
1948	USA 3:10.4	FRA 3:14.8	SWE 3:16.0
1952	JAM 3:03.9	USA 3:04.0	GER 3:06.6
1956	USA 3:04.8	AUS 3:06.2	GBR 3:07.2
1960	USA 3:02.2	GER 3:02.7	ANT 3:04.0
1964	USA 3:00.7	GBR 3:01.6	TRI 3:01.7
1968	USA 2:56.1	KEN 2:59.6	FRG 3:00.5
1972	KEN 2:59.8	GBR 3:00.5	FRA 3:00.7
1976	USA 2:58.65	POL 3:01.43	FRG 3:01.98
1980	URS 3:01.08	GDR 3:01.26	ITA 3:04.3

High Jump

			Distance
1948	1	J. Winter (AUS)	1.98m (6ft 6in)
	2	B. Paulsen (NOR)	1.95m (6ft 4¾in)
	3	G. Stanich (USA)	1.95m (6ft 4¾in)
1952	1	W. Davis (USA)	2.04m (6ft 8⅜in)
	2	K. Wiesner (USA)	2.01m (6ft 7⅛in)
	3	J. Telles da Conceição (BRA)	1.98m (6ft 6in)
1956	1	C. Dumas (USA)	2.12m (6ft 11½in)
	2	C. Porter (AUS)	2.10m (6ft 10⅝in)
	3	I. Kashkarov (USA)	2.08m (6ft 9⅞in)
1960	1	R. Shaveakadze (URS)	2.16m (7ft 1⅛in)
	2	V. Brumel (URS)	2.16m (7ft 1⅛in)
	3	J. Thomas (USA)	2.14m (7ft 0¼in)
1964	1	V. Brumel (URS)	2.18m (7ft 1¾in)
	2	J. Thomas (USA)	2.18m (7ft 1¾in)
	3	J. Rambo (USA)	2.16m (7ft 1in)
1968	1	R. Fosbury (USA)	2.24m (7ft 4¼in)
	2	E. Caruthers (USA)	2.22m (7ft 3½in)
	3	V. Gavrilov (URS)	2.20m (7ft 2⅝in)

1972	1	Y. Tarmak (URS)	2.23m (7ft 3¾in)
	2	S. Junge (GDR)	2.21m (7ft 3in)
	3	D. Stones (USA)	2.21m (7ft 3in)
1976	1	J. Wszola (POL)	2.25m (7ft 4½in)
	2	G. Joy (CAN)	2.23m (7ft 3¾in)
	3	D. Stones (USA)	2.21m (7ft 3in)
1980	1	G. Wessig (GDR)	2.36m (7ft 8¾in)
	2	J. Wszola (POL)	2.31m (7ft 7in)
	3	J. Freimuth (GDR)	2.31m (7ft 7in)

Long jump

			Distance
1948	1	W. Steele (USA)	7.82m (25ft 8in)
	2	T. Bruce (AUS)	7.55m (24ft 9¼in)
	3	H. Douglas (USA)	7.54m (24ft 9in)
1952	1	J. Biffle (USA)	7.57m (24ft 10in)
	2	M. Gourdine (USA)	7.53m (24ft 8½in)
	3	O. Földessy (HUN)	7.30m (23ft 11½in)
1956	1	G. Bell (USA)	7.83m (25ft 8¼in)
	2	J. Bennett (USA)	7.68m (25ft 2¼in)
	3	J. Valkama (FIN)	7.48m (24ft 6½in)
1960	1	R. Boston (USA)	8.12m (26ft 7¾in)
	2	I. Roberson (USA)	8.11m (26ft 7¼in)
	3	I. Ter-Ovanesyan (URS)	8.04m (26ft 4½in)
1964	1	L. Davies (GBR)	8.07m (26ft 5¾in)
	2	R. Boston (USA)	8.03m (26ft 4¼in)
	3	I. Ter-Ovanesyan (URS)	7.99m (26ft 2¾in)
1968	1	R. Beamon (USA)	8.90m (29ft 2½in)
	2	K. Beer (GDR)	8.19m (26ft 10½in)
	3	R. Boston (USA)	8.16m (26ft 9¼in)
1972	1	R. Williams (USA)	8.24m (27ft 0½in)
	2	H. Baumgärtner (FRG)	8.18m (26ft 10in)
	3	A. Robinson (USA)	8.03m (26ft 4¼in)
1976	1	A. Robinson (USA)	8.35m (27ft 4¾in)
	2	R. Williams (USA)	8.11m (26ft 7¼in)
	3	F. Wartenberg (GDR)	8.02m (26ft 3¾in)
1980	1	L. Dombrowski (GDR)	8.54m (28ft 0¼in)
	2	F. Paschek (GDR)	8.21m (26ft 11¼in)
	3	V. Podluzhny (URS)	8.18m (26ft 10in)

Triple jump

			Distance
1948	1	A. Åhman (SWE)	15.40 (50ft 6¼in)
	2	G. Avery (AUS)	15.37m (50ft 5in)
	3	R. Sarialp (TUR)	15.02m (49ft 3½in)
1952	1	A.F. da Silva (BRA)	16.22m (53ft 2½in)
	2	L. Shcherbakov (URS)	15.98m (52ft 5¼in)
	3	A. Devonish (VEN)	15.52m (50ft 11in)

1956	1	A.F. da Silva (BRA)	16.35m (53ft 7¾in)
	2	V. Einarsson (ISL)	16.26m (53ft 4¼in)
	3	V. Kreyer (URS)	16.02m (52ft 6¾in)
1960	1	J. Szmidt (POL)	16.81m (55ft 1¾in)
	2	V. Goryayev (URS)	16.63m (54ft 6¾in)
	3	V. Kreyer (URS)	16.43m (53ft 10¾in)
1964	1	J. Szmidt (POL)	16.85m (55ft 3½in)
	2	O. Fedoseyev (URS)	16.58m (54ft 4¾in)
	3	V. Kravchenko (URS)	16.57m (54ft 4¼in)
1968	1	V. Saneyev (URS)	17.39m (57ft 0¾in)
	2	N. Prudencio (BRA)	17.27m (56ft 8in)
	3	G. Gentile (ITA)	17.22m (56ft 6in)
1972	1	V. Saneyev (URS)	17.35m (56ft 11¼in)
	2	J. Drehmel (GDR)	17.31m (56ft 9½in)
	3	N. Prudencio (BRA)	17.05m (55ft 11¼in)
1976	1	V. Saneyev (URS)	17.29m (56ft 8¾in)
	2	J. Butts (USA)	17.18m (56ft 4⅜in)
	3	J.C. de Oliviera (BRA)	16.90m (55ft 5⅜in)
1980	1	J. Uudmäe (URS)	17.35m (56ft 11¼in)
	2	V. Saneyev (URS)	17.24m (56ft 6¾in)
	3	J.C. de Oliveira (BRA)	17.22m (56ft 6in)

Pole vault

			Distance
1948	1	O.G. Smith (USA)	4.30m (14ft 1¼in)
	2	E. Kataja (FIN)	4.20m (13ft 9½in)
	3	R. Richards (USA)	4.20m (13ft 9½in)
1952	1	R. Richards (USA)	4.55m (14ft 11¼in)
	2	D. Laz (USA)	4.50m (14ft 9¼in)
	3	R. Lundberg (SWE)	4.40m (14ft 5¼in)
1956	1	R. Richards (USA)	4.56m (14ft 11½in)
	2	R. Gutowski (USA)	4.53m (14ft 10¼in)
	3	G. Roubanis (GRE)	4.50m (14ft 9¼in)
1960	1	D. Bragg (USA)	4.70m (15ft 5in)
	2	R. Morris (USA)	4.60m (15ft 1¼in)
	3	E. Landström (FIN)	4.55m (14ft 11¼in)
1964	1	F. Hansen (USA)	5.10m (16ft 8¾in)
	2	W. Reinhardt (GER)	5.05m (16ft 6¾in)
	3	K. Lehnertz (GER)	5.00m (16ft 5in)
1968	1	R. Seagren (USA)	5.40m (17ft 8½in)
	2	C. Schiprowski (FRG)	5.40m (17ft 8½in)
	3	W. Nordwig (GDR)	5.40m (17ft 8½in)
1972	1	W. Nordwig (GDR)	5.50m (18ft 0½in)
	2	R. Seagren (USA)	5.40m (17ft 8½in)
	3	J. Johnson (USA)	5.35m (17ft 6½in)

1976	1	T. Slusarski (POL)	5.50m (18ft 0½in)
	2	A. Kalliomaki (FIN)	5.50m (18ft 0½in)
	3	D. Roberts (USA)	5.50m (18ft 0½in)
1980	1	W. Kozakiewicz (POL)	5.78m (18ft 11½in)
	2	T. Slusarski (POL)	5.65m (18ft 6½in)
		K. Volkov (URS)	5.65m (18ft 6½in)

Shot

			Distance
1948	1	W. Thompson (USA)	17.12m (56ft 2in)
	2	J. Delaney (USA)	16.68m (54ft 8¾in)
	3	J. Fuchs (USA)	16.42m (53ft 10½in)
1952	1	P. O'Brien (USA)	17.41m (57ft 1½in)
	2	D. Hooper (USA)	17.39m (57ft 0¾in)
	3	J. Fuchs (USA)	17.06m (55ft 11¾in)
1956	1	P. O'Brien (USA)	18.57m (60ft 11¼in)
	2	W. Nieder (USA)	18.18m (59ft 7¾in)
	3	J. Skobla (TCH)	17.65m (57ft 11in)
1960	1	W. Nieder (USA)	19.68m (64ft 6¾in)
	2	P. O'Brien (USA)	19.11m (62ft 8¼in)
	3	D. Long (USA)	19.01m (62ft 4¼in)
1964	1	D. Long (USA)	20.33m (66ft 8½in)
	2	R. Matson (USA)	20.20m (66ft 3¼in
	3	V. Varju (HUN)	19.39m (63ft 7½in)
1968	1	R. Matson (USA)	20.54m (67ft 4¾in)
	2	G. Woods (USA)	20.12m (66ft 0¼in)
	3	E. Gushchin (URS)	20.09m (65ft 11in)
1972	1	W. Komar (POL)	21.18m (69ft 6in)
	2	G. Woods (USA)	21.17m (69ft 5½in)
	3	H. Briesenick (GDR)	21.14m (69ft 4¼in)
1976	1	U. Beyer (GDR)	21.05m (69ft 0¾in)
	2	E. Mironov (URS)	21.03m (69ft 0in)
	3	A. Barishnikov (URS)	21.00m (68ft 10¾in)
1980	1	V. Kiselyev (URS)	21.35m (70ft 0½in)
	2	A. Baryshnikov (URS)	21.08m (69ft 2in)
	3	U. Beyer (GDR)	21.06m (69ft 1½in)

Discus

			Distance
1948	1	A. Consolin (ITA)	52.78m (172ft 2in)
	2	G. Tosi (ITA)	51.78m (169ft 10½in)
	3	F. Gordien (USA)	50.77m (166ft 7in)
1952	1	S. Iness (USA)	55.03m (180ft 6½in)
	2	A. Consolini (ITA)	53.78m (176ft 5in)
	3	J. Dillion (USA)	53.28m (174ft 9½in)
1956	1	A. Oerter (USA)	56.36m (184ft 11in)
	2	F. Gordien (USA)	54.81m (179ft 9in)
	3	D. Koch (USA)	54.40m (178ft 5½in)

1960	1	A. Oerter (USA)	59.18m (194ft 1¾in)
	2	R. Babka (USA)	58.01m (190ft 4¼in)
	3	R. Cochran (USA)	57.16m (187ft 6¼in)
1964	1	A. Oerter (USA)	61.00m (200ft 1½in)
	2	L. Danek (TCH)	60.52m (198ft 6½in)
	3	D. Weill (USA)	59.49m (195ft 2in)
1968	1	A. Oerter (USA)	64.78m (212ft 6½in)
	2	L. Milde (GDR)	63.08m (206ft 11½in)
	3	L. Danek (TCH)	62.92m (206ft 5in)
1972	1	L. Danek (TCH)	64.40m (211ft 3in)
	2	L.J. Silvester (USA)	63.50m (208ft 4in)
	3	R. Bruch (SWE)	63.40m (208ft 0in)
1976	1	M. Wilkins (USA)	67.50m (221ft 5½in)
	2	W. Schmidt (GDR)	66.22m (217ft 3in)
	3	J. Powell (USA)	65.70m (215ft 6⅝in)
1980	1	V. Rashchupkin (URS)	66.64m (218ft 8in)
	2	I. Bugár (TCH)	66.38m (217ft 9in)
	3	L. Delis (CUB)	66.32m (217ft 7in)

Hammer

			Distance
1948	1	I. Németh (HUN)	56.07m (183ft 11½in)
	2	I. Gubijan (YUG)	54.27m (178ft 0½in)
	3	R. Bennett (USA)	53.73m (176ft 3½in)
1952	1	J. Csermák (HUN)	60.34m (197ft 11½in)
	2	K. Storch (GER)	58.86m (193ft 1in)
	3	I. Németh (HUN)	57.74m (189ft 5in)
1956	1	H. Connolly (USA)	63.19m (207ft 3½in)
	2	M. Krivonosov (URS)	63.03m (206ft 9½in)
	3	A. Samotsvetov (URS)	62.56m (205ft 3in)
1960	1	V. Rudenkov (URS)	67.10m (220ft 1¾in)
	2	H. Zsivótzky (HUN)	65.79m (215ft 10in)
	3	T. Rut (POL)	65.64m (215ft 4½in)
1964	1	R. Klim (URS)	69.74m (228ft 10in)
	2	G. Zsivótzky (HUN)	69.09m (226ft 8in)
	3	U. Beyer (GER)	68.09m (223ft 4½in)
1968	1	G. Zsivótzky (HUN)	73.36m (240ft 8in)
	2	R. Klim (URS)	73.28m (240ft 5in)
	3	L. Lovász (HUN)	69.78m (228ft 11in)
1972	1	A. Bondarchuk (URS)	75.50m (247ft 8in)
	2	J. Sachse (GDR)	74.96m (245ft 11in)
	3	V. Khmelevski (URS)	74.04m (242ft 11in)
1976	1	Y. Sedykh (URS)	77.52m (254ft 4in)
	2	A. Spiridonov (URS)	76.08m (249ft 7½in)
	3	A. Bondarchuk (URS)	75.48m (247ft 7¾in)

1980	1	Y. Sedykh (URS)	81.80m
			(268ft 4in)
	2	S. Litvinov (URS)	80.64m
			(264ft 7in)
	3	Y. Tamm (URS)	78.96m
			(259ft 1in)

Javelin

			Distance
1948	1	T. Rautavaara (FIN)	69.77m
			(228ft 11in)
	2	S. Seymour (USA)	67.56m
			(221ft 8in)
	0	J. Várszegi (HUN)	67.03m
			(219ft 11in)
1952	1	C. Young (USA)	73.78m
			(242ft 0½in)
	2	W. Miller (USA)	72.46m
			(237ft 8½in)
	3	T. Hyytiäinen (FIN)	71.89m
			(235ft 10½in)
1956	1	E. Danielsen (NOR)	85.71m
			(281ft 2½in)
	2	J. Sidlo (POL)	79.98m
			(262ft 4½in)
	3	V. Tsibulenko (URS)	79.50m
			(260ft 10in)
1960	1	V. Tsibulenko (URS)	84.64m
			(277ft 8in)
	2	W. Krüger (GER)	79.36m
			(260ft 4½in)
	3	G. Kulcsár (HUN)	78.57m
			(257ft 9½in)
1964	1	P. Nevala (FIN)	82.66m
			(271ft 2in)
	2	G. Kulcsár (HUN)	82.32m
			(270ft 0½in)
	3	Y. Lusis (URS)	80.57m
			(264ft 4½in)
1968	1	Y. Lusis (URS)	90.10m
			(295ft 7in)
	2	J. Kinnunen (FIN)	88.58m
			(290ft 7½in)
	3	G. Kulcsár (HUN)	87.06m
			(285ft 7½in)

1972	1	K. Wolfermann (FRG)	90.48m
			(296ft 10in)
	2	Y. Lusis (URS)	90.46m
			(296ft 9in)
	3	W. Schmidt (USA)	84.42m
			(276ft 11in)
1976	1	M. Németh (HUN)	94.58m
			(310ft 3⅞in)
	2	H. Siitonen (FIN)	87.92m
			(288ft 5½in)
	3	G. Megelea (ROM)	87.16m
			(285ft 11⅞in)
1980	1	D. Kula (URS)	91.20m
			(299ft 2in)
	2	A. Makarov (URS)	89.64m
			(294ft 1in)
	3	W. Hanisch (GDR)	86.72m
			(284ft 6in)

Decathlon

There are ten events over two days. The first day's events are: 100 metres, long jump, shot, high jump and 400 metres. The 110 metres hurdles, discus, pole vault, javelin and 1500 metres are held on the second day.

			Points
1948	1	R. Mathias (USA)	7139
	2	I. Heinrich (FRA)	6974
	3	F. Simmons (USA)	6950
1952	1	R. Mathias (USA)	7887
	2	M. Campbell (USA)	6975
	3	F. Simmons (USA)	6788
1956	1	M. Campbell (USA)	7937
	2	R. Johnson (USA)	7587
	3	V. Kuznetsov (URS)	7465
1960	1	R. Johnson (USA)	8392
	2	C.K. Yang (ROC)	8334
	3	V. Kuznetsov (URS)	7809
1964	1	W. Holdorf (GER)	7887
	2	R. Aun (URS)	7842
	3	H.J. Walde (GER)	7809

1968	1	B. Toomey (USA)	8193
	2	H.J. Walde (FRG)	8111
	3	K. Bendlin (FRG)	8064
1972	1	N. Avilov (URS)	8454
	2	L. Litvinenko (URS)	8035
	3	R. Katus (POL)	7984
1976	1	B. Jenner (USA)	8618
	2	G. Kratschmer (FRG)	8411
	3	N. Avilov (URS)	8369
1980	1	D. Thompson (GBR)	8495
	2	Y. Kutsenko (URS)	8331
	3	S. Zhelanov (URS)	8135

Athletics (women)
100 metres

			Time
1948	1	F. Blankers-Koen (HOL)	11.9
	2	D. Manley (GBR)	12.2
	3	S. Strickland (AUS)	12.2
1952	1	M. Jackson (AUS)	11.5
	2	D. Hasenjager (SAF)	11.8
	3	S. Strickland (AUS)	11.9
1956	1	B. Cuthbert (AUS)	11.5
	2	C. Stubnick (GER)	11.7
	3	M. Matthews (AUS)	11.7
1960	1	W. Rudolph (USA)	11.0
	2	D. Hyman (GBR)	11.3
	3	G. Leone (ITA)	11.3
1964	1	W. Tyus (USA)	11.4
	2	E. Maguire (USA)	11.6
	3	E. Klobukowska (POL)	11.6
1968	1	W. Tyus (USA)	11.0
	2	B. Ferrell (USA)	11.1
	3	I. Kirzenstein-Szewinska (POL)	11.1
1972	1	R. Stecher (GDR)	11.07
	2	R. Boyle (AUS)	11.23
	3	S. Chivas (CUB)	11.24
1976	1	A. Richter (GDR)	11.08
	2	R. Stecher (GDR)	11.13
	3	I. Helten (FRG)	11.17
1980	1	L. Kondratyeva (URS)	11.06
	2	M. Göhr (GDR)	11.07
	3	I. Auerswald (GDR)	11.14

200 metres

			Time
1948	1	F. Blankers-Koen (HOL)	24.4
	2	A. Williamson (GBR)	25.1
	3	A. Patterson (USA)	25.2
1952	1	M. Jackson (AUS)	23.7
	2	B. Brouwer (HOL)	24.2
	3	N. Khnykina (URS)	24.2

1956	1	B. Cuthbert (AUS)	23.4
	2	C. Stubnick (GER)	23.7
	3	M. Matthews (AUS)	23.8
1960	1	W. Rudolph (USA)	24.0
	2	J. Heine (GER)	24.4
	3	D. Hyman (GBR)	24.7
1964	1	E. Maguire (USA)	23.0
	2	I. Kirszenstein (POL)	23.1
	3	M. Black (AUS)	23.1
1968	1	I. Kirzenstein-Szewinska (POL)	22.5
	2	R. Boyle (AUS)	22.7
	3	J. Lamy (AUS)	22.8
1972	1	R. Stecher (GDR)	22.40
	2	R. Boyle (AUS)	22.45
	3	I. Kirzenstein-Szewinska (POL)	22.74
1976	1	B. Eckert (GDR)	22.37
	2	A. Richter (FRG)	22.39
	3	R. Stecher (GDR)	22.47
1980	1	B. Wöckel (GDR)	22.03
	2	N. Bochina (URS)	22.19
	3	M. Ottey (JAM)	22.20

400 metres

			Time
1964	1	B. Cuthbert (AUS)	52.0
	2	A. Packer (GBR)	52.2
	3	J. Amoore (AUS)	53.4
1968	1	C. Besson (FRA)	52.0
	2	L. Board (GBR)	52.1
	3	N. Pechenkina (URS)	52.2
1972	1	M. Zehrt (GDR)	51.08
	2	R. Wilden (FRG)	51.21
	3	K. Hammond (USA)	51.64
1976	1	I. Kirzenstein-Szewinska (POL)	49.29
	2	C. Brehmer (GDR)	50.51
	3	E. Streidt (GDR)	50.55
1980	1	M. Koch (GDR)	48.88
	2	J. Kratochvilova (TCH)	49.46
	3	C. Lathan (GDR)	49.66

800 metres

			Time
1960	1	L. Shevtsova (URS)	2:04.3
	2	B. Jones (AUS)	2:04.4
	3	U. Donath (GER)	2:05.6
1964	1	A. Packer (GBR)	2:01.1
	2	M. Dupureur (FRA)	2:01.9
	3	M. Chamberlain (NZL)	2:02.8
1968	1	M. Manning (USA)	2:00.9
	2	I. Silai (ROM)	2:02.5
	3	M. Gommers (HOL)	2:02.6
1972	1	H. Falck (FRG)	1:58.6
	2	N. Sabaite (URS)	1:58.7
	3	G. Hoffmeister (GDR)	1:59.2
1976	1	T. Kazankina (URS)	1:54.94
	2	H. Chtereva (BUL)	1:55.42
	3	E. Zinn (GDR)	1:55.60
1980	1	N. Olizarenko (URS)	1:53.5
	2	O. Mineyeva (URS)	1:54.9
	3	T. Providokhina (URS)	1:55.5

1500 metres

			Time
1972	1	L. Bragina (URS)	4:01.4
	2	G. Hoffmeister (GDR)	4:02.8
	3	P. Cacchi (ITA)	4:02.9
1976	1	T. Kazankina (URS)	4:05.48
	2	G. Hoffmeister (GDR)	4:06.22
	3	H. Klapezynski (GDR)	4:06.09
1980	1	T. Kazankina (URS)	3:56.6
	2	C. Wartenberg (GDR)	3:57.8
	3	N. Olizarenko (URS)	3:59.6

80 metres hurdles
(Became 100 metres hurdles in 1972)

			Time
1948	1	F. Blankers-Koen (HOL)	11.2
	2	M. Gardner (GBR)	11.2
	3	S. Strickland de la Hunty (AUS)	11.4

1952	1	S. (Strickland) de la Hunty (AUS)	10.9
	2	M. Golubnichaya (URS)	11.1
	3	M. Sander (GER)	11.1
1956	1	S. (Strickland) de la Hunty (AUS)	10.7
	2	G. (Köhler) Birkemeyer (GER)	10.9
	3	N. Thrower (AUS)	11.0
1960	1	I. Press (URS)	10.8
	2	C. Quinton (GBR)	10.9
	3	G. (Köhler) Birkemeyer (GER)	11.0
1964	1	K. Balzer (GER)	10.5
	2	T. Ciepla (POL)	10.5
	3	P. Kilborn (AUS)	10.5
1968	1	M. Caird (AUS)	10.3
	2	P. Kilborn (AUS)	10.4
	3	C. Cheng (ROC)	10.4

100 metres hurdles

			Time
1972	1	A. Ehrhardt (GDR)	12.59
	2	V. Bufanu (ROM)	12.84
	3	K. Balzer (GDR)	12.90
1976	1	J. Schaller (GDR)	12.77
	2	T. Anisimova (URS)	12.78
	3	N. Lebedeva (URS)	12.80
1980	1	V. Komisova (URS)	12.56
	2	J. (Scheller) Klier (GDR)	12.63
	3	L. Langer (POL)	12.65

4 x 100 metres relay

	Gold	Silver	Bronze
1948	HOL 47.5	AUS 47.6	CAN 47.8
1952	USA 45.9	GER 45.9	GBR 46.2
1956	AUS 44.5	GBR 44.7	USA 44.9
1960	USA 44.5	GER 44.8	POL 45.0
1964	POL 43.6	USA 43.9	GBR 44.0
1968	USA 42.8	CUB 43.3	URS 43.4
1972	FRG 42.81	GDR 42.95	CUB 43.36
1976	GDR 42.55	FRG 42.59	URS 43.09
1980	GDR 41.60	URS 42.10	GBR 42.43

4 x 400 metres relay

	Gold	Silver	Bronze
1972	GDR 3:23.0	USA 3:25.2	FRG 3:26.5
1976	GDR 3:19.23	USA 3:22.81	URS 3:24.24
1980	URS 3:20.12	GDR 3:20.35	GBR 3:27.5

High jump

			Distance
1948	1	A. Coachman (USA)	1.68m (5ft 6¼in)
	2	D.(Odam) Tyler (GBR)	1.68m (5ft 6¼in)
	3	M. Ostermeyer (FRA)	1.61m (5ft 3¼in)
1952	1	E. Brand (SAF)	1.67m (5ft 5¾in)
	2	S. Lerwill (GBR)	1.65m (5ft 5¼in)
	3	A. Chudina (URS)	1.63m (5ft 4in)
1956	1	M. McDaniel (USA)	1.76m (5ft 9¼in)
	2	T. Hopkins (GBR) M. Pisaryeva (URS)	1.67m (5ft 5¾in)
1960	1	I. Balaş (ROM)	1.85m (6ft 0¾in)
	2	J. Jóźwiakowska (POL) D. Shirley (GBR)	1.71m (5ft 7¼in)
1964	1	I. Balaş (ROM)	1.90m (6ft 2¾in)
	2	M. Brown (AUS)	1.80m (5ft 11in)
	3	T. Chenchik (URS)	1.78m (5ft 10in)
1968	1	M. Rezková (TCH)	1.82m (5ft 11¾in)
	2	A. Okorokova (URS)	1.80m (5ft 10¾in)
	3	V. Kozyr (URS)	1.80m (5ft 10¾in)
1972	1	U. Meyfarth (FRG)	1.92m (6ft 3½in)
	2	Y. Blagoyeva (BUL)	1.88m (6ft 2in)
	3	I. Gusenbauer (AUT)	1.88m (6ft 2in)
1976	1	R. Ackermann (GDR)	1.93m (6ft 4in)
	2	S. Simeoni (ITA)	1.91m (6ft 3¼in)
	3	Y. Blagoyeva (BUL)	1.91m (6ft 3¼in)
1980	1	S. Simeoni (ITA)	1.97m (6ft 5½in)
	2	U. Kielan (POL)	1.94m (6ft 4¼in)
	3	J. Kirst (GDR)	1.94m (6ft 4¼in)

Long jump

			Distance
1948	1	O. Gyarmati (HUN)	5.70m (18ft 8¼in)
	2	N.S. de Portela (ARG)	5.60m (18ft 4½in)
	3	A. Leyman (SWE)	5.58m (18ft 3¾in)
1952	1	Y. Williams (NZL)	6.24m (20ft 5½in)
	2	A. Chudina (URS)	6.14m (20ft 1¾in)
	3	S. Cawley (GBR)	5.92m (19ft 5in)
1956	1	E. Krzesinska (POL)	6.35m (20ft 10in)
	2	W. White (USA)	6.09m (19ft 11¾in)
	3	N. (Khnykina) Dvalishvili (URS)	6.07m (19ft 11in)
1960	1	V. Krepkina (URS)	6.37m (20ft 10¾in)
	2	E. Krzesinska (POL)	6.27m (20ft 6¾in)
	3	H. Claus (GER)	6.21m (20ft 4½in)
1964	1	M. Rand (GBR)	6.76m (22ft 2¼in)
	2	I. Kirszenstein Szewińska (POL)	6.60m (21ft 7¾in)
	3	T. Shchelkanova (URS)	6.42m (21ft 0¾in)

1968	1	V. Viscopoleanu (ROM)	6.82m (22ft 4½in)
	2	S. Sherwood (GBR)	6.68m (21ft 11in)
	3	T. Talysheva (URS)	6.66m (21ft 10¼in)
1972	1	H. Rosendahl (FRG)	6.78m (22ft 3in)
	2	D. Yorgova (BUL)	6.77m (22ft 2½in)
	3	E. Suranová (TCH)	6.67m (21ft 10¾in)
1976	1	A. Voigt (GDR)	6.72m (22ft 0¾in)
	2	K. McMillan (USA)	6.66m (21ft 10⅛in)
	3	L. Alfeeva (URS)	6.60m (21ft 7¾in)
1980	1	T. Kolpakova (URS)	7.06m (23ft 2in)
	2	B. Wujak (GDR)	7.04m (23ft 1¼in)
	3	T. Skatchko (URS)	7.01m (23ft 0in)

Shot

			Distance
1948	1	M. Ostermeyer (FRA)	13.75m (45ft 1½in)
	2	A. Piccinini (ITA)	13.10m (42ft 11¼in)
	3	I. Schäffer (AUT)	13.08m (42ft 10¾in)
1952	1	G. Zybina (URS)	15.28m (50ft 1½in)
	2	M. Werner (GER)	14.57m (47ft 9½in)
	3	K. Tochenova (URS)	14.50m (47ft 6¾in)
1956	1	T. Tyshkevich (URS)	16.59m (54ft 5in)
	2	G. Zybina (URS)	16.53m (54ft 2¾in)
	3	M. Werner (GER)	15.61m (51ft 2½in)
1960	1	T. Press (URS)	17.32m (56ft 10in)
	2	J. Lüttge (GER)	16.61m (54ft 6in)
	3	E. Brown (USA)	16.42m (53ft 10½in)
1964	1	T. Press (URS)	18.14m (59ft 6in)
	2	R. Garisch (GER)	17.61m (57ft 9¼in)
	3	G. Zybina (URS)	17.45m (57ft 3in)
1968	1	M. Gummel (GDR)	19.61m (64ft 4in)
	2	M. Lange (GDR)	18.78m (61ft 7½in)
	3	N. Chizhova (URS)	18.19m (59ft 8¼in)
1972	1	N. Chizhova (URS)	21.03m (69ft 0in)
	2	M. Gummel (GDR)	20.22m (66ft 4¼in)
	3	I. Khristova (BUL)	19.35m (63ft 6in)
1976	1	I. Christova (BUL)	21.16m (69ft 5⅛in)
	2	N. Chizhova (URS)	20.96m (68ft 9¼in)
	3	H. Fibingerova (TCH)	20.67m (67ft 9¾in)
1980	1	I. Slupianek (GDR)	22.41m (73ft 6¼in)
	2	S. Krachevskaya (URS)	21.42m (70ft 3½in)
	3	M. Pufe (GDR)	21.20m (69ft 6¾in)

Discus

			Distance
1948	1	M. Ostermeyer (FRA)	41.92m (137ft 6⅛in)
	2	E. Gentile Cordiale (ITA)	41.17m (135ft 0⅞in)
	3	J. Mazeas (FRA)	40.47m (132ft 9½in)

1952	1	N. Romashkova (URS)	51.42m (168ft 8½in)
	2	Y. Bagryantseva (URS)	47.08m (154ft 5⅝in)
	3	N. Dumbadze (URS)	46.29m (151ft 10½in)
1956	1	O. Fikotová (TCH)	53.69m (176ft 1½in)
	2	I. Beglyakova (URS)	52.54m (172ft 4½in)
	3	N. Ponomareva (URS)	52.02m (170ft 8in)
1960	1	N. Ponomareva (URS)	55.10m (180ft 9¼in)
	2	T. Press (URS)	52.59m (172ft 6½in)
	3	L. Manoliu (ROM)	52.36m (171ft 9½in)
1964	1	T. Press (URS)	57.27m (187ft 10½in)
	2	I. Lotz (GER)	57.21m (187ft 8½in)
	3	L. Manoliu (ROM)	56.97m (186ft 11in)
1968	1	L. Manoliu (ROM)	58.28m (191ft 2½in)
	2	L. Westermann (FRG)	57.76m (189ft 6in)
	3	J. Kleiber (HUN)	54.90m (180ft 1½in)
1972	1	F. Melnik (URS)	66.62m (218ft 7in)
	2	A. Menis (ROM)	65.06m (213ft 5in)
	3	V. Stoeva (BUL)	64.34m (211ft 1in)
1976	1	E. Schlaak (GDR)	69.00m (226ft 4⅜in)
	2	M. Vergova (BUL)	67.30m (220ft 9⅝in)
	3	G. Hinzmann (GDR)	66.84m (219ft 5⅝in)
1980	1	E. Jahl (GDR)	69.96m (229ft 6in)
	2	M. Petkova (BUL)	67.90m (222ft 9in)
	3	T. Lesovaya (URS)	67.40m (221ft 1in)

Javelin

			Distance
1948	1	H. Bauma (AUT)	45.57m (149ft 6in)
	2	K. Parviänen (FIN)	43.79m (143ft 8⅛in)
	3	L. Carlstedt (DEN)	42.80m (140ft 5⅛in)
1952	1	D. Zátopková (TCH)	50.47m (165ft 7in)
	2	A. Chudina (URS)	50.01m (164ft 0⅞in)
	3	T. Gorchakova (URS)	49.76m (163ft 3⅛in)
1956	1	I. Yaunzeme (URS)	53.86m (176ft 8½in)
	2	M. Ahrens (CHI)	50.38m (165ft 3½in)
	3	N. Konyaeva (URS)	50.28m (164ft 11½in)
1960	1	E. Ozolina (URS)	55.98m (183ft 8in)
	2	D. Zátopková (TCH)	53.78m (176ft 5¼in)
	3	B. Kalediene (URS)	53.45m (175ft 4½in)
1964	1	M. Penes (ROM)	60.54 (198ft 7½in)
	2	M. Rudas (HUN)	58.27m (191ft 2in)
	3	Y. Gorchakova (URS)	57.06m (187ft 2½in)
1968	1	A. Németh (HUN)	60.36m (198ft 0½in)
	2	M. Penes (ROM)	59.92m (196ft 7in)
	3	E. Janko (AUT)	58.04m (190ft 5in)

1972	1	R. Fuchs (GDR)	63.88m
			(209ft 7in)
	2	J. Todten (GDR)	62.54m
			(205ft 2in)
	3	K. Schmidt (USA)	59.94m
			(196ft 8in)
1976	1	R. Fuchs (GDR)	65.94m
			(216ft 4¼in)
	2	M. Becker (FRG)	64.70m
			(212ft 3¼in)
	3	K. Schmidt (USA)	63.96m
			(209ft 10¼in)
1980	1	M. Colon (CUB)	68.40m
			(224ft 5in)
	2	S. Gunba (URS)	67.76m
			(222ft 4in)
	3	U. Hommola (GDR)	66.56m
			(218ft 4in)

Pentathlon

There are five events over two days. The first day's events are: 80 metres hurdles (100 metres hurdles after 1968), shot, high jump. Long jump and 200 metres are held on the second day.

			Points
1964	1	I. Press (URS)	5246
	2	M. Rand (GBR)	5035
	3	G. Bystrova (URS)	4956
1968	1	I. Becker (FRG)	5098
	2	L. Prokop (AUT)	4966
	3	A. Toth (HUN)	4959
1972	1	M. Peters (GBR)	4801
	2	H. Rosendahl (FRG)	4791
	3	B. Pollak (GDR)	4768
1976	1	S. Siegl (GDR)	4745
	2	C. Laser (GDR)	4745
	3	B. Pollak (GDR)	4740
1980	1	N. Tkachenko (URS)	5083
	2	O. Rukavishnikova (URS)	4937
	3	O. Kuragina (URS)	4875

Basketball (women)

	Gold	Silver	Bronze
1976	URS	USA	BUL
1980	URS	BUL	YUG

Basketball (men)

	Gold	Silver	Bronze
1948	USA	FRA	BRA
1952	USA	URS	URU
1956	USA	URS	URU
1960	USA	URS	BRA
1964	USA	URS	BRA
1968	USA	YUG	URS
1972	URS	USA	CUB
1976	USA	YUG	URS
1980	YUG	ITA	URS

Boxing
(Since 1952 losing semi-finalists are awarded bronze medals)

Light flyweight
Weight limit 48kg (105lb 13oz)

1968	1	F. Rodriguez (VEN)
	2	Y.J. Jee (KOR)
	3	H. Marbley (USA)
		H. Skrzypczak (POL)

1972	1	G. Gedo (HUN)
	2	U.G. Kim (PRK)
	3	R. Evans (GBR)
		E. Rodriguez (ESP)

1976	1	U. Hernandez (CUB)
	2	B.U. Li (PRK)
	3	P. Pooltarat (THA)
		O. Maldonado (PUR)

1980	1	S. Sabirov (URS)
	2	H. Ramos (CUB)
	3	B. Uk Li (PRK)
		I. Moustafov (BUL)

Flyweight
Weight limit 51kg (112lb 6oz)

1948	1	P. Perez (ARG)
	2	S. Bandinelli (ITA)
	3	S.A. Han (KOR)

1952	1	N. Brooks (USA)
	2	E. Basel (GER)
	3	A. Bulakov (URS)
		W. Toweel (SAF)

1956	1	T. Spinks (GBR)
	2	M. Dobrescu (ROM)
	3	J. Caldwell (IRL)
		R. Libeer (FRA)

1960	1	G. Török (HUN)
	2	S. Sivko (URS)
	3	K. Tanabe (JPN)
		A. Elgviodi (UAR)

1964	2	F. Atzori (ITA)
	2	A. Olech (POL)
	3	S. Sorokin (URS)
		R. Carmody (USA)

1968	1	R. Delgado (MEX)
	2	A. Olech (POL)
	3	S. de Oliveira (BRA)
		L. Rwabwogo (UGA)

1972	1	G. Kostadinov (BUL)
	2	L. Rwabwogo (UGA)
	3	I. Blażyński (POL)
		D. Rodriguez (CUB)

1976	1	L. Randolph (USA)
	2	R. Duvalon (CUB)
	3	D. Torosyan (URS)
		L. Blażyński (POL)

1980	1	P. Lessov (BUL)
	2	V. Miroshnichenko (URS)
	3	H. Russell (IRL)
		J. Varadi (HUN)

Bantamweight
Weight limit 54kg (119lb)

1948	1	T. Csik (HUN)
	2	G. Zuddas (ITA)
	3	J. Venegas (PUR)

1952	1	P. Hämäläinen (FIN)
	2	J. McNally (IRL)
	3	G. Garbuzov (URS)
		J.H. Kang (KOR)

1956	1	W. Behrendt (GER)
	2	S.C. Song (KOR)
	3	F. Gilroy (IRL)
		C. Barrientos (CHI)

1960	1	O. Grigoriev (URS)
	2	P. Zamparini (ITA)
	3	O. Taylor (AUS)
		B. Bendig (POL)

1964	1	T. Sakurai (JPN)
	2	S.C. Chung (KOR)
	3	B.J. Fabila (MEX)
		W. Rodriguez (URU)

1968	1	V. Sokolov (URS)
	2	E. Mukwanga (UGA)
	3	E. Morioka (JPN)
		K.C. Chang (KOR)

1972   1 O. Martinez (CUB)
       2 A. Zamora (MEX)
       3 G. Turpin (GBR)
          R. Carreras (USA)

1976   1 Y.J. Gu (PRK)
       2 C. Mooney (USA)
       3 P. Cowdell (GBR)
          V. Rybakov (URS)

1980   1 J. Hernandez (CUB)
       2 B. Pinango (VEN)
       3 D. Cipere (ROM)
          M. Anthony (GUY)

Featherweight

Weight limit 57kg (125lb 10½oz) — 58kg (127lb 14oz) in 1948

1948   1 E. Formenti (ITA)
       2 D. Shepherd (SAF)
       3 A. Antkiewicz (POL)

1952   1 J. Zachara (TCH)
       2 S. Caprari (ITA)
       3 L. Leisching (SAF)
          J. Ventaja (FRA)

1956   1 V. Safronov (URS)
       2 T. Nicholls (GBR)
       3 H. Niedźwiedzki (POL)
          P. Hämäläinen (FIN)

1960   1 F. Musso (ITA)
       2 J. Adamski (POL)
       3 W. Meyers (SAF)
          J. Limmonen (FIN)

1964   1 S. Stepashkin (URS)
       2 A. Villanueva (PHI)
       3 C. Brown (USA)
          H. Schulz (GER)

1968   1 A. Roldan (MEX)
       2 A. Robinson (USA)
       3 P. Waruinge (KEN)
          I. Mikhailov (BUL)

1972   1 B. Kusnetsov (URS)
       K P. Waruinge (KEN)
       3 C. Rojas (COL)
          A. Botos (HUN)

1976   1 A. Herrera (CUB)
       2 R. Nowakowski (GDR)
       3 J. Paredes (MEX)
          L. Kosedowski (POL)

1980   1 R. Fink (GDR)
       2 A. Horta (CUB)
       3 V. Rybakov (URS)
          K. Kosedowski (POL)

Lightweight

Weight limit 60kg (132lb 4½oz) — 62kg (136lb 11oz) in 1948

1948   1 G. Dreyer (SAF)
       2 J. Vissers (BEL)
       3 S. Wad (DEN)

1952   1 A. Bolognesi (ITA)
       2 A. Antkiewicz (POL)
       3 G. Fiat (ROM)
          E. Pakkanen (FIN)

1956   1 R. McTaggart (GBR)
       2 H. Kurschat (GER)
       X A. Byrne (IRL)
          A. Lagetko (URS)

1960   1 K. Pázdzior (POL)
       K S. Lopopolo (ITA)
       3 R. McTaggart (GBR)
          A. Laudonio (ARG)

1964   1 J. Grudzién (POL)
       2 V. Baranikov (URS)
       3 R. Harris (USA)
       C . McCourt (IRL)

1968   1 R. Harris (USA)
       2 J. Grudzién (POL)
       X V. Wdel G, Y
          Z. Vujin (YUG)

1972   2 J. Szczepanski (POL)
       2 L. Orban (HUN)
       3 S. Mbugua (KEN)
          A. Pérez (COL)

1976   1 H. Davis (USA)
       K S. Cutov (ROM)
       3 A. Rusevski (YUG)
          V. Solomin (URS)

1980　1　A. Herrera (CUB)
　　　　2　V. Dernianenko (URS)
　　　　3　K. Adach (POL)
　　　　　　R. Nowakowski (GDR)

Light welterweight
Weight limit 63.5kg (140lb)

1952　1　C. Adkins (USA)
　　　　2　V. Mednov (URS)
　　　　3　E. Mallenius (FIN)
　　　　　　B. Visintin (ITA)

1956　1　V. Yengibaryan (URS)
　　　　2　F. Nenci (ITA)
　　　　3　H. Loubscher (SAF)
　　　　　　C. Dumitrescu (ROM)

1960　1　B. Nemecek (TCH)
　　　　2　C. Quartey (GHA)
　　　　3　Q. Daniels (USA)
　　　　　　M. Kasprzyk (POL)

1964　1　J. Kulej (POL)
　　　　2　Y. Frolov (URS)
　　　　3　E. Blay (GHA)
　　　　　　H. Galhia (TUN)

1968　1　J. Kulej (POL)
　　　　2　E. Regueiferos (CUB)
　　　　3　A. Nilsson (FIN)
　　　　　　J. Wallington (USA)

1972　1　R. Seales (USA)
　　　　2　A. Anghelov (BUL)
　　　　3　Z. Vujin (YUG)
　　　　　　I. Daborg (NIG)

1976　1　R. Leonard (USA)
　　　　2　A. Aldama (CUB)
　　　　3　V. Kolev (BUL)
　　　　　　K. Szczerba (POL)

1980　1　P. Oliva (ITA)
　　　　2　S. Konakbayev (URS)
　　　　3　J. Aguilar (CUB)
　　　　　　A. Willis (GBR)

Welterweight
*Weight limit 67kg (147lb 11½oz) — 66.68kg
(147lb) before 1968*

1948　1　J. Torma (TCH)
　　　　2　H. Herring (USA)
　　　　3　A. d'Ottavio (ITA)

1952　1　Z. Chychla (POL)
　　　　2　S. Shcherbakov (URS)
　　　　3　J. Jørgensen (DEN)
　　　　　　G. Heidemann (GER)

1956　1　N. Linca (ROM)
　　　　2　F. Tiedt (IRL)
　　　　3　K. Hogarth (AUS)
　　　　　　N. Gargano (GER)

1960　1　G. Benvenuti (ITA)
　　　　2　Y. Radonyak (URS)
　　　　3　L. Drogosz (POL)
　　　　　　J. Lloyd (GBR)

1964　1　M. Kasprzyk (POL)
　　　　2　R. Tamulis (URS)
　　　　3　P. Purhonen (FIN)
　　　　　　S. Bertini (ITA)

1968　1　M. Wolke (GDR)
　　　　2　J. Bessala (CMR)
　　　　3　V. Masalimov (URS)
　　　　　　M. Guilloti González (ARG)

1972　1　E. Correa (CUB)
　　　　2　J. Kajdi (HUN)
　　　　3　D. Murunga (KEN)
　　　　　　J. Valdez (USA)

1976　1　J. Bachfield (GDR)
　　　　2　P.J. Gamarro (VEN)
　　　　3　R. Skricek (FRG)
　　　　　　V. Zilberman (ROM)

1980　1　A. Aldama (CUB)
　　　　2　M. Mugabi (UGA)
　　　　3　K-H. Krüger (GDR)
　　　　　　K. Szczerba (POL)

Light middleweight
Weight limit 71kg (156lb 8½oz)

1952 1 L. Papp (HUN)
     2 T. van Schalkwyk (SAF)
     3 B. Tishin (URS)
       E. Herrera (ARG)

1956 1 L. Papp (HUN)
     2 J. Torres (USA)
     3 J. McCormack (GBR)
       Z. Pietrzykowski (POL)

1960 1 W. McClure (USA)
     2 C. Bossi (ITA)
     3 B. Lagutin (URS)
       W. Fisher (GBR)

1964 1 B. Lagutin (URS)
     2 J. Gonzales (FRA)
     3 N. Maiyegun (NGR)
       J. Grzesiak (POL)

1968 1 B. Lagutin (URS)
     2 R. Garbey (CUB)
     3 J. Baldwin (USA)
       G. Meier (FRG)

1972 1 D. Kottysch (FRG)
     2 W. Rudkowski (POL)
     3 A. Minter (GBR)
       P. Tiepold (GDR)

1976 1 J. Rybicki (POL)
     2 T. Kacar (YUG)
     3 R. Garbey (CUB)
       V. Savchenko (URS)

1980 1 A. Martinez (CUB)
     2 A. Koshkin (URS)
     3 J. Franck (TCH)
       D. Kastner (GDR)

Middleweight
*Weight limit 75kg (165lb 5⅓oz) — 73kg
(169lb 15oz) before 1952*

1948 1 L. Papp (HUN)
     2 J. Wright (GBR)
     3 I. Fontana (ITA)

1952 1 F. Patterson (USA)
     2 V. Tita (ROM)
     3 B. Nikolov (BUL)
       K. Sjölin (SWE)

1956 1 G. Shatkov (URS)
     2 R. Tapia (CHI)
     3 G. Chapron (FRA)
       V. Zalazar (ARG)

1960 1 E. Crook (USA)
     2 T. Walasek (POL)
     3 I. Monea (ROM)
       Y. Feofanov (URS)

1964 1 V. Popenchenko (URS)
     2 E. Schulz (GER)
     3 F. Valla (ITA)
       T. Walasek (POL)

1968 1 C. Finnegan (GBR)
     2 A. Kiselyov (URS)
     3 Z. Zaragoza (MEX)
       A. Jones (USA)

1972 1 V. Lemechev (URS)
     2 R. Virtanen (FIN)
     3 P. Amartey (GHA)
       M. Johnson (USA)

1976 1 M. Spinks (USA)
     2 R. Riskiev (URS)
     3 A. Nastac (ROM)
       L. Martinez (CUB)

1980 1 J. Gomez (CUB)
     2 V. Savchenko (URS)
     3 J. Rybicki (POL)
       V. Silaghi (ROM)

Light heavyweight
*Weight limit 81kg (178lb 9oz) — 80kg
(176lb 6oz) before 1952*

1948 1 G. Hunter (SAF)
     2 D. Scott (GBR)
     3 M. Cia (ARG)

1952 1 N. Lee (USA)
     2 A. Pacenza (ARG)
     3 A. Perov (URS)
       H. Siljander (FIN)

1956 1 J. Boyd (USA)
      2 G. Negrea (ROM)
      3 C. Lucas (CHI)
        R. Murauskas (URS)

1960 1 C. Clay (USA)
      2 Z. Pietrzykowski (POL)
      3 A. Madigan (AUS)
        G. Saraudi (ITA)

1964 1 C. Pinto (ITA)
      2 A. Kiselyov (URS)
      3 A. Nicolov (BUL)
        Z. Pietrzykowski (POL)

1968 1 D. Poznyak (URS)
      2 I. Monea (ROM)
      3 G. Stankov (BUL)
        S. Dragan (POL)

1972 1 M. Parlov (YUG)
      2 G. Carrillo (CUB)
      3 I. Ikhouria (NGR)
        J. Gortat (POL)

1976 1 L. Spinks (USA)
      2 S. Soria (CUB)
      3 C. Dafinioiu (ROM)
        J. Gortat (POL)

1980 1 S. Kacar (YUG)
      2 P. Skrzecz (POL)
      3 H. Bauch (GDR)
        R. Rojas (CUB)

1960 1 F. de Piccoli (ITA)
      2 D. Bekker (SAF)
      3 J. Nemec (TCH)
        G. Siegmund (GER)

1964 1 J. Frazier (USA)
      2 H. Huber (GER)
      3 G. Ros (ITA)
        V. Yemelyanov (URS)

1968 1 G. Foreman (USA)
      2 I. Chepulis (URS)
      3 G. Bambini (ITA)
        J. Rocha (MEX)

1972 1 T. Stevenson (CUB)
      2 I. Alexe (ROM)
      3 P. Hussing (FRG)
        H. Thomsen (SWE)

1976 1 T. Stevenson (CUB)
      2 M. Simon (ROM)
      3 J. Tate (USA)
        C. Hill (BER)

1980 1 T. Stevenson (CUB)
      2 P. Zayev (URS)
      3 J. Fanghanel (GDR)
        I. Levai (HUN)

Heavyweight
*Weight limit 81kg (178lb 9oz) — 80kg
(176lb 6oz) before 1952*

1948 1 R. Iglesias (ARG)
      2 G. Nilsson (SWE)
      3 J. Arthur (SAF)

1952 1 H.E. Sanders (USA)
      2 Not awarded
      3 A. Nieman (SAF)
        I. Koski (FIN)

1956 1 T.P. Rademacher (USA)
      2 L. Mukhin (URS)
      3 D. Bekker (SAF)
        G. Bozzano (ITA)

Canoeing (men)
Canadian singles, 500 metres

1	S. Postrekhin (URS)	1:53.37
2	L. Lubenov (BUL)	1:53.49
3	O. Heukrodt (GDR)	1:54.38
4	T. Wichman (HUN)	1:54.58
5	M. Lbik (POL)	1:55.90
6	T. Gronlund (FIN)	1:55.94
7	L. Varabiev (ROM)	1:56.80
8	R. Blazik (TCH)	1:56.83
9	M. Ljubek (YUG)	2:03.43

Canadian pairs, 500 metres

1	L. Foltan, I. Vaskuti (HUN)	1:43.39
2	I. Potzaichin, P. Capustal (ROM)	1:44.12
3	B. Ananiev, N. Ilkov (BUL)	1:44.83
4	M. Wisla, J. Dunajski (POL)	1:45.10
5	J. Vrdlovec, P. Kubicek (TCH)	1:46.48
6	S. Petrenko, A. Vinogradov (URS)	1:46.95
7	N. Suarez, S. Magaz (ESP)	1:48.18
8	B. Lindelof, E. Zeidlitz (SWE)	1:48.69
9	F. Lambert, P. Langlois (FRA)	1:50.33

Kayak singles, 500 metres

1	V. Parfenovich (URS)	1:43.43
2	J. Sumegi (AUS)	1:44.12
3	V. Diba (ROM)	1:44.90
4	M. Janic (YUG)	1:45.63
5	F-P Bischof (GDR)	1:45.97
6	A. Andersson (SWE)	1:46.32
7	I. G. Ferguson (NZL)	1:47.36
8	F. Masar (TCH)	1:48.18
9	Z. Sztaniti (HUN)	1:48.34

Kayak pairs, 500 metres

1	V. Parfenovich, S. Chukhrai (URS)	1:32.38
2	H. Menendez, G. Del Riego (ESP)	1:33.65
3	R. Helm, B. Olbricht (GDR)	1:34.00
4	F. Hervieu, A. Lebas (FRA)	1:36.22
5	B. Kelly, R. Lee (AUS)	1:36.45
6	A. Giura, I. Birladeanu (ROM)	1:36.96

Canadian singles
Course 1000m (1094 yd)

			Time
1948	1	J. Holecek (TCH)	5:42.0
	2	D. Bennett (CAN)	5:53.3
	3	R. Boutigny (FRA)	5:55.9
1952	1	J. Holecek (TCH)	4:56.3
	2	J. Parti (HUN)	5:03.6
	3	O. Ojanperä (FIN)	5:08.5
1956	1	L. Rotman (ROM)	5:05.3
	2	I. Hernel (HUN)	5:06.2
	3	G. Bukharin (URS)	5:12.7
1960	1	J. Parti (HUN)	4:33.93
	2	A. Silayev (URS)	4:34.41
	3	L. Rotman (ROM)	4:35.87
1964	1	J. Eschert (GER)	4:35.14
	2	A. Igorov (ROM)	4:37.89
	3	Y. Penyaev (URS)	4:38.31
1968	1	T. Tatai (HUN)	4:36.14
	2	D. Lewe (FRG)	4:38.31
	3	V. Galkov (URS)	4:40.42
1972	1	I. Patzaichin (ROM)	4:08.94
	2	T. Wichmann (HUN)	4:12.42
	3	D. Lewe (FRG)	4:13.63
1976	1	M. Ljubek (YUG)	4:09.51
	2	V. Urchenko (URS)	4:12.57
	3	T. Wichmann (HUN)	4:14.11
1980	1	L. Lubenov (BUL)	4:12.38
	2	S. Postrekin (URS)	4:13.53
	3	E. Leve (GDR)	4:15.02

Kayak singles
Course 1000m (1094 yd)

			Time
1948	1	G. Fredriksson (SWE)	4:33.2
	2	J.F. Kobberup (DEN)	4:39.9
	3	H. Eberhardt (FRA)	4:41.4
1952	1	G. Fredriksson (SWE)	4:07.9
	2	T. Strömberg (FIN)	4:09.7
	3	L. Gantois (FRA)	4:20.1
1956	1	G. Fredriksson (SWE)	4:12.8
	2	I. Pisarev (URS)	4:15.3
	3	L. Kiss (HUN)	4:16.2
1960	1	E. Hansen (DEN)	3:53.0
	2	I. Szöllosi (HUN)	3:54.02
	3	G. Fredriksson (SWE)	3:55.89

1964	1	R. Peterson (SWE)	3:57.13
	2	M. Hesz (HUN)	3:57.28
	3	A. Vernescu (ROM)	4:00.77
1968	1	M. Hesz (HUN)	4:02.63
	2	A. Shaparenko (URS)	4:03.58
	3	E. Hansen (DEN)	4:04.39
1972	1	A. Shaparenko (URS)	3:48.06
	2	R. Peterson (SWE)	3:48.35
	3	G. Csapo (HUN)	3:49.38
1976	1	R. Helm (GDR)	3:48.20
	2	G. Csapo (HUN)	3:48.84
	3	V. Diba (ROM)	3:49.65
1980	1	R. Helm (GDR)	3:48.77
	2	A. Lebas (FRA)	3:50.20
	3	I. Birladeanu (ROM)	3:50.49

Canadian pairs
Course 1000m (1094yd)

	Gold	Silver	Bronze
1948	TCH 5:07.1	USA 5:08.2	FRA 5:15.2
1952	DEN 4:38.3	TCH 4:42.9	GER 4:48.3
1956	ROM 4:47.4	URS 4:48.6	HUN 4:54.3
1960	URS 4:17.94	ITA 4:20.77	HUN 4:20.89
1964	URS 4:04.64	FRA 4:06.52	DEN 4:07.48
1968	ROM 4:07.18	HUN 4:08.77	URS 4:11.30
1972	URS 3:52.60	ROM 3:52.63	BUL 3:58.10
1976	URS 3:52.76	ROM 3:54.28	HUN 3:55.66
1980	ROM 3:47.65	GDR 3:49.93	URS 3:51.28

Kayak pairs
Course 1000m (1094yd)

	Gold	Silver	Bronze
1948	SWE 4:07.3	DEN 4:07.5	FIN 4:08.7
1952	FIN 3:51.1	SWE 3:51.1	AUT 3:51.4
1956	GER 3:49.6	URS 3:51.4	AUT 3:55.8
1960	SWE 3:34.73	HUN 3:34.91	POL 3:37.34
1964	SWE 3:38.54	HOL 3:39.30	GER 3:40.69
1968	URS 3:37.54	HUN 3:38.44	AUT 3:40.71
1972	URS 3:31.23	HUN 3:32.00	POL 3:33.83
1976	URS 3:29.01	GDR 3:29.33	HUN 3:30.36
1980	URS 3:26.72	HUN 3:28.49	ESP 3:28.66

Kayak fours
Course 1000m (1094yd)

			Time
1964	1	URS	3:14.67
	2	GER	3:15.39
	3	ROM	3:15.51
1968	1	NOR	3:14.38
	2	ROM	3:14.81
	3	HUN	3:15.10
1972	1	URS	3:14.02
	2	ROM	3:15.07
	3	NOR	3:15.27
1976	1	URS	3:08.69
	2	ESP	3:08.95
	3	GDR	3:10.76
1980	1	GDR	3:13.76
	2	ROM	3:15.35
	3	BUL	3:15.46

Slalom – kayak singles
Not held before 1972.

			Points
1972	1	A. Bahmann (GDR)	364.50
	2	G. Grothaus (FRG)	398.15
	3	M. Wunderlich (FRG)	400.50
1976	*Not held.*		
1980	*Not held.*		

Canoeing (women)
Kayak singles
Course 500m (547yd)

			Time
1948	1	K. Hoff (DEN)	2:31.9
	2	A. van der Anker-Deodans (HOL)	2:32.8
	3	F. Schwingl (AUT)	2:32.9
1952	1	S. Saimo (FIN)	2:18.4
	2	G. Liebhart (AUT)	2:18.8
	3	N. Savina (URS)	2:21.6
1956	1	E. Dementieva (URS)	2:18.9
	2	T. Zenz (GER)	2:19.6
	3	T. Søby (DEN)	2:22.3
1960	1	A. Seredina (URS)	2:08.08
	2	T. Zenz (GER)	2:08.22
	3	D. Walkowiak (POL)	2:10.46
1964	1	L. Khvedosyuk (URS)	2:12.87
	2	H. Lauer (ROM)	2:15.35
	3	M. Jones (USA)	2:15.68
1968	1	L. Pinaeva (URS)	2:11.09
	2	R. Breuer (FRG)	2:12.71
	3	V. Dumitru (ROM)	2:13.22
1972	1	Y. Ryabchinskaya (URS)	2:03.17
	2	M. Jaapies (HOL)	2:04.03
	3	A. Pfeffer (HUN)	2:05.50
1976	1	C. Zirzow (GDR)	2:01.05
	2	T. Korshunova (URS)	2:03.07
	3	K. Rajnai (HUN)	2:05.01
1980	1	B. Fischer (GDR)	1:57.96
	2	V. Ghecheva (BUL)	1:59.48
	3	A. Melnikova (URS)	1:59.66

Kayak pairs
Course 500m (547yd)

1960	URS 1:54.76	GER 1:56.66	HUN 1:58.22
1964	GER 1:56.95	USA 1:59.16	ROM 2:00.25
1968	FRG 1:56.44	HUN 1:58.60	URS 1:58.61
1972	URS 1:53.50	GDR 1:54.30	ROM 1:55.01
1976	URS 1:51.15	HUN 1:51.69	GDR 1:51.81
1980	GDR 1:43.88	URS 1:46.91	HUN 1:47.95

Cycling
1000 metres sprint
(Times given are for the last 200m)

			Time
1948	1	M. Ghella (ITA)	12.0
	2	R. Harris (GBR)	
	3	A. Schandorff (DEN)	
1952	1	E. Sacchi (ITA)	12.0
	2	L. Cox (AUS)	
	3	W. Potzernheim (GER)	
1956	1	M. Rousseau (FRA)	11.4
	2	G. Pesenti (ITA)	
	3	R. Ploog (AUS)	
1960	1	S. Gaiardoni (ITA)	11.1
	2	L. Sterckx (BEL)	
	3	V. Gasparella (ITA)	
1964	1	G. Pettenella (ITA)	13.69
	2	S. Bianchetto (ITA)	
	3	D. Morelon (FRA)	
1968	1	D. Morelon (FRA)	10.68
	2	G. Turrini (ITA)	
	3	P. Trentin (FRA)	
1972	1	D. Morelon (FRA)	11.69
	2	J. Nicholson (AUS)	
	3	O. Pkhakadze (URS)	
1976	1	A. Tkac (TCH)	
	2	D. Morelon (FRA)	
	3	H.J. Geschke (GDR)	
1980	1	L. Hesslich (GDR)	11.40
	2	Y. Cahard (FRA)	
	3	S. Kopylov (URS)	

1000 metres time trial

			Time
1948	1	J. Dupont (FRA)	1:13.5
	2	P. Nihant (BEL)	1:14.5
	3	T. Godwin (GBR)	1:15.0
1952	1	R. Mockridge (AUS)	1:11.1
	2	M. Morettini (ITA)	1:12.7
	3	R. Robinson (SAF)	1:13.0

1956	1	L. Faggin (ITA)	1:09.8
	2	L. Foucek (TCH)	1:11.4
	3	A. Swift (SAF)	1:11.6
1960	1	S. Gaiardoni (ITA)	1:07.27
	2	D. Gieseler (GER)	1:08.75
	3	R. Vargashkin (URS)	1:08.86
1964	1	P. Sercu (BEL)	1:09.59
	2	G. Pettenella (ITA)	1:10.09
	3	P. Trentin (FRA)	1:10.42
1968	1	P. Trentin (FRA)	1:03.91
	2	N.C. Fredborg (DEN)	1:04.61
	3	J. Kierzkowski (POL)	1:04.63
1972	1	N.C. Fredborg (DEN)	1:06.44
	2	D. Clark (AUS)	1:06.87
	3	J. Schütze (GDR)	1:07.02
1976	1	K.J. Grunke (GDR)	1:05.927
	2	M. Vaarten (BEL)	1:07.516
	3	N.C. Fredborg (DEN)	1:07.617
1980	1	L. Thoms (GDR)	1:02.955
	2	A. Pantilov (URS)	1:04.845
	3	D. Weller (JAM)	1:05.241

4000 metres pursuit (individual)

			Time
1964	1	J. Daler (TCH)	5:04.75
	2	G. Ursi (ITA)	5:05.96
	3	P. Isaksson (DEN)	5:01.90
1968	1	D. Rebillard (FRA)	4:41.71
	2	M.F. Jensen (DEN)	4:42.43
	3	X. Kurmann (SUI)	4:39.42
1972	1	K. Knudsen (NOR)	4:45.74
	2	X. Kurmann (SUI)	4:51.96
	3	H. Lutz (FRG)	4:50.80
1976	1	G. Braun (FRG)	4:47.61
	2	H. Ponsteen (HOL)	4:49.72
	3	T. Huschke (GDR)	4:52.71
1980	1	R. Dill-Bundi (SUI)	4:35.66
	2	A. Bondue (FRA)	4:42.96
	3	H.H. Örsted (DEN)	4:36.54

Road race (individual)

Distance in 1948 194.6km (121 miles); in 1952 190.4km (118 miles); in 1956 187.7km (117 miles); in 1960 175.4km (109 miles); in 1964 194.8km (121 miles); in 1968 196.2km (122 miles); in 1972 182.4km (113 miles).

			Time
1948	1	J. Beyaert (FRA)	5h 18:12.6
	2	G.P. Voorting (HOL)	5h 18:16.2
	3	L. Wouters (BEL)	5h 18:16.2
1952	1	A. Noyelle (BEL)	5h 06:03.4
	2	R. Grondelaers (BEL)	5h 06:51.2
	3	E. Ziegler (GER)	5h 07:47.5
1956	1	E. Baldini (ITA)	5h 21:17.0
	2	A. Geyre (FRA)	5h 23:16.0
	3	A. Jackson (GBR)	5h 23:16.0
1960	1	V. Kapitonov (URS)	4h 20:37.0
	2	L. Trapé (ITA)	4h 20:37.0
	3	W. van den Berghen (BEL)	4h 20:57.0
1964	1	M. Zanin (ITA)	4h 39:51.63
	2	K.A. Rodian (DEN)	4h 39:51.65
	3	W. Godefroot (BEL)	4h 39:51.74
1968	1	P. Vianelli (ITA)	4h 41:25.24
	2	L. Mortensen (DEN)	4h 42:49.71
	3	G. Pettersson (SWE)	4h 43:15.24
1972	1	H. Kuiper (HOL)	4h 14:37.0
	2	K.C. Sefton (AUS)	4h 15:04.0
	3	*Bronze not awarded*	
1976	1	B. Johansson (SWE)	4h 46:52.0
	2	G. Martinelli (ITA)	4h 47:23.0
	3	M. Nowicki (POL)	4h 47:23.0
1980	1	S. Sukhoruchenkov (URS)	4h 48:28.9
	2	C. Lane (POL)	4h 51:26.9
	3	Y. Barinov (URS)	4h 51:26.9

2000 metres tandem

Times given are for the last 200m

	Gold	Silver	Bronze
1948	ITA 11.3	GBR	FRA
1952	AUS 11.0	SAF	ITA
1956	AUS 10.8	TCH	ITA
1960	ITA 10.7	GER	URS
1964	ITA 10.75	URS	GER
1968	FRA 9.83	HOL	BEL
1972	URS 10.52	GDR	POL
1976	*Not held*		
1980	*Not held*		

4000 metres pursuit (team)

	Gold	Silver	Bronze
1948	FRA 4:57.8	ITA 5:36.7	GBR 5:55.8
1952	ITA 4:46.1	SAF 4:53.6	GBR 4:51.5
1956	ITA 4:37.4	FRA 4:39.4	GBR 4:42.2
1960	ITA 4:30.90	GER 4:35.78	URS 4:34.05
1964	GER 4:35.67	ITA 4:35.74	HOL 4:38.99
1968	DEN 4:22.44	FRG 4:18.94	ITA 4:18.35
1972	FRG 4:22.14	GDR 4:25.25	GBR 4:23.78
1976	FRG 4:21.06	URS 4:27.15	GBR 4:22.41
1980	URS 4:15.70	GDR 4:19.67	TCH *

* Promoted to bronze medallists when Italy were disqualified

Road race (team)

Distance from 1960 100km (62 miles).

			Time
1948	1	BEL	15h 58:17.4
	2	GBR	16h 03:31.6
	3	FRA	16h 08:19.4
1952	1	BEL	15h 20:46.6
	2	ITA	15h 33:27.3
	3	FRA	15h 38:58.1
1956	1	FRA 22 pts	16h 10:36
	2	GBR 23 pts	16h 10:46
	3	GER 27 pts	16h 11:10
1960	1	ITA	2h 14:33.53
	2	GER	2h 16:56.31
	3	URS	2h 18:41.67
1964	1	HOL	2h 26:31.19
	2	ITA	2h 26:55.39
	3	SWE	2h 27:11.52
1968	1	HOL	2h 07:49.06
	2	SWE	2h 09:26.60
	3	ITA	2h 10:18.74
1972	1	URS	2h 11:17.8
	2	POL	2h 11:47.5
	3	*Bronze not awarded*	
1976	1	URS	2h 08:53.0
	2	POL	2h 09:13.0
	3	DEN	2h 12:20.0
1980	1	URS	2h 01:21.7
	2	GDR	2h 02:53.2
	3	TCH	2h 02:53.9

Equestrianism
Dressage (individual)

			Points
1948	1	H. Moser (SUI) *Hummer*	492.5
	2	A. Jousseaume (FRA) *Harpagon*	480.0
	3	G.A. Boltenstern (SWE) *Trumpf*	447.5
1952	1	H. St Cyr (SWE) *Master Rufus*	561.0
	2	L. Hartel (DEN) *Jubilee*	541.5
	3	A. Jousseaume (FRA) *Harpagon*	541.0
1956	1	H. St Cyr (SWE) *Juli*	860
	2	L. Hartel (DEN) *Jubilee*	850
	3	L. Linsenhoff (GER) *Adular*	832
1960	1	S. Filatov (URS) *Absent*	2144
	2	G. Fischer (SUI) *Wald*	2087
	3	J. Neckermann (GER) *Asbach*	2082
1964	1	H. Chammartin (SUI) *Woermann*	1504
	2	H. Boldt (GER) *Remus*	1503
	3	S. Filatov (URS) *Absent*	1486
1968	1	I. Kizimov (URS) *Ikhor*	1572
	2	J. Neckermann (FRG) *Mariano*	1546
	3	R. Klimke (FRG) *Dux*	1537
1972	1	L. Linsenhoff (FRG) *Piaff*	1229
	2	E. Petushkova (URS) *Pepel*	1185
	3	J. Neckermann (FRG) *Venetia*	1177

1976	1	E. Stueckelberger (SUI)	1486
		Granat	
	2	H. Boldt (FRG)	1435
		Woycek	
	3	R. Klimke (FRG)	1395
		Mehmed	

1980	1	E. Theurer (AUT)	1370
		Mon Cherie	
	2	Y. Kovshov (URS)	1300
		Igrok	
	3	V. Ugryumov (URS)	1234
		Shkval	

Three-day event (individual)

			Faults
1948	1	B. Chevalier (FRA)	4 pts
		Aiglonne	
	2	F. Henry (USA)	21
		Swing Low	
	3	R. Selfelt (SWE)	25
		Claque	

1952	1	H. von Blixen-Finecke (SWE)	28.33
		Jubal	
	2	C. Lefrant (FRA)	54.50
		Verdun	
	3	W. Büsing (GER)	55.50
		Hubertus	

1956	1	P. Kastenman (SWE)	66.53
		Iluster	
	2	A. Lütke-Westhues (GER)	84.87
		Trux von Kamax	
	3	F. Weldon (GBR)	85.48
		Kilbarry	

1960	1	L. Morgan (AUS)	7.15 pts
		Salad Days	
	2	N. Lavis (AUS)	16.50
		Mirrabooka	
	3	A. Bühler (SUI)	51.21
		Gay Spark	

1964	1	M. Checcoli (ITA)	64.40 pts
		Surbean	
	2	C. Moratorio (ARG)	56.40 pts
		Chalan	
	3	F. Ligges (GER)	49.20 pts
		Donkosak	

1968	1	J.J. Guyon (FRA)	38.86
		Pitou	
	2	D. Allhusen (GBR)	41.61
		Lochinvar	
	3	M. Page (USA)	52.31
		Foster	

1972	1	R. Meade (GBR)	57.73 pts
		Laurieston	
	2	A. Argenton (ITA)	43.33 pts
		Woodland	
	3	J. Jonsson (SWE)	39.67 pts
		Sarajevo	

1976	1	E. Coffin (USA)	114.99
		Bally-Cor	
	2	M. Plumb (USA)	125.85
		Better & Better	
	3	K. Schultz (FRG)	129.45
		Madrigal	

1980	1	F. Roman (ITA)	108.60 pts
		Rossinan	
	2	A. Blinov (URS)	120.80 pts
		Galzun	
	3	Y. Salnikov (URS)	151.60 pts
		Pintset	

Show jumping (individual)

			Faults
1948	1	H. Mariles-Cortés (MEX)	6.25
		Arete	
	2	R. Uriza (MEX)	8
		Harvey	
	3	J. F. d'Orgiex (FRA)	8
		Sucre de Pomme	

1952	1	P.J. d'Oriola (FRA)	8
		Ali Baba	
	2	O. Cristi (CHI)	8
		Bambi	
	3	F. Thiedemann (GER)	8
		Meteor	

1956	1	H.G. Winkler (GER)	4
		Halla	
	2	R. d'Inzeo (ITA)	8
		Merano	
	3	P. d'Inzeo (ITA)	11
		Uruguay	
1960	1	R. d'Inzeo (ITA)	12
		Posillipo	
	2	P. d'Inzeo (ITA)	16
		The Rock	
	3	D. Broome (GBR)	23
		Sunsalve	
1964	1	P.J. d'Oriola (FRA)	9
		Lutteur	
	2	H. Schridde (GER)	13.75
		Dozent	
	3	P. Robeson (GBR)	16
		Firecrest	
1968	1	W. Steinkraus (USA)	4
		Snowbound	
	2	M. Coakes (GBR)	8
		Stroller	
	3	D. Broome (GBR)	12
		Mister Softee	

1972	1	G. Mancinelli (ITA)	8
		Ambassador	
	2	A. Moore (GBR)	8
		Psalm	
	3	N. Shapiro (USA)	8
		Sloopy	
1976	1	A. Schockemoehle (FRG)	0
		Warwick Rex	
	2	M. Vaillancourt (CAN)	12
		Branch County	
	3	F. Mathy (BEL)	12
		Gai Luron	
1980	1	J. Kuwalczyk (POL)	8
		Artemor	
	2	N. Korolkov (URS)	9.50
		Espadron	
	3	J. Peres-Heras (MEX)	12
		Alymony	

Dressage (team)

	Gold	Silver	Bronze
1948	FRA 1269 pts	USA 1256 pts	POR 1182 pts
1952	SWE 1597.5 pts	SUI 1579.0 pts	GER 1501.0 pts
1956	SWE 2475 pts	GER 2346 pts	SUI 2346 pts
1960	*Not held*		
1964	GER 2558 pts	SUI 2526 pts	URS 2311 pts
1968	FRG 2699 pts	URS 2657 pts	SUI 2547 pts
1972	URS 5095 pts	FRG 5083 pts	SWE 4849 pts
1976	FRG 5155 pts	SUI 4684 pts	USA 4647 pts
1980	URS 4383 pts	BUL 3580 pts	ROM 3346 pts

Three-day event (team)

	Gold	Silver	Bronze
1948	USA 161.50 flts	SWE 165.00 flts	MEX 305.25 flts
1952	SWE 221.94 flts	GER 235.49 flts	USA 587.16 flts
1956	GBR 355.48 flts	GER 475.91 flts	CAN 572.72 flts
1960	AUS 128.18 flts	SUI 386.02 flts	FRA 515.71 flts
1964	ITA 85.80 pts	USA 65.86 pts	GER 56.73 pts
1968	GBR 175.93 flts	USA 245.87 flts	AUS 331.26 flts
1972	GBR 95.53 pts	USA 10.81 pts	FRG -18.00 flts
1976	USA 441.00 flts	FRG 584.60 flts	AUS 599.64 flts
1980	URS 457.00 pts	ITA 656.20 pts	MEX 1172.85 pts

Show jumping (team)

	Gold	Silver	Bronze
1948	MEX 34.25 flts	ESP 56.5 flts	GBR 67 flts
1952	GBR 40.75 flts	CHI 45.75 flts	USA 52.25 flts
1956	GER 40 flts	ITA 66 flts	GBR 69 flts
1960	GER 46.5 flts	USA 66 flts	ITA 80.5 flts
1964	GER 68.50 flts	FRA 77.75 flts	ITA 88.50 flts
1968	CAN 102.75 flts	FRA 110.50 flts	FRG 117.25 flts
1972	FRG 32.00 flts	USA 32.25 flts	ITA 48.00 flts
1976	FRA 40 flts	FRG 44 flts	BEL 63 flts
1980	URS 16 flts	POL 32 flts	MEX 39.25 flts

Fencing (men)
Foil (individual)

			Wins
1948	1	J. Buhan (FRA)	7
	2	C. d'Oriola (FRA)	5
	3	L. Maszlay (HUN)	4
1952	1	C. d'Oriola (FRA)	8
	2	E. Mangiarotti (ITA)	6
	3	M. di Rosa (ITA)	5
1956	1	C. d'Oriola (FRA)	6
	2	G. Bergamini (ITA)	5
	3	A. Spallino (ITA)	5
1960	1	V. Zhdanovich (URS)	7
	2	Y. Siskin (URS)	4
	3	A. Axelrod (USA)	3
1964	1	E. Franke (POL)	3
	2	J.C. Magnan (FRA)	2
	3	D. Revenu (FRA)	1
1968	1	I. Drimba (ROM)	4
	2	J. Kamut (HUN)	3
	3	D. Revenu (FRA)	3
1972	1	W. Woyda (POL)	5
	2	J. Kamuti (HUN)	4
	3	C. Noël (FRA)	2
1976	1	F. Dal Zotto (ITA)	4
	2	A. Romankov (URS)	4
	3	B. Talvard (FRA)	3
1980	1	V. Smirnov (URS)	5
	2	P. Jolyot (FRA)	5
	3	A. Romankov (URS)	5

Epée (Individual)

			Wins
1948	1	L. Cantone (ITA)	7
	2	O. Zappelli (SUI)	5
	3	E. Mangiarotti (ITA)	5
1952	1	E. Mangiarotti (ITA)	7
	2	D. Mangiarotti (ITA)	6
	3	O. Zappelli (SUI)	6
1956	1	C. Pavesi (ITA)	5
	2	G. Delfino (ITA)	5
	3	E. Mangiarotti (ITA)	5
1960	1	G. Delfino (ITA)	5
	2	A. Jay (GBR)	5
	3	B. Khabarov (URS)	4
1964	1	G. Kriss (URS)	2
	2	W. Hoskyns (GBR)	2
	3	G. Kostava (URS)	1
1968	1	G. Kulcsár (HUN)	4
	2	G. Kriss (URS)	4
	3	G. Saccaro (ITA)	4
1972	1	C. Fenyvesi (HUN)	2
	2	J. La Degaillerie (FRA)	2
	3	G. Kulcsár (HUN)	1
1976	1	A. Pusch (FRG)	3
	2	J. Hehn (FRG)	3
	3	E. Kulcsár (HUN)	3
1980	1	J. Harmenberg (SWE)	4
	2	E. Kolczonay (HUN)	3
	3	P. Riboud (FRA)	3

Foil (team)

	Gold	Silver	Bronze
1948	FRA	ITA	BEL
1952	FRA	ITA	HUN
1956	ITA	FRA	HUN
1960	URS	ITA	GER
1964	URS	POL	FRA
1968	FRA	URS	POL
1972	POL	URS	FRA
1976	FRG	ITA	FRA
1980	FRA	URS	POL

Epée (team)

	Gold	Silver	Bronze
1948	FRA	ITA	SWE
1952	ITA	SWE	SUI
1956	ITA	HUN	FRA
1960	ITA	GBR	URS
1964	HUN	ITA	FRA
1968	HUN	URS	POL
1972	HUN	SUI	URS
1976	SWE	FRG	SUI
1980	FRA	POL	URS

Sabre (Individual)

			Wins
1948	1	A. Gerevich (HUN)	7
	2	V. Pinton (ITA)	5
	3	P. Kovács (HUN)	5
1952	1	P. Kovács (HUN)	8
	2	A. Gerevich (HUN)	7
	3	T. Berczelly (HUN)	5
1956	1	R. Kárpáti (HUN)	6
	2	J. Pawlowski (POL)	5
	3	L. Kuznetsov (URS)	4
1960	1	R. Kárpáti (HUN)	5
	2	Z. Horváth (HUN)	4
	3	W. Calarese (ITA)	4
1964	1	T. Pézsa (HUN)	2
	2	C. Arabo (FRA)	2
	3	U. Mavlikhanov (URS)	1
1968	1	J. Pawlowski (POL)	4
	2	M. Rakita (URS)	4
	3	T. Pésza (HUN)	3
1972	1	V. Sidiak (URS)	4
	2	P. Maroth (HUN)	3
	3	V. Nazlymov (URS)	3
1976	1	V. Krovopouskov (URS)	5
	2	V. Nazlymov (URS)	4
	3	V. Sidiak (URS)	3
1980	1	V. Krovopouskov (URS)	5
	2	M. Burtsev (URS)	4
	3	I. Gedovari (HUN)	3

Fencing (women)
Foil (Individual)

			Wins
1948	1	I. Elek (HUN)	6
	2	K. Lachmann (DEN)	5
	3	E. (Preis) Müller (AUT)	5
1952	1	I. Camber (ITA)	5
	2	I. Elek (HUN)	5
	3	K. Lachmann (DEN)	4
1956	1	G. Sheen (GBR)	6
	2	O. Orban (ROM)	6
	3	R. Garilhe (FRA)	5
1960	1	H. Schmid (GER)	6
	2	V. Rastvorova (URS)	5
	3	M. Vicol (ROM)	4
1964	1	I. (Ujlakil) Rejtö (HUN)	2
	2	H. Mees (GER)	2
	3	A. Ragno (ITA)	2
1968	1	Y. Novikova (URS)	4
	2	P. Roldan (MEX)	3
	3	I. (Ujlakil) Rejtö (HUN)	3
1972	1	A. (Ragno) Lonzi (ITA)	4
	2	I. Bobis (HUN)	3
	3	G. Gorokhova (URS)	3
1976	1	I. Schwarczenberger (HUN)	4
	2	M. Collino (ITA)	4
	3	E. Belova (URS)	3
1980	1	P. Trinquet (FRA)	4
	2	M. Maros (HUN)	3
	3	B. Wysoczanska (POL)	3

Sabre (team)

	Gold	Silver	Bronze
1948	HUN	ITA	USA
1952	HUN	ITA	FRA
1956	HUN	POL	URS
1960	HUN	POL	ITA
1964	URS	ITA	POL
1968	URS	ITA	HUN
1972	ITA	URS	HUN
1976	URS	ITA	ROM
1980	URS	ITA	HUN

Foil (team)

	Gold	Silver	Bronze
1960	URS	HUN	ITA
1964	HUN	URS	GER
1968	URS	HUN	ROM
1972	URS	HUN	ROM
1976	URS	FRA	HUN
1980	FRA	URS	HUN

Gymnastics (men)
Combined exercises (Individual)

			Points
1948	1	V. Huhtanen (FIN)	229.7
	2	W. Lehmann (SUI)	229.0
	3	P. Aaltonen (FIN)	228.8
1952	1	V. Chukarin (URS)	115.70
	2	G. Shaginyan (URS)	114.95
	3	J. Stalder (SUI)	114.75
1956	1	V. Chukarin (URS)	114.25
	2	T. Ono (JPN)	114.20
	3	Y. Titov (URS)	113.80
1960	1	B. Shakhlin (URS)	115.95
	2	T. Ono (JPN)	115.90
	3	Y. Titov (URS)	115.60
1964	1	Y. Endo (JPN)	115.95
	2	S. Tsurumi (JPN), B. Shakhlin (URS) & V. Lisitski (URS)	115.40
1968	1	S. Kato (JPN)	115.90
	2	M. Voronin (URS)	115.85
	3	A. Nakayama (JPN)	115.65
1972	1	S. Kato (JPN)	114.650
	2	E. Kenmotsu (JPN)	114.575
	3	A. Nakayama (JPN)	114.325
1976	1	N. Andrianov (URS)	116.650
	2	S. Kato (JPN)	115.650
	3	M. Tsukahara (JPN)	115.575
1980	1	A. Ditiatin (URS)	118.650
	2	N. Andrianov (URS)	118.225
	3	S. Deltchev (BUL)	118.000

Parallel bars

			Points
1948	1	M. Reusch (SUI)	39.50
	2	V. Huhtanen (FIN)	39.30
	3	C. Kipfer (SUI)	
		J. Stalder (SUI)	39.10
1952	1	H. Eugster (SUI)	19.65
	2	V. Chukarin (URS)	19.60
	3	J. Stalder (SUI)	19.50
1956	1	V. Chukarin (URS)	19.20
	2	M. Kubota (JPN)	19.15
	3	T. Ono (JPN)	
		M. Takemoto (JPN)	19.10
1960	1	B. Shakhlin (URS)	19.40
	2	G. Carminucci (ITA)	19.375
	3	T. Ono (JPN)	19.35
1964	1	Y. Endo (JPN)	19.675
	2	S. Tsurumi (JPN)	19.45
	3	F. Menichelli (ITA)	19.35
1968	1	A. Nakayama (JPN)	19.475
	2	M. Voronin (URS)	19.425
	3	V. Klimenko (URS)	19.225
1972	1	S. Kato (JPN)	19.475
	2	S. Kasamatsu (JPN)	19.375
	3	E. Kenmotsu (JPN)	19.250
1976	1	S. Kato (JPN)	19.675
	2	N. Andrianov (URS)	19.500
	3	M. Tsukahara (JPN)	19.475
1980	1	A. Tkachev (URS)	19.775
	2	A. Ditiatin (URS)	19.750
	3	R. Brückner (GDR)	19.650

Combined exercises (team)

	Gold	Silver	Bronze
1948	FIN 1358.30	SUI 1356.70	HUN 1330.35
1952	URS 574.40	SUI 567.50	FIN 564.20
1956	URS 568.25	JPN 566.40	FIN 555.95
1960	JPN 575.20	URS 572.70	ITA 559.05
1964	JPN 577.95	URS 575.45	GER 565.10
1968	JPN 575.90	URS 571.10	GDR 557.15
1972	JPN 571.25	URS 564.05	GDR 559.70
1976	JPN 576.85	URS 576.45	GDR 564.65
1980	URS 589.60	GDR 581.15	HUN 575.00

Horizontal Bar

			Points
1948	1	J. Stalder (SUI)	39.7
	2	W. Lehmann (SUI)	39.4
	3	V. Huhtanen (FIN)	39.2
1952	1	J. Günthard (SUI)	19.55
	2	J. Stalder (SUI)	
		A. Schwarzmann (GER)	19.50
1956	1	T. Ono (JPN)	19.60
	2	Y. Titov (URS)	19.40
	3	M. Takemoto (JPN)	19.30
1960	1	T. Ono (JPN)	19.60
	2	M. Takemoto (JPN)	19.52
	3	B. Shakhlin (URS)	19.475
1964	1	B. Shakhlin (URS)	19.625
	2	Y. Titov (URS)	19.55
	3	M. Cerar (YUG)	19.50
1968	1	M. Votonin (URS)	
		A. Nakayama (JPN)	19.550
	3	E. Kenmotsu (JPN)	19.375
1972	1	M. Tsukahara (JPN)	19.725
	2	S. Kato (JPN)	19.525
	3	S. Kasamatsu (JPN)	19.450
1976	1	M. Tsukahara (JPN)	19.675
	2	E. Kenmotsu (JPN)	19.500
	3	E. Gienger (FRG)	19.475
1980	1	S. Deltchev (BUL)	19.825
	2	A. Ditiatin (URS)	19.750
	3	N. Andrianov (URS)	19.675

Horse

			Points
1948	1	P. Aaltonen (FIN),	
		V. Huhtanen (FIN)	
		H. Savolainen (FIN)	38.7
	2	L. Zanetti (ITA)	38.30
	3	G. Figone (ITA)	38.20
1952	1	V Chukarin (URS)	19.50
	2	Y. Korolkov (URS)	
		G. Shaginyan (URS)	19.40
1956	1	B. Shakhlin (URS)	19.25
	2	T. Ono (JPN)	19.20
	3	V. Chukarin (URS)	19.10

1960	1	E. Ekman (FIN)	
		B. Shakhlin (URS)	19.375
	3	S. Tsurumi (JPN)	19.150
1964	1	M. Cerar (YUG)	19.525
	2	S. Tsurumi (JPN)	19.325
	3	Y. Tsapenko (URS)	19.20
1968	1	M. Cerar (YUG)	19.325
	2	O. Laiho (FIN)	19.225
	3	M. Voronin (URS)	19.200
1972	1	V. Klimenko (URS)	19.125
	2	S. Kato (JPN)	19.000
	3	E. Kenmotsu (JPN)	18.950
1976	1	Z. Magyar (HUN)	19.700
	2	E. Kenmotsu (JPN)	19.575
	3	N. Adrianov (URS)	19.525
1980	1	Z. Magyar (HUN)	19.95
	2	A. Ditiatin (URS)	19.800
	3	M. Nikolay (GDR)	19.775

Vault

			Points
1948	1	P. Aaltonen (FIN)	39.1
	2	O. Rove (FIN)	39.0
	3	J. Mogyorsi-Klencs	
		(HUN)	
		F. Pataki (HUN)	
		L. Sotornik (TCH)	38.5
1952	1	V. Chukarin (URS)	19.20
	2	M. Takemoto (JPN)	19.15
	3	T. Uesako (JPN)	
		T. Ono (JPN)	19.10
1956	1	H. Bantz (GER)	
		V. Muratov (URS)	18.85
	3	Y. Titov (URS)	18.75
1960	1	T. Ono (JPN)	
		B. Shakhlin (URS)	19.35
	3	V. Portnoi (URS)	19.225
1964	1	H. Yamashita (JPN)	19.660
	2	V. Lisitski (URS)	19.325
	3	H. Rantakari (FIN)	19.300
1968	1	M. Voronin (URS)	19.000
	2	Y. Endo (JPN)	18.950
	3	S. Diomidov (URS)	18.925

1972	1 K. Köste (GDR)	18.850
	2 V. Klimenko (URS)	18.825
	3 N. Andrianov (URS)	18,800

1976	1 N. Andrianov (URS)	19.450
	2 M. Tsukahara (JPN)	19.375
	3 H. Kajiyama (JPN)	19.275

1980	1 N. Andrianov (URS)	19.825
	2 A. Ditiatin (URS)	19.800
	3 R. Brückner (GDR)	19.775

Rings

		Points
1948	1 K. Frei (SUI)	39.6
	2 M. Reusch (SUI)	39.1
	3 Z. Ruzicka (TCH)	38.5

1952	1 G. Shaginyan (URS)	19.75
	2 V. Chukarin (URS)	19.55
	3 D. Leonkin (URS)	
	H. Eugster (SUI)	19.40

1956	1 A. Azarian (URS)	19.35
	2 V. Muratov (URS)	19.15
	3 M. Takemoto (JPN)	
	M. Kubota (JPN)	19.10

1960	1 A. Azarian (URS)	19.725
	2 B. Shakhlin (URS)	19.500
	3 V. Kapsazov (BUL)	
	T. Ono (JPN)	19.425

1964	1 T. Hayata (JPN)	19.475
	2 F. Menichelli (ITA)	19.425
	3 B. Shakhlin (URS)	19.400

1968	1 A. Nakayama (JPN)	19.450
	2 M. Voronin (URS)	19.325
	3 S. Kato (JPN	19.225

1972	1 A. Nakayama (JPN)	19.350
	2 M. Voronin (URS)	19.275
	3 M. Tsukahara (JPN)	19.225

1976	1 N. Andrianov (URS)	19.650
	2 A. Ditiatin (URS)	19.550
	3 D. Greco (ROM)	19.500

1980	1 A. Ditiatin (URS)	19.875
	2 A. Tkachev (URS)	19.725
	3 J. Tabak (TCH)	19.600

Floor exercises

		Points
1948	1 F. Pataki (HUN)	38.70
	2 J. Mogyorósi-	38.40
	Klencs (HUN)	
	3 Z. Ruzicka (TCH)	38.10

1952	1 W. Thoresson (SWE)	19.25
	2 T. Uesako (JPN)	
	J. Jokiel (POL)	19.15

1956	1 V. Muratov (URS)	19.20
	2 N. Aihara (JPN)	
	W. Thoresson (SWE)	
	V. Chukarin (URS)	19.10

1960	1 N. Aihara (JPN)	19.45
	2 Y. Titov (URS)	19.325
	3 F. Menichelli (ITA)	19.275

1964	1 F. Menichelli (ITA)	19.45
	2 V. Lisitski (URS)	19.35
	3 Y. Endo (JPN)	19.35

1968	1 S. Kato (JPN)	19.475
	2 A. Nakayama (JPN)	19.400
	3 T. Kato (JPN)	19.275

1972	1 N. Andrianov (URS)	19.175
	2 A. Nakayama (JPN)	19.125
	3 S. Kasamatsu (JPN)	19.025

1976	1 N. Andrianov (URS)	19.450
	2 V. Marchenko (URS)	19.425
	3 P. Kormann (USA)	19.300

1980	1 R. Bruckner (GDR)	19.750
	2 N. Andrianov (URS)	19.725
	3 A. Ditiatin (URS)	19.700

Gymnastics (women)
Combined exercises (individual)

			Points
1952	1	M. Gorokhovskaya (URS)	76.78
	2	N. Bocharova (URS)	75.94
	3	M. Korondi (HUN)	75.82
1956	1	L. Latynina (URS)	74.933
	2	A. Keleti (HUN)	74.633
	3	S. Muratova (URS)	74.466
1960	1	L. Latynina (URS)	77.031
	2	S. Muratova (URS)	76.696
	3	P. Astakhova (URS)	76.164
1964	1	V. Cáslavská (TCH)	77.564
	2	L. Latynina (URS)	76.998
	3	P. Astakhova (URS)	76.965
1968	1	V. Cáslavská (TCH)	78.25
	2	Z. Voronina (URS)	76.85
	3	N. Kuchinskaya (URS)	76.75
1972	1	L. Turisheva (URS)	77.025
	2	K. Janz (GDR)	76.875
	3	T. Lazakovich (URS)	76.850
1976	1	N. Comaneci (ROM)	79.275
	2	N. Kim (URS)	78.675
	3	L. Turisheva (URS)	78.625
1980	1	E. Davydova (URS)	79.150
	2	M. Gnauck (GDR)	
		N. Comaneci (ROM)	79.075

Asymmetrical bars

			Points
1952	1	M. Korondi (HUN)	19.40
	2	M. Gorokhovskaya (URS)	19.26
	3	A. Keleti (HUN)	19.16
1956	1	A. Keleti (HUN)	18.966
	2	L. Latynina (URS)	18.833
	3	S. Muratova (URS)	18.800
1960	1	P. Astakhova (URS)	19.616
	2	L. Latynina (URS)	19.416
	3	T. Lyukhina (URS)	19.399
1964	1	P. Astakhova (URS)	19.332
	2	K. Makray (HUN)	19.216
	3	L. Latynina (URS)	19.199
1968	1	V. Cáslavská (TCH)	19.650
	2	K. Janz (GDR)	19.500
	3	Z. Voronina (URS)	19.425
1972	1	K. Janz (GDR)	19.675
	2	O. Korbut (URS)	
		E. Zuchold (GDR)	19.450
1976	1	N. Comaneci (ROM)	20.000
	2	T. Ungureanu (ROM)	19.800
	3	M. Egervari (HUN)	19.775
1980	1	M. Gnauck (GDR)	19.875
	2	E. Eberle (ROM)	19.850
	3	S. Kräker (GDR)	
		M. Rühn (ROM)	
		M. Filatova (URS)	19.775

Combined exercises (team)

	Gold	Silver	Bronze
1948	TCH 445.45	HUN 440.55	USA 422.63
1952	URS 527.03	HUN 520.96	TCH 503.32
1956	URS 444.80	HUN 443.50	ROM 438.20
1960	URS 382.320	TCH 373.323	ROM 372.053
1964	URS 380.890	TCH 379.989	JPN 377.889
1968	URS 382.85	TCH 382.20	GDR 379.10
1972	URS 380.50	GDR 376.55	HUN 368.25
1976	URS 390.50	ROM 387.15	GDR 385.10
1980	URS 394.90	ROM 393.50	GDR 392.55

Beam

			Points
1952	1	N. Bocharova (URS)	19.22
	2	M. Gorokhovskaya (URS)	19.13
	3	M. Korondi (HUN)	19.02
1956	1	Á. Keleti (HUN)	18.800
	2	E. Bosáková (TCH) T. Manina (URS)	18.633
1960	1	E. Bosáková (TCH)	19.283
	2	L. Latynina (URS)	19.233
	3	S. Muratova (URS)	19.232
1904	1	V. Cáslavoká (TCH)	19.449
	2	T. Manina (URS)	19.399
	3	L. Latynina (URS)	19.382
1968	1	N. Kuchinskaya (URS)	19.650
	2	V. Cáslavská (TCH)	19.575
	3	L. Petrik (URS)	19.250
1972	1	O. Korbut (URS)	19.400
	2	T. Lazakovich (URS)	19.375
	3	K. Janz (GDR)	18.975
1976	1	N. Comaneci (ROM)	19.950
	2	O. Korbut (URS)	19.725
	3	T. Ungureanu (ROM)	19.700
1980	1	N. Comaneci (ROM)	19.800
	2	E. Davydova (URS)	19.750
	3	N. Shaposhnikova (URS)	19.725

Horse vault

			Points
1952	1	Y. Kalinchuk (URS)	19.20
	2	M. Gorokhovskaya (URS)	19.19
	3	G. Minaicheva (URS)	19.16
1956	1	L. Latynina (URS)	18.833
	2	T. Manina (URS)	18.800
	3	A.S. Colling (SWE) O. Tass (HUN)	18.733
1960	1	M. Nikolaeva (URS)	19.316
	2	S. Muratova (URS)	19.049
	3	L. Latynina (URS)	19.016

1964	1	V. Cáslavská (TCH)	19.483
	2	L. Latynina (URS) B. Radochia (GER)	19.283
1968	1	V. Cáslavská (TCH)	19.775
	2	E. Zuchold (GDR)	19.625
	3	Z. Voronina (URS)	19.500
1972	1	K. Janz (GDR)	19.525
	2	E. Zuchold (GDR)	19.275
	3	L. Turischeva (URS)	19.250
1976	1	N. Kim (URS)	19.800
	2	L. Turischeva (URS) C. Dombeck (GDR)	19.650
1980	1	N. Shaposhnikova (URS)	19.725
	2	S. Kräker (GDR)	19.675
	3	M. Rühn (ROM)	19.650

Floor exercises

			Points
1952	1	A. Keleti (HUN)	19.36
	2	M. Gorokhovskaya (URS)	19.20
	3	M. Korondi (HUN)	19.00
1956	1	L. Latynina (URS) A. Keleti (HUN)	18.733
	3	E. Leustean (ROM)	18.700
1960	1	L. Latynina (URS)	19.583
	2	P. Astakhova (URS)	19.532
	3	T. Lyukhina (URS)	19.449
1964	1	L. Latynina (URS)	19.599
	2	P. Astakhova (URS)	19.500
	3	A. Jánosi (HUN)	19.300
1968	1	V. Cáslavská (TCH) L. Petrik (URS)	19.675
	3	N. Kuchinskaya (URS)	19.650
1972	1	O. Korbut (URS)	19.575
	2	L. Turischeva (URS)	19.550
	3	T. Lazakovich (URS)	19.450
1976	1	N. Kim (URS)	19.850
	2	L. Turischeva (URS)	19.825
	3	N. Comaneci (ROM)	19.750

1980	1	N. Kim (URS)	
		N. Comaneci (ROM)	19.875
	3	N. Shaposhnikova (URS)	
		M. Gnauck (GDR)	19.825

Handball
Handball (men)

	Gold	Silver	Bronze
1972	YUG	TCH	ROM
1976	URS	ROM	POL
1980	GDR	URS	ROM

Handball (women)

	Gold	Silver	Bronze
1976	URS	GDR	HUN
1980	URS	YUG	GDR

Hockey
Hockey (men)

	Gold	Silver	Bronze
1948	IND	GBR	HOL
1952	IND	HOL	GBR
1956	IND	PAK	GER
1960	PAK	IND	ESP
1964	IND	PAK	AUS
1968	PAK	AUS	IND
1972	FRG	PAK	IND
1976	NZL	AUS	PAK
1980	IND	ESP	URS

Hockey (women)

	Gold	Silver	Bronze
1980	ZIM	TCH	URS

Judo

Lightweight
Weight limit 63kg (138lb 14½oz) —
before 1972. 68kg (149lb 14½oz)

1964 1 T. Nakatani (JPN)
　　2 E. Hänni (SUI)
　　3 O. Stepanov (URS)
　　　A. Bogolubov (URS)

1968 *Not held*

1972 1 T. Kawaguchi (JPN)
　　2 *Not awarded*
　　3 Y.I. Kim (PRK)
　　　J.J. Mounier (FRA)

1976 1 H. Rodriguez (CUB)
　　2 E. Chang (KOR)
　　3 F. Mariani (ITA)
　　　J. Tuncsik (HUN)

Welterweight
Weight limit 70kg (154lb 5oz)

1972 1 T. Nomura (JPN)
　　2 A. Zajkowski (POL)
　　3 D. Hoetger (GDR)
　　　A. Novikov (URS)

1976 1 V. Nevzorov (URS)
　　2 K. Kuramoto (JPN)
　　3 P. Vial (FRA)
　　　M. Talaj (POL)

Middleweight
Weight limit 80kg (176lb 6oz)

1964 1 I. Okano (JPN)
　　2 W. Hofmann (GER)
　　3 J. Bregman (USA)
　　　E.T. Kim (KOR)

1968 *Not held*

1972 1 S. Sekine (JPN)
　　2 S.L. Oh (PRK)
　　3 B. Jacks (GBR)
　　　J.P. Cochet (FRA)

1976 1 I. Sonoda (JPN)
　　2 V. Dvoinikov (URS)
　　3 S. Obadov (YUG)
　　　Y.C. Park (KOR)

Light heavyweight
Weight limit 93kg (205lb 0½oz)

1972 1 S. Chochoshvili (URS)
　　2 D.C. Starbrook (GBR)
　　3 P. Barth (FRG)
　　　C. Ishii (BRA)

1976 1 K. Ninomiya (JPN)
　　2 R. Harshiladze (URS)
　　3 D. Starbrook (GBR)
　　　J. Roethlisberger (SUI)

Heavyweight
Weight limit over 93kg (205lb 0½oz) —
before 1972 over 80kg (176lb 6oz)

1964 1 I. Inokuma (JPN)
　　2 A.H. Rogers (CAN)
　　3 A. Kiknadze (URS)
　　　P. Chikviladze (URS)

1968 *Not held*

1972 1 W. Ruska (HOL)
　　2 K. Glahn (FRG)
　　3 G. Onashvili (URS)
　　　M. Nishimura (JPN)

1976 1 S. Novikov (URS)
　　2 G. Neureuther (FRG)
　　3 S. Endo (JPN)
　　　A. Coage (USA)

Open
No weight limit

1964 1 A. Geesink (HOL)
　　2 A. Kaminaga (JPN)
　　3 K. Glahn (GER)
　　　T. Boronovskis (AUS)

1968 *Not held*

1972   1   W. Ruska (HOL)
      2   V. Kusnetsov (URS)
      3   A. Paris (GBR)
         J.C. Brondani (FRA)

1976   1   H. Uemura (JPN)
      2   K. Remfry (GBR)
      3   S. Chochoshvili (URS)
         J. Cho (KOR)

1980   1   D. Lorenz (GDR)
      2   A. Parisi (FRA)
      3   A. Ozsvar (HUN)
         A. Mapp (GBR)

*In 1980 weights were revised
to introduce two new categories.*
Up to 60kg

1980   1   T. Rey (FRA)
      2   R. Carbonell (CUB)
      3   T. Kincses (HUN)
         A. Emizh (URS)

Up to 65kg

1980   1   N. Solodukhin (URS)
      2   T. Damdin (MGL)
      3   I. Nedkov (BUL)
         J. Pawlowski (POL)

Up to 71kg

1980   1   E. Gamba (ITA)
      2   N. Adams (GBR)
      3   K. Lehmann (GDR)
         R. Davaadalai (MGL)

Up to 78kg

1980   1   S. Khabaleri (URS)
      2   J. La Hera (CUB)
      3   H. Heinke (GDR)
         B. Tchouillouyan (FRA)

Up to 86kg

1980   1   J. Roethlisberger (SUI)
      2   I. Oliva (CUB)
      3   D. Ultsch (GDR)
         A. Yatskevich (URS)

Up to 95kg

1980   1   R. Van de Walle (BEL)
      2   T. Khubuluri (URS)
      3   D. Lorenz (GDR)
         H. Numan (HOL)

Over 95kg

1980   1   A. Parisi (FRA)
      2   D. Zaprianov (BUL)
      3   V. Kocman (TCH)
         R. Kovacevic (YUG)

Modern Pentathlon

Modern pentathlon (Individual)
The five events are: horse-riding, fencing, pistol shooting, swimming and cross-country running.

1948	W. Grut (SWE)	G. Moore (USA)	A. Gärdin (SWE)
	16 pts	47 pts	49 pts
1952	L. Hall (SWE)	G. Benedek (HUN)	I. Szondi (HUN)
	32 pts	39 pts	41 pts
1956	L. Hall (SWE)	O. Mannonen (FIN)	V. Korhonen (FIN)
	4833 pts	4774.5 pts	4750 pts
1960	F. Németh (HUN)	I. Nagy (HUN)	R. Beck (USA)
	5024 pts	4988 pts	4981 pts
1964	F. Török (HUN)	I. Novikov (URS)	A. Mokeyev (URS)
	5116 pts	5067 pts	5039 pts
1968	B. Ferm (SWE)	A. Balczó (HUN)	P. Lednev (URS)
	4964 pts	4953 pts	4795 pts
1972	A. Balczó (HUN)	B. Onishenko (URS)	P. Lednev (URS)
	5412 pts	5335 pts	5328 pts
1976	J. Pyciak-Peciak (POL)	P. Lednev (URS)	J. Bartu (TCH)
	5520 pts	5485 pts	5466 pts
1980	A. Starostin (URS)	T. Szombathelyi (HUN)	P. Lednev (URS)
	5568 pts	5502 pts	5382 pts

Modern pentathlon (team)

	Gold	Silver	Bronze
1952	HUN 166	SWE 182	FIN 213
1956	URS 13690.5	USA 13482.0	FIN 13185.5
1960	HUN 14863	URS 14309	USA 14192
1964	URS 14961	USA 14189	HUN 14173
1968	HUN 14325	URS 14248	FRA 13289
1972	URS 15968	HUN 15348	FIN 14812
1976	GBR 15559	TCH 15451	HUN 15395
1980	URS 16126	HUN 15912	SWE 15845

Rowing (men)
Single sculls
Distance: 2000m (1mile 427yd)
In 1948 distance was 1880m

			Time
1948	1	M. Wood (AUS)	7:24.4
	2	E. Risso (URU)	7:38.2
	3	R. Catasta (ITA)	7:51.4
1952	1	Y. Tyukalov (URS)	8:12.8
	2	M. Wood (AUS)	8:14.5
	3	T. Kocerka (POL)	8:19.4
1956	1	V. Ivanov (URS)	8:02.5
	2	S. Mackenzie (AUS)	8:07.7
	3	J. Kelly (USA)	8:11.8
1960	1	V. Ivanov (URS)	7:13.96
	2	A. Hill (GER)	7:20.21
	3	T. Kocerka (POL)	7:21.26

1964	1	V. Ivanov (URS)	8:22.51
	2	A. Hill (GER)	8:26.24
	3	G. Kottman (SUI)	8:29.68
1968	1	H.J. Wienese (HOL)	7:47.80
	2	J. Meissner (FRG)	7:52.00
	3	A. Demiddi (ARG)	7:57.19
1972	1	Y. Malyshev (URS)	7:10.12
	2	A. Demiddi (ARG)	7:11.53
	3	W. Güldenpfennig (GDR)	7:14.45
1976	1	P. Karppinen (FIN)	7:29.03
	2	P.M. Kolbe (FRG)	7:31.67
	3	J. Dreifke (GDR)	7:38.03
1980	1	P. Karppinen (FIN)	7:09.61
	2	V. Yakusha (URS)	7:11.66
	3	P. Kersten (GDR)	7:14.88

Double sculls

	Gold	Silver	Bronze
1948	GBR 6:51.3	DEN 6:55.3	URU 7:12.4
1952	ARG 7:32.2	URS 7:38.2	URU 7:43.7
1956	URS 7:24.0	USA 7:32.2	AUS 7:37.4
1960	TCH 6:47.50	URS 6:50.49	SUI 6:50.59
1964	URS 7:10.66	USA 7:13.16	TCH 7:14.23
1968	URS 6:51.82	HOL 6:52.80	USA 6:54.21
1972	URS 7:01.77	NOR 7:02.58	GDR 7:05.55
1976	NOR 7:13.20	GBR 7:15.26	GDR 7:17.45
1980	GDR 6:24.33	YUG 6:26.34	TCH 6:29.07

Coxless pairs

	Gold	Silver	Bronze
1948	GBR 7:21.1	SUI 7:23.9	ITA 7:31.5
1952	USA 8:20.7	BEL 8:23.5	SUI 8:32.7
1956	USA 7:55.4	URS 8:03.9	AUT 8:11.8
1960	URS 7:02.00	AUT 7:03.69	FIN 7:03.80
1964	CAN 7:32.94	HOL 7:33.40	GER 7:38.63
1968	GDR 7:26.56	USA 7:26.71	DEN 7:31.84
1972	GDR 6:53.16	SUI 6:57.06	HOL 6:58.70
1976	GDR 7:23.31	USA 7:26.73	FRG 7:30.03
1980	GDR 6:48.01	URS 6:50.50	GBR 6:51.47

Coxed pairs

	Gold	Silver	Bronze
	Gold	*Silver*	*Bronze*
1948	DEN 8:00.5	ITA 8:12.2	HUN 8:25.2
1952	FRA 8:28.6	GER 8:32.1	DEN 8:34.9
1956	USA 8:26.1	GER 8:29.2	URS 8:31.0
1960	GER 7:29.14	URS 7:30.17	USA 7:34.58
1964	USA 8:21.23	FRA 8:23.15	HOL 8:23.42
1968	ITA 8:04.81	HOL 8:06.80	DEN 8:08.07
1972	GDR 7:17.25	TCH 7:19.57	ROM 7:21.36
1976	GDR 7:58.99	URS 8:01.82	TCH 8:03.28
1980	GDR 7:02.54	URS 7:03.35	YUG 7:04.92

Coxless fours

	Gold	Silver	Bronze
	Gold	*Silver*	*Bronze*
1948	ITA 6:39.0	DEN 6:43.5	USA 6:47.7
1952	YUG 7:16.0	FRA 7:18.9	FIN 7:23.3
1956	CAN 7:08.8	USA 7:18.4	FRA 7:20.9
1960	USA 6:26.26	ITA 6:28.78	URS 6:29.62
1964	DEN 6:59.30	GBR 7:00.47	USA 7:01.37
1968	GDR 6:39.18	HUN 6:41.64	ITA 6:44.01
1972	GDR 6:24.27	NZL 6:25.64	FRG 6:28.41
1976	GDR 6:37.42	NOR 6:41.22	URS 6:42.52
1980	GDR 6:08.17	URS 6:11.81	GBR 6:16.58

Coxed fours

	Gold	Silver	Bronze
	Gold	*Silver*	*Bronze*
1948	USA 6:50.3	SUI 6:53.3	DEN 6:58.6
1952	TCH 7:33.4	SUI 7:36.5	USA 7:37.0
1956	ITA 7:19.4	SWE 7:22.4	FIN 7:30.9
1960	GER 6:39.12	FRA 6:41.62	ITA 6:43.12
1964	GER 7:00.44	ITA 7:02.84	HOL 7:06.46
1968	NZL 6:45.62	GDR 6:48.20	SUI 6:49.04
1972	FRG 6:31.85	GDR 6:33.30	TCH 6:35.64
1976	URS 6:40.22	GDR 6:42.70	FRG 6:46.96
1980	GDR 6:14.51	URS 6:19.05	POL 6:22.52

Coxless quadruple sculls

	Gold	Silver	Bronze
	Gold	*Silver*	*Bronze*
1976	GDR 6:18.65	URS 6:19.89	TCH 6:21.77
1980	GDR 5:49.81	URS 5:51.47	BUL 5:52.38

Eights

	Gold	Silver	Bronze
1948	USA 5:46.7	GBR 6:06.9	NOR 6:10.3
1952	USA 6:25.9	URS 6:31.2	AUS 6:33.1
1956	USA 6:35.2	CAN 6:37.1	AUS 6:39.2
1960	GER 5:57.18	CAN 6:01.52	TCH 6:04.84
1964	USA 6:18.23	GER 6:23.29	TCH 6:25.11
1968	FRG 6:07.00	AUS 6:07.98	URS 6:09.11
1972	NZL 6:08.94	USA 6:11.61	GDR 6:11.67
1976	GDR 5:58.29	GBR 6:00.82	NZL 6:03.51
1980	GDR 5:49.05	GBR 5:51.92	URS 5:52.66

Rowing (women)

Single sculls (1000m)

			Time
1976	1	C. Scheiblich (GDR)	4:05.56
	2	J. Lind (USA)	4:06.21
	3	E. Antonova (URS)	4:10.24
1980	1	S. Toma (ROM)	3:40.69
	2	A. Makhina (URS)	3:41.65
	3	M. Schröter (GDR)	3:43.54

Coxed quadruple sculls

			Time
1976	1	GDR	3:29.99
	2	URS	3:32.49
	3	ROM	3:32.76
1980	1	GDR	3:15.32
	2	URS	3:15.73
	3	BUL	3:16.10

Double sculls (1000m)

			Time
1976	1	BUL	3:44.36
	2	GDR	3:47.86
	3	URS	3:49.93
1980	1	URS	3:16.27
	2	GDR	3:17.63
	3	ROM	3:18.91

Coxed fours

			Time
1976	1	GDR	3:45.08
	2	BUL	3:48.24
	3	URS	3:49.38
1980	1	GDR	3:19.27
	2	BUL	3:20.75
	3	URS	3:20.92

Coxless pairs

			Time
1976	1	BUL	4:01.22
	2	GDR	4:01.64
	3	FRG	4:02.35
1980	1	GDR	3:30.49
	2	POL	3:30.95
	3	BUL	3:32.39

Eights

			Time
1976	1	GDR	3:33.32
	2	URS	3:36.17
	3	USA	3:38.68
1980	1	GDR	3:03.32
	2	URS	3:04.29
	3	ROM	3:05.63

Shooting
Free pistol
Range 50m

			Points
1948	1	E. Vasquez Cam (PER)	545
	2	R. Schnyder (SUI)	539
	3	T. Ullman (SWE)	539
1952	1	H. Benner (USA)	553
	2	A. de Gozalo (ESP)	550
	3	A. Balogh (HUN)	549
1956	1	P. Linnosvuo (FIN)	556
	2	M. Umarov (URS)	556
	3	O. Pinion (USA)	551
1960	1	A. Gushchin (URS)	560
	2	M. Umarov (URS)	552
	3	Y. Yoshikawa (JPN)	552
1964	1	V. Markkanen (FIN)	560
	2	F. Green (USA)	557
	3	Y. Yoshikawa (JPN)	554
1968	1	G. Kosykh (URS)	562
	2	H. Mertel (FRG)	562
	3	H. Vollmar (GDR)	560
1972	1	R. Skanåker (SWE)	567
	2	D. Iuga (ROM)	562
	3	R. Dollinger (AUT)	560
1976	1	U. Potteck (GDR)	573
	2	H. Vollmar (GDR)	567
	3	R. Dollinger (AUT)	562
1980	1	A. Melentyev (URS)	581
	2	H. Vollmar (GDR)	568
	3	L. Diakov (URS)	565

Running game
Range 50m

			Points
1972	1	L. Zhelezniak (URS)	569
	2	H. Bellingrodt (COL)	565
	3	K. Kynoch (GBR)	562
1976	1	A. Gazov (URS)	579
	2	A. Kedyarov (URS)	576
	3	J. Greszkiewicz (POL)	571

1980	1	I. Sokolov (URS)	589
	2	T. Pfeffer (GDR)	589
	3	A. Gasov (URS)	587

Rapid fire pistol
Range 25m

			Points
1948	1	K. Takács (HUN)	580
	2	C.E. Diaz Sáenz Valiente (ARG)	571
	3	S. Lundqvist (SWE)	569
1952	1	K. Takács (HUN)	579
	2	S. Kun (HUN)	570
	3	G. Lichiardopol (ROM)	578
1956	1	S. Petrescu (ROM)	587
	2	Y. Cherkassov (URS)	585
	3	G. Lichiardopol (ROM)	581
1960	1	W. McMillan (USA)	587
	2	P. Linnosvuo (FIN)	587
	3	A. Zabelin (URS)	587
1964	1	P. Linnosvuo (FIN)	592
	2	I. Tripşa (ROM)	591
	3	L. Nacovsky (TCH)	590
1968	1	J. Zapedski (POL)	593
	2	M. Roşca (ROM)	591
	3	R. Suleimanov (URS)	591
1972	1	J. Zapedski (POL)	595
	2	L. Falta (TCH)	594
	3	V. Torshin (URS)	593
1976	1	N. Klaar (GDR)	597
	2	J. Wiefel (GDR)	596
	3	R. Ferraris (ITA)	595
1980	1	C. Ion (ROM)	596
	2	J. Wiefel (GDR)	596
	3	G. Petrisch (AUT)	596

Free rifle
Range 300m

			Points
1948	1	E. Grünig (SUI)	1120
	2	P. Janhonen (FIN)	1114
	3	W. Røgeberg (NOR)	1112

1952	1	A. Bogdanov (URS)	1123
	2	R. Bürchler (SUI)	1120
	3	L. Vainshtain (URS)	1109

1956	1	V. Borisov (URS)	1138
	2	A. Erdman (URS)	1137
	3	Y. Ylönen (FIN)	1128

1960	1	H. Hammere (AUT)	1129
	2	H. Spillmann (SUI)	1127
	3	V. Borisov (URS)	1127

1964	1	G. Anderson (USA)	1153
	2	S. Kveliashvili (URS)	1144
	3	M. Gunnarsson (USA)	1136

1968	1	G. Anderson (USA)	1157
	2	V. Kornev (URS)	1151
	3	K. Müller (SUI)	1148

1972	1	L. Wigger (USA)	1155
	2	B. Melnik (URS)	1155
	3	L. Pap (HUN)	1149

Event not held in 1976 or 1980

Smallbore rifle (prone)
Range 50m

			Points
1948	1	A. Cook (USA)	599
	2	W. Tomsen (USA)	599
	3	J. Jonsson (SWE)	597

1952	1	I. Sarbu (ROM)	400
	2	B. Andreev (URS)	400
	3	A. Jackson (USA)	399

1956	1	G.R. Ouellette (CAN)	600
	2	V. Borisov (URS)	599
	3	G.S. Boa (CAN)	598

1960	1	P. Kohnke (GER)	590
	2	J. Hill (USA)	589
	3	E. Forcella Pelliccioni (VEN)	587

1964	1	L. Hammerl (HUN)	597
	2	L. Wigger (USA)	597
	3	T. Pool (USA)	596

1968	1	J. Kurka (TCH)	598
	2	L. Hammerl (HUN)	598
	3	I. Ballinger (NZL)	597

1972	1	Ho Jun Li (PRK)	599
	2	V. Auer (USA)	598
	3	N. Rotaru (ROM)	598

1976	1	K. Smieszek (FRG)	599
	2	U. Lind (FRG)	597
	3	G. Lushchikov (URS)	595

1980	1	K. Varga (HUN)	599
	2	H. Heilfort (GDR)	599
	3	R. Zapianov (BUL)	598

Smallbore rifle (three positions)
Range 50m: standing, kneeling, prone.

			Points
1952	1	E. Kongshaug (NOR)	1164
	2	V. Ylönen (FIN)	1164
	3	B. Andreev (URS)	1163

1956	1	A. Bogdanov (URS)	1172
	2	O. Horinek (TCH)	1172
	3	N.J. Sundberg (SWE)	1167

1960	1	V. Shamburkin (URS)	1149
	2	M. Niasov (URS)	1145
	3	K. Zähringer (GER)	1139

1964	1	L. Wigger (USA)	1164
	2	V. Khristov (BUL)	1152
	3	L. Hammerl (HUN)	1151

1968	1	B. Klingner (FRG)	1157
	2	J. Writer (USA)	1156
	3	V. Parkhimovich (URS)	1154

1972	1	J. Writer (USA)	1166
	2	L. Bassham (USA)	1157
	3	W. Lippoldt (GDR)	1153

1976	1	L. Bassham (USA)	1162
	2	M. Murdoch (USA)	1162
	3	W. Seibold (FRG)	1160

1980	1	V. Vlasov (URS)	1173
	2	B. Hartstein (GDR)	1166
	3	S. Johansson (SWE)	1165

Trap shooting
200 pigeons

			Points
1952	1	G.P. Généreux (CAN)	192
	2	K. Holmqvist (SWE)	191
	3	H. Liljedahl (SWE)	190
1956	1	G. Rossini (ITA)	195
	2	A. Smelczyński (POL)	190
	3	A. Ciceri (ITA)	188
1960	1	I. Dumitrescu (ROM)	192
	2	G. Rossini (ITA)	191
	3	S. Kalinin (URS)	190
1964	1	E. Mattarelli (ITA)	198
	2	P. Senichev (URS)	194
	3	W. Morris (USA)	194
1968	1	J.R. Braithwaite (GBR)	198
	2	T. Garrigus (USA)	196
	3	K. Czekalla (GDR)	196
1972	1	A. Scalzone (ITA)	199
	2	M. Carrega (FRA)	198
	3	S. Basagni (ITA)	195
1976	1	D. Haldeman (USA)	190
	2	A. Silva Marques (POR)	189
	3	U. Baldi (ITA)	189
1980	1	L. Giovanetti (ITA)	198
	2	R. Yambulatov (URS)	196
	3	J. Damme (GDR)	196

Skeet

			Points
1968	1	Y. Petrov (URS)	198
	2	R. Garagnani (ITA)	198
	3	K. Wirnhier (FRG)	198
1972	1	K. Wirnhier (FRG)	195
	2	Y. Petrov (URS)	195
	3	M. Buchheim (GDR)	195
1976	1	J. Panacek (TCH)	198
	2	E. Swinkels (HOL)	198
	3	W. Gawlikowski (POL)	196
1980	1	H.J. Rasmussen (DEN)	196
	2	L.G. Carlsson (SWE)	196
	3	R. Garcia (CUB)	196

Swimming and diving
(men)
100 metres freestyle

			Points
1948	1	W. Ris (USA)	57.3
	2	A. Ford (USA)	57.8
	3	G. Kádas (HUN)	58.1
1952	1	C. Scholes (USA)	57.4
	2	H. Suzuki (JPN)	57.4
	3	G. Larsson (SWE)	58.2
1956	1	J. Henricks (AUS)	55.4
	2	J. Devitt (AUS)	55.8
	3	G. Chapman (AUS)	56.7
1960	1	J. Devitt (AUS)	55.2
	2	L. Larson (USA)	55.2
	3	M. Dos Santos (BRA)	55.4
1964	1	D. Schollander (USA)	53.4
	2	R. McGregor (GBR)	53.5
	3	H.J. Klein (GER)	54.0
1968	1	M. Wenden (AUS)	52.2
	2	K. Walsh (USA)	52.8
	3	M. Spitz (USA)	53.0
1972	1	M. Spitz (USA)	51.22
	2	J. Heidenreich (USA)	51.65
	3	V. Bure (URS)	51.77
1976	1	J. Montgomery (USA)	49.99
	2	J. Babashoff (USA)	50.81
	3	P. Nocke (FRG)	51.31
1980	1	J. Woithe (GDR)	50.40
	2	P. Holmertz (SWE)	50.91
	3	P. Johansson (SWE)	51.29

200 metres freestyle

			Time
1968	1	M. Wenden (AUS)	1:55.2
	2	D. Schollander (USA)	1:55.8
	3	J. Nelson (USA)	1:58.1
1972	1	M. Spitz (USA)	1:52.78
	2	S. Genter (USA)	1:53.73
	3	W. Lampe (FRG)	1:53.99

1976	1	B. Furniss (USA)	1:50.29
	2	J. Naber (USA)	1:50.50
	3	J. Montgomery (USA)	1:50.58
1980	1	S. Kopliakov (URS)	1:49.81
	2	A. Krylov (URS)	1:50.76
	3	G. Brewer (AUS)	1:51.60

400 metres freestyle

			Time
1948	1	W. Smith (USA)	4:41.0
	2	J. McLane (USA)	4:43.4
	3	J. Marshall (AUS)	4:47.4
1952	1	J. Boiteux (FRA)	4:30.7
	2	F. Konno (USA)	4:31.3
	3	P.O. Östrand (SWE)	4:35.2
1956	1	M. Rose (AUS)	4:27.3
	2	T. Yamanaka (JPN)	4:30.4
	3	G. Breen (USA)	4:32.5
1960	1	M. Rose (AUS)	4:18.3
	2	T. Yamanaka (JPN)	4:21.4
	3	J. Konrads (AUS)	4:21.8
1964	1	D. Schollander (USA)	4:12.2
	2	F. Wiegand (GER)	4:14.9
	3	A. Wood (AUS)	4:15.1
1968	1	M. Burton (USA)	4:09.0
	2	R. Hutton (CAN)	4:11.7
	3	A. Mosconi (FRA)	4:13.3
1972	1	B. Cooper (AUS)	4:00.27
	2	S. Genter (USA)	4:01.94
	3	T. McBreen (USA)	4:02.64
1976	1	B. Goodell (USA)	3:51.93
	2	T. Shaw (USA)	3:52.54
	3	V. Raskatov (URS)	3:55.76
1980	1	V. Salnikov (URS)	3:51.31
	2	A. Krylov (URS)	3:53.24
	3	I. Stukolkin (URS)	3:53.95

1500 metres freestyle

			Time
1948	1	J. McLane (USA)	19:18.5
	2	J. Marshall (AUS)	19:31.3
	3	G. Mitró (HUN)	19:43.2
1952	1	F. Konno (USA)	18:30.3
	2	S. Hashizume (JPN)	18:41.4
	3	T. Okamoto (BRA)	18:51.3
1956	1	M. Rose (AUS)	17:58.9
	2	T. Yamanaka (JPN)	18:00.3
	3	G. Breen (USA)	18:08.2
1960	1	J. Konrads (AUS)	17:19.6
	2	M. Rose (AUS)	17:21.7
	3	G. Breen (USA)	17:30.6
1964	1	R. Windle (AUS)	17:01.7
	2	J. Nelson (USA)	17:03.0
	3	A. Wood (AUS)	17:07.7
1968	1	M. Burton (USA)	16:38.9
	2	J. Kinsella (USA)	16:57.3
	3	G. Brough (AUS)	17:04.7
1972	1	M. Burton (USA)	15:52.58
	2	G. Windeatt (AUS)	15:58.48
	3	D. Northway (USA)	16:09.25
1976	1	B. Goodell (USA)	15:02.40
	2	B. Hackett (USA)	15:03.91
	3	S. Holland (AUS)	15:04.66
1980	1	V. Salnikov (URS)	14:58.27
	2	A. Chaev (URS)	15:14.30
	3	M. Metzker (AUS)	15:14.49

100 metres backstroke

			Time
1948	1	A. Stack (USA)	1:06.4
	2	R. Cowell (USA)	1:06.5
	3	G. Vallerey (FRA)	1:07.8
1952	1	Y. Oyakawa (USA)	1:05.4
	2	G. Bozon (FRA)	1:06.2
	3	J. Taylor (USA)	1:06.4
1956	1	D. Theile (AUS)	1:02.2
	2	J. Monckton (AUS)	1:03.2
	3	F. McKinney (USA)	1:04.5

1960	1	D. Theile (AUS)	1:01.9
	2	F. McKinney (USA)	1:02.1
	3	R. Bennett (USA)	1:02.3

1964 *Event not held.*

1968	1	R. Matthes (GDR)	58.7
	2	C. Hickcox (USA)	1:00.2
	3	R. Mills (USA)	1:00.5

1972	1	R. Matthes (GDR)	56.58
	2	M. Stamm (USA)	57.70
	3	J. Murphy (USA)	58.35

1976	1	J. Naber (USA)	55.49
	2	P. Rocca (USA)	56.34
	3	R. Matthes (GDR)	57.22

1980	1	B. Baron (SWE)	56.53
	2	V. Kuznetsov (URS)	56.99
	3	V. Dolgov (URS)	57.63

200 metres backstroke

			Points
1964	1	J. Graef (USA)	2:10.3
	2	G. Dilley (USA)	2:10.5
	3	R. Bennett (USA)	2:13.1

1968	1	R. Matthes (GDR)	2:09.6
	2	M. Ivey (USA)	2:10.6
	3	J. Horsley (USA)	2:10.9

1972	1	R. Matthes (GDR)	2:02.82
	2	M. Stamm (USA)	2:04.09
	3	M. Ivey (USA)	2:04.33

1976	1	J. Naber (USA)	1:59.19
	2	P. Rocca (USA)	2:00.55
	3	D. Harrigan (USA)	2:01.35

1980	1	S. Wladar (HUN)	2:01.93
	2	Z. Verraszto (HUN)	2:02.40
	3	M. Kerry (AUS)	2:03.14

100 metres breaststroke

			Time
1968	1	D. McKenzie (USA)	1:07.7
	2	V. Kosinski (URS)	1:08.0
		N. Pankin (URS)	1:08.0

1972	1	N. Taguchi (JPN)	1:04.94
	2	T. Bruce (USA)	1:05.43
	3	J. Hencken (USA)	1:05.61

1976	1	J. Hencken (USA)	1:03.11
	2	D. Wilkie (GBR)	1:03.43
	3	A. Ivozaytis (URS)	1:04.23

1980	1	D. Goodhew (GBR)	1:03.34
	2	A. Muskarov (URS)	1:03.82
	3	P. Evans (AUS)	1:03.96

200 metres breaststroke

			Time
1948	1	J. Verdeur (USA)	2:39.3
	2	K. Carter (USA)	2:40.2
	3	R. Sohl (USA)	2:43.9

1952	1	J. Davies (AUS)	2:34.4
	2	B. Stassforth (USA)	2:34.7
	3	H. Klein (GER)	2:35.9

1956	1	M. Furukawa (JPN)	2:34.7
	2	M. Yoshimura (JPN)	2:36.7
	3	K. Yunichev (URS)	2:36.8

1960	1	W. Mulliken (USA)	2:37.4
	2	Y. Osaki (JPN)	2:38.0
	3	W. Mensonides (HOL)	2:39.7

1964	1	I. O'Brien (AUS)	2:27.8
	2	G. Prokopenko (URS)	2:28.2
	3	C. Jastremski (USA)	2:29.6

1968	1	M. Muñoz (MEX)	2:28.7
	2	V. Kosinski (URS)	2:29.2
	3	B. Job (USA)	2:29.9

1972	1	J. Hencken (USA)	2:21.55
	2	D. Wilkie (GBR)	2:23.67
	3	N. Taguchi (JPN)	2:23.88

1976	1	D. Wilkie (GBR)	2:15.11
	2	C. Keating (USA)	2:17.26
	3	R. Colella (USA)	2:19.20

1980	1	R. Shulpa (URS)	2:15.85
	2	A. Vermes (HUN)	2:16.93
	3	A. Miskarov (URS)	2:17.28

100 metres butterfly

			Points
1968	1	D. Russell (USA)	55.9
	2	M. Spitz (USA)	56.4
	3	R. Wales (USA)	57.2
1972	1	M. Spitz (USA)	54.27
	2	B. Robertson (CAN)	55.56
	3	J. Heidenreich (USA)	55.74
1976	1	M. Vogel (USA)	54.35
	2	J. Bottom (USA)	54.50
	3	G. Hall (USA)	54.65
1980	1	P. Arvidsson (SWE)	54.92
	2	R. Pyttel (GDR)	54.94
	3	D. Lopez (ESP)	55.13

200 metres butterfly

			Points
1956	1	W. Yorzyk (USA)	2:19.3
	2	T. Ishimoto (JPN)	2:23.8
	3	G. Tumpek (HUN)	2:23.9
1960	1	M. Troy (USA)	2:12.8
	2	N. Hayes (AUS)	2:14.6
	3	D. Gillanders (USA)	2:15.3
1964	1	K. Berry (AUS)	2:06.6
	2	G. Robie (USA)	2:07.5
	3	F. Schmidt (USA)	2:09.3
1968	1	C. Robie (USA)	2:08.7
	2	M. Woodroffe (GBR)	2:09.0
	3	J. Ferris (USA)	2:09.3
1972	1	M. Spitz (USA)	2:00.70
	2	G. Hall (USA)	2:02.86
	3	R. Backhaus (USA)	2:03.23
1976	1	M. Bruner (USA)	1:59.23
	2	S. Gregg (USA)	1:59.54
	3	B. Forrester (USA)	1:59.96
1980	1	S. Fesenko (URS)	1:59.76
	2	R. Hubble (GBR)	2:01.20
	3	R. Pyttel (GDR)	2:01.39

200 metres individual medley

Order of strokes: butterfly, backstroke, breaststroke, freestyle.

			Time
1968	1	C. Hickcox (USA)	2:12.0
	2	G. Buckingham (USA)	2:13.0
	3	J. Ferris (USA)	2:13.3
1972	1	G. Larsson (SWE)	2:07.17
	2	T. McKee (USA)	2:08.37
	3	S. Furniss (USA)	2:08.45

Event not held in 1976 and 1980

400 metres individual medley

Order of strokes: butterfly, backstroke, breaststroke, freestyle.

			Time
1964	1	R. Roth (USA)	4:45.4
	2	R. Saari (USA)	4:47.1
	3	G. Hetz (GER)	4:51.0
1968	1	C. Hickcox (USA)	4:48.4
	2	G. Hall (USA)	4:48.7
	3	M. Holthaus (FRG)	4:51.4
1972	1	G. Larsson (SWE)	4:31.98
	2	T. McKee (USA)	4:31.98
	3	A. Hargitay (HUN)	4:32.70
1976	1	R. Strachan (USA)	4:23.68
	2	T. McKee (USA)	4:24.62
	3	A. Smirnov (URS)	4:26.90
1980	1	A. Sidorenko (URS)	4:22.89
	2	S. Fesenko (URS)	4:23.43
	3	Z. Verraszto (HUN)	4:24.24

4 x 100 metres freestyle relay

	Gold	Silver	Bronze
1964	USA 3:33.2	GER 3:37.2	AUS 3:39.1
1968	USA 3:31.7	URS 3:34.2	AUS 3:34.7
1972	USA 3:26.42	URS 3:29.72	GDR 3:32.42

Event not held in 1976 and 1980

4 x 200 metres freestyle relay

	Gold	Silver	Bronze
1948	USA 8:46.0	HUN 8:48.4	FRA 9:08.0
1952	USA 8:31.1	JPN 8:33.5	FRA 8:45.9
1956	AUS 8:23.6	USA 8:31.5	URS 8:34.7
1960	USA 8:10.2	JPN 8:13.2	AUS 8:13.8
1964	USA 7:52.1	GER 7:59.3	JPN 8:03.8
1968	USA 7:52.3	AUS 7:53.7	URS 8:01.6
1972	USA 7:35.78	FRG 7:41.69	URS 7:45.76
1976	USA 7:23.22	URS 7:27.97	GBR 7:32.11
1980	URS 7:23.50	GDR 7:28.60	BRA 7:29.30

4 x 100 metres medley relay

Order of strokes: backstroke, breaststroke, butterfly, freestyle.

	Gold	Silver	Bronze
1960	USA 4:05.4	AUS 4:12.0	JPN 4:12.2
1964	USA 3:58.4	GER 4:01.6	AUS 4:02.3
1968	USA 3:54.9	GDR 3:57.5	URS 4:00.7
1972	USA 3:48.16	GDR 3:52.1	CAN 3:52.26
1976	USA 3:42.22	CAN 3:45.94	FRG 3:47.29
1980	AUS 3:45.70	URS 3:45.92	GBR 3:47.71

Highboard diving

			Points
1948	1	S. Lee (USA)	130.05
	2	B. Harlan (USA)	122.30
	3	J. Capilla Pérez (MEX)	113.52
1952	1	S. Lee (USA)	156.28
	2	J. Capilla Pérez (MEX)	145.21
	3	G. Haase (GER)	141.31
1956	1	J. Capilla Pérez (MEX)	152.44
	2	G. Tobian (USA)	152.41
	3	R. Connor (USA)	149.79
1960	1	R. Webster (USA)	165.56
	2	G. Tobian (USA)	165.25
	3	B. Phelps (GBR)	157.13
1964	1	R. Webster (USA)	148.58

	2	K. Dibias (ITA)	147.54
	3	T. Gompf (USA)	146.57
1968	1	K. Dibiasi (ITA)	164.18
	2	A. Gaxiola (MEX)	154.49
	3	E. Young (USA)	153.93
1972	1	K. Dibiasi (ITA)	504.12
	2	R. Rydze (USA)	480.75
	3	F. Cagnotto (ITA)	475.83
1976	1	K. Dibiasi (ITA)	600.51
	2	G. Louganis (USA)	576.99
	3	V. Aleynik (URS)	548.61
1980	1	F. Hoffmann (GDR)	835.65
	2	V. Heynik (URS)	819.71
	3	D. Ambartsumyan (URS)	817.44

Springboard diving

			Points
1948	1	B. Harlan (USA)	163.64
	2	M. Anderson (USA)	157.29
	3	S. Lee (USA)	145.52
1952	1	D. Browning (USA)	205.29
	2	M. Anderson (USA)	199.84
	3	R. Clotworthy (USA)	184.92
1956	1	R. Clotworthy (USA)	159.56
	2	D. Harper (USA)	156.23
	3	J. Capilla Pérez (MEX)	150.69
1960	1	G. Tobian (USA)	170.00
	2	S. Hall (USA)	167.08
	3	J. Botella (MEX)	162.30
1964	1	K. Sitzberger (USA)	159.90
	2	F. Gorman (USA)	157.63
	3	L. Andreasen (USA)	143.77
1968	1	B. Wrightson (USA)	170.15
	2	K. Dibiasi (ITA)	159.74
	3	J. Henry (USA)	158.09
1972	1	V. Vasin (URS)	594.08
	2	F. Cagnotto (ITA)	591.63
	3	C. Lincoln (USA)	577.29
1976	1	P. Boggs (USA)	619.05
	2	F. Cagnotto (ITA)	570.40
	3	A. Kosenkov (URS)	567.24
1980	1	A. Portnov (URS)	905.025
	2	G. Giron (MEX)	892.140
	3	F. Cagnotto (ITA)	871.500

Water polo

1948	1	ITA
	2	HUN
	3	HOL
1952	1	HUN
	2	YUG
	3	ITA
1956	1	HUN
	2	YUG
	3	URS
1960	1	ITA
	2	URS
	3	HUN
1964	1	HUN
	2	YUG
	3	URS
1968	1	YUG
	2	URS
	3	HUN
1972	1	URS
	2	HUN
	3	USA
1976	1	HUN
	2	ITA
	3	HOL
1980	1	URS
	2	YUG
	3	HUN

Swimming and diving (women)

100 metres freestyle

			Time
1948	1	G. Andersen (DEN)	1:06.3
	2	A. Curtis (USA)	1:06.5
	3	M.L. Vaessen (HOL)	1:07.6
1952	1	K. Szoke (HUN)	1:06.8
	2	J. Termeulen (HOL)	1:07.0
	3	J. Temes (HUN)	1:07.1
1956	1	D. Fraser (AUS)	1:02.0
	2	L. Crapp (AUS)	1:02.3
	3	F. Leech (AUS)	1:05.1
1960	1	D. Fraser (AUS)	1:01.2
	2	C. Von Saltza (USA)	1:02.8
	3	N. Steward (GBR)	1:03.1
1964	1	D. Fraser (AUS)	59.5
	2	S. Stouder (USA)	59.9
	3	K. Ellis (USA)	1:00.8
1968	1	J. Henne (USA)	1:00.0
	2	S. Pedersen (USA)	1:00.3
	3	L. Gustavson (USA)	1:00.3
1972	1	S. Neilson (USA)	58.59
	2	S. Babashoff (USA)	59.02
	3	S. Gould (AUS)	59.06
1976	1	K. Ender (GDR)	55.65
	2	P. Priemer (GDR)	56.49
	3	E. Brigitha (HOL)	56.65
1980	1	B. Krause (GDR)	54.79
	2	C. Metschuck (GDR)	55.16
	3	I. Diers (GDR)	55.65

200 metres freestyle

			Points
1968	1	D. Meyer (USA)	2:10.5
	2	J. Henne (USA)	2:11.0
	3	J. Barkman (USA)	2:11.2
1972	1	S. Gould (AUS)	2:03.56
	2	S. Babashoff (USA)	2:04.33
	3	K. Rothhammer (USA)	2:04.92

1976	1	K. Ender (GDR)	1:59.26
	2	S. Babashoff (USA)	2:01.22
	3	E. Brigitha (HOL)	2:01.40
1980	1	B. Krause (GDR)	1:58.33
	2	I. Diers (GDR)	1:59.64
	3	C. Schmidt (GDR)	2:01.44

400 metres freestyle

			Points
1948	1	A. Curtis (USA)	5:17.8
	2	K.M. Harup (DEN)	5:21.2
	3	C. Gibson (GBR)	5:22.5
1952	1	V. Gyenge (HUN)	5:12.1
	2	E. Novák (HUN)	5:13.7
	3	E. Kawamoto (USA)	5:14.6
1956	1	L. Crapp (AUS)	4:54.6
	2	D. Fraser (AUS)	5:02.5
	3	S. Ruuska (USA)	5:07.1
1960	1	C. Von Saltza (USA)	4:50.6
	2	J. Cederqvist (SWE)	4:53.9
	3	C. Lagerberg (HOL)	4:56.9
1964	1	V. Duenkel (USA)	4:43.3
	2	M. Ramenofsky (USA)	4:44.6
	3	T. Stickles (USA)	4:47.2
1968	1	D. Meyer (USA)	4:31.8
	2	L. Gustavson (USA)	4:35.5
	3	K. Moras (AUS)	4:37.0
1972	1	S. Gould (AUS)	4:19.04
	2	N. Calligaris (ITA)	4:22.44
	3	G. Wegner (GDR)	4:23.11
1976	1	P. Thumer (GDR)	4:09.89
	2	S. Babashoff (USA)	4:10.46
	3	S. Smith (CAN)	4:14.60
1980	1	I. Diers (GDR)	4:08.76
	2	P. Schneider (GDR)	4:09.16
	3	C. Schmidt (GDR)	4:10.86

800 metres freestyle

			Time
1968	1	D. Meyer (USA)	9:24.0
	2	P. Kruse (USA)	9:35.7
	3	M. Ramirez (MEX)	9:38.5
1972	1	K. Rothhammer (USA)	8:53.68
	2	S. Gould (AUS)	8:56.39
	3	N. Calligaris (ITA)	8:57.46
1976	1	P. Thumer (GDR)	8:37.14
	2	S. Babashoff (USA)	8:37.59
	3	W. Weinberg (USA)	8:42.60
1980	1	M. Ford (AUS)	8:28.90
	2	I. Diers (GDR)	8:32.55
	3	H. Dähne (GDR)	8:33.48

100 metres backstroke

			Time
1948	1	K.M. Harup (DEN)	1:14.4
	2	S. Zimmerman (USA)	1:16.0
	3	J.J. Davies (AUS)	1:16.7
1952	1	J. Harrison (SAF)	1:14.3
	2	G. Wielema (HOL)	1:14.5
	3	J. Stewart (NZL)	1:15.8
1956	1	J. Grinham (GBR)	1:12.9
	2	C. Cone (USA)	1:12.9
	3	M. Edwards (GBR)	1:13.1
1960	1	L. Burke (USA)	1:09.3
	2	N. Steward (GBR)	1:10.8
	3	S. Tanaka (JPN)	1:11.4
1964	1	C. Ferguson (USA)	1:07.7
	2	C. Caron (FRA)	1:07.9
	3	V. Duenkel (USA)	1:08.0
1968	1	K. Hall (USA)	1:06.2
	2	E. Tanner (CAN)	1:06.7
	3	J. Swagerty (USA)	1:08.1
1972	1	M. Belote (USA)	1:05.78
	2	A. Gyarmati (HUN)	1:06.26
	3	S. Atwood (USA)	1:06.34
1976	1	U. Richter (GDR)	1:01.83
	2	B. Treiber (GDR)	1:03.41
	3	N. Garapick (CAN)	1:03.71

1980	1	R. Reinisch (GDR)	1:00.86
	2	I. Kleber (GDR)	1:02.07
	2	P. Riedel (GDR)	1:02.64

200 metres backstroke

			Time
1968	1	L. Watson (USA)	2:24.8
	2	E. Tanner (CAN)	2:27.4
	3	K. Hall (USA)	2:28.9
1972	1	M. Belote (USA)	2:19.19
	2	S. Atwood (USA)	2:20.38
	3	D.M. Gurr (CAN)	2:23.22
1976	1	U. Richter (GDR)	2:13.43
	2	B. Treiber (GDR)	2:14.97
	3	N. Garapick (CAN)	2:15.60
1980	1	R. Reinisch (GDR)	2:11.77
	2	C. Pilot (GDR)	2:13.75
	3	B. Treiber (GDR)	2:14.14

100 metres breaststroke

			Time
1968	1	D. Bjedov (YUG)	1:15.8
	2	G. Prozumenshchikova (URS)	1:15.9
	3	S. Wichman (USA)	1:16.1
1972	1	C. Carr (USA)	1:13.58
	2	G. Stepanova (URS)	1:14.99
	3	B. Whitfield (AUS)	1:15.73
1976	1	H. Anka (GDR)	1:11.16
	2	L. Rusanov (URS)	1:13.04
	3	M. Koshevaia (URS)	1:13.30
1980	1	U. Geweniger (GDR)	1:10.22
	2	E. Vasilkova (URS)	1:10.41
	3	S. Nielsson (DEN)	1:11.16

200 metres breaststroke

			Time
1948	1	P. van Vliet (HOL)	2:57.2
	2	B. Lyons (AUS)	2:57.7
	3	E. Novák (HUN)	3:00.2

1952	1	É. Székely (HUN)	2:51.7
	2	R. Novák (HUN)	2:54.4
	3	H. Gordon (GBR)	2:57.6
1956	1	U. Happe (GER)	2:53.1
	2	É. Székely (HUN)	2:54.8
	3	E.M. ten Elsen (GER)	2:55.1
1960	1	A. Lonsbrough (GBR)	2:49.5
	2	W. Urselmann (GER)	2:50.0
	3	B. Gobel (GER)	2:53.6
1964	1	G. Prozumenshchikova (URS)	2:46.4
	2	C. Kolb (USA)	2:47.6
	3	S. Babanina (URS)	2:18.6
1968	1	S. Wichman (USA)	2:44.4
	2	D. Bjedov (YUG)	2:46.4
	3	G. Prozumenshchikova (URS)	2:47.0
1972	1	B. Whitfield (AUS)	2:41.71
	2	D. Schoenfield (USA)	2:42.05
	3	G. Stepanova (URS)	2:42.36
1976	1	M. Koshevaia (URS)	2:33.35
	2	M. Iurchenia (URS)	2:36.08
	3	L. Rusanov (URS)	2:36.22
1980	1	L. Kachushite (URS)	2:29.54
	2	S. Varganova (URS)	2:29.61
	3	Y. Bogdanova (URS)	2:32.39

100 metres butterfly

			Time
1956	1	S. Mann (USA)	1:11.0
	2	N. Ramey (USA)	1:11.9
	3	M. Sears (USA)	1:14.4
1960	1	C. Schuler (USA)	1:09.5
	2	M. Heemskerk (HOL)	1:10.4
	3	J. Andrew (AUS)	1:12.2
1964	1	S. Stouder (USA)	1:04.7
	2	A. Kok (HOL)	1:05.6
	3	K. Ellis (USA)	1:06.0
1968	1	L. McClements (AUS)	1:05.5
	2	E. Daniel (USA)	1:05.8
	3	S. Shields (USA)	1:06.2

1972	1	M. Aoki (JPN)	1:03.34
	2	R. Beier (GDR)	1:03.61
	3	A. Gyarmati (HUN)	1:03.73
1976	1	K. Ender (GDR)	1:00.13
	2	A. Pollack (GDR)	1:00.98
	3	W. Boglioli (USA)	1:01.17
1980	1	C. Metschuck (GDR)	1:00.42
	2	A. Pollack (GDR)	1:00.90
	3	C. Knacke (GDR)	1:01.44

200 metres butterfly

			Time
1968	1	A. Kok (HOL)	2:24.7
	2	H. Lindner (GDR)	2:24.8
	3	E. Daniel (USA)	2:25.9
1972	1	K. Moe (USA)	2:15.57
	2	L. Colella (USA)	2:16.34
	3	E. Daniel (USA)	2:16.74
1976	1	A. Pollack (GDR)	2:11.41
	2	U. Tauber (GDR)	2:12.50
	3	R. Gabriel (GDR)	2:12.86
1980	1	I. Geissler (GDR)	2:10.44
	2	S. Schönrock (GDR)	2:10.45
	3	M. Ford (AUS)	2:11.66

200 metres individual medley

Order of strokes: butterfly, backstroke, breaststroke, freestyle.

			Time
1968	1	C. Kolb (USA)	2:24.7
	2	S. Pedersen (USA)	2:28.8
	3	J. Henne (USA)	2:31.4
1972	1	S. Gould (AUS)	2:23.07
	2	K. Ender (GDR)	2:23.59
	3	L. Vidali (USA)	2:24.06

Event not held in 1976 and 1980

400 metres individual medley

Order of strokes: butterfly, backstroke, breaststroke, freestyle.

			Time
1964	1	D. De Varona (USA)	5:18.7
	2	S. Finneran (USA)	5:24.1
	3	M. Randall (USA)	5:24.2
1968	1	C. Kolb (USA)	5:08.5
	2	L. Vidali (USA)	5:22.2
	3	S. Steinbach (GDR)	5:25.3
1972	1	G. Neall (AUS)	5:02.97
	2	L. Cliff (CAN)	5:03.57
	3	N. Calligaris (ITA)	5:03.99
1976	1	U. Tauber (GDR)	4:42.77
	2	C. Gibson (CAN)	4:48.10
	3	B. Smith (CAN)	4:50.48
1980	1	P. Schneider (GDR)	4:36.29
	2	S. Davies (GBR)	4:46.83
	3	A. Czopek (POL)	4:48.17

4 x 100 metres freestyle relay

	Gold	Silver	Bronze
1948	USA 4:29.2	DEN 4:29.6	HOL 4:31.6
1952	HUN 4:24.4	HOL 4:29.0	USA 4:30.1
1956	AUS 4:17.1	USA 4:19.2	SAF 4:25.7
1960	USA 4:08.9	AUS 4:11.3	GER 4:19.7
1964	USA 4:03.8	AUS 4:06.9	HOL 4:12.0
1968	USA 4:02.5	GDR 4:05.7	CAN 4:07.2
1972	USA 3:55.19	GDR 3:55.55	FRG 3:57.93
1976	USA 3:44.82	GDR 3:45.50	CAN 3:48.81
1980	GDR 3:42.71	SWE 3:48.93	HOL 3:49.51

4 x 100 metres medley relay

Order of strokes: backstroke, breaststroke, butterfly, freestyle.

	Gold	Silver	Bronze
1960	USA 4:41.1	AUS 4:45.9	GER 4:47.6
1964	USA 4:33.9	HOL 4:37.0	URS 4:39.2
1968	USA 4:28.3	AUS 4:30.0	FRG 4:36.4
1972	USA 4:20.75	GDR 4:24.91	FRG 4:26.46
1976	GDR 4:07.95	USA 4:14.55	CAN 4:15.22
1980	GDR 4:06.67	GBR 4:12.24	URS 4:13.61

Highboard diving

			Points
1948	1	V. Draves (USA)	68.87
	2	P. Elsener (USA)	66.28
	3	B. Christoffersen (DEN)	66.04
1952	1	P. McCormick (USA)	79.37
	2	P. Myers (USA)	71.63
	3	J. Irwin (USA)	70.49
1956	1	P. McCormick (USA)	84.85
	2	J. Irwin (USA)	81.64
	3	P. Myers (USA)	81.58
1960	1	I. (Krämer) Engel (GER)	91.28
	2	P. (Myers) Pope (USA)	88.94
	3	N. Krutova (URS)	86.99

1964	1 L. Bush (USA)	99.80
	2 I. (Krämer) Engel (GER)	98.45
	3 G. Alekseeva (URS)	97.60

1968	1 M. Duchková (TCH)	109.59
	2 N. Lobanova (URS)	105.14
	3 A. Peterson (USA)	101.11

1972	1 U. Knape (SWE)	390.00
	2 M. Duchkova (TCH)	370.92
	3 M. Janicke (GDR)	360.54

1976	1 E. Vaytsekhovskaya (URS)	406.59
	2 U. Knape (SWE)	402.60
	3 D. Wilson (USA)	401.07

1980	1 M. Jáschke (GDR)	596.250
	2 S. Emirzyan (URS)	576.465
	3 L. Tsotadze (URS)	575.925

1972	1 M. King (USA)	450.03
	2 U. Knape (SWE)	434.19
	3 M. Janicke (GDR)	430.92

1976	1 J. Chandler (USA)	506.19
	2 C. Kohler (GDR)	469.41
	3 C. McIngvale (USA)	466.83

1980	1 I. Kalinina (URS)	725.910
	2 M. Proeber (GDR)	698.895
	3 K. Guthke (GDR)	685.245

Springboard diving

		Points
1948	1 V. Draves (USA)	108.74
	2 Z.A. (Olsen) Jensen (USA)	108.23
	3 P. Elsener (USA)	101.30

1952	1 P. McCormick (USA)	147.30
	2 M. Moreau (FRA)	139.34
	3 Z.A. (Olsen) Jensen (USA)	127.57

1956	1 P. McCormick (USA)	142.36
	2 J. Stunyo (USA)	125.89
	3 I. MacDonald (CAN)	121.40

1960	1 I. (Krämer) Engel (GER)	155.81
	2 P.J. (Myers) Pope (USA)	141.24
	3 E. Ferris (GBR)	139.09

1964	1 I. (Krämer) Engel (GER)	145.00
	2 J. Collier (USA)	138.36
	3 P. Willard (USA)	138.18

1968	1 S. Gossick (USA)	150.77
	2 T. Pogosheva (URS)	145.30
	3 K. O'Sullivan (USA)	145.23

Volleyball (men)

	Gold	Silver	Bronze
1964	URS	TCH	JPN
1968	URS	JPN	TCH
1972	JPN	GDR	URS
1976	POL	URS	CUB
1980	URS	BUL	ROM

Volleyball (women)

	Gold	Silver	Bronze
1964	JPN	URS	POL
1968	URS	JPN	POL
1972	URS	JPN	PRK
1976	JPN	URS	KOR
1980	URS	GDR	BUL

Weightlifting

Flyweight

Weight limit 52kg (114½lb)

1972	1	Z. Smalcerz (POL) 337.5kg (744lb)
	2	L. Szvecs (HUN) 330.00kg (727½lb)
	3	S. Holczreiter (HUN) 327.5kg (722lb)
1976	1	A. Voronin (URS) 242.5kg (534¼lb)
	2	G. Koszegi (HUN) 237.5kg (523¼lb)
	3	M. Nassiri (IRN) 235.0kg (517¾lb)
1980	1	K. Osmonoliev (URS) 245kg (540¼lb)
	2	B.C. Ho (PRK) 245kg (540¼lb)
	3	G. Si Han (PRK) 245kg (540¼lb)

Bantamweight

Weight limit 56kg (123¼lb)

1948	1	J. De Pietro (USA) 307.5kg (677¾lb)
	2	J. Creus (GBR) 297.5kg (655¾lb)
	3	R. Tom (USA) 295.0kg (650¼lb)
1952	1	I. Udodov (URS) 315.0kg (694¼lb)
	2	M. Namdjou (IRN) 307.5kg (677¾lb)
	3	A. Mirzai (IRN) 300.0kg (661¼lb)
1956	1	C. Vinci (USA) 342.5kg (755lb)
	2	V. Stogov (URS) 337.5kg (744lb)
	3	M. Namdjou (IRN) 332.5kg (733lb)

1960 1 C. Vinci (USA)
345.0kg (760½lb)
2 Yoshinobu Miyake (JPN)
337.5kg (744lb)
3 E. Elmkhah (IRN)
330.0kg (727½lb)

1964 1 A. Vakhonin (URS)
357.5kg (788lb)
2 I. Foldi (HUN)
355.0kg (782½lb)
3 S. Ichinoseki (JPN)
347.5kg (766lb)

1968 1 M. Nassiri (IRN)
367.5kg (810lb)
2 I. Foldi (HUN)
367.5kg (810lb)
3 H. Trebick (POL)
357.5kg (788lb)

1972 1 I. Foldi (HUN)
377.5kg (832lb)
2 M. Nassiri (IRN)
370.0kg (815½lb)
3 G. Chetin (URS)
367.5kg (810lb)

1976 1 N. Nurikyan (BUL)
262.0kg (578½lb)
2 G. Cziura (POL)
252.0kg (554½lb)
3 K. Ando (JPN)
250.0kg (551lb)

1980 1 D. Nunez (CUB)
275kg (606½lb)
2 Y. Sarkisian (URS)
270kg (595½lb)
3 T. Dembonczyk (POL)
265kg (584½lb)

Featherweight
Weight limit 60kg (132½lb)

1948 1 M. Fayad (EGY)
332.5kg (733lb)
2 R. Wilkes (TRI)
317.5kg (699½lb)
3 J. Salmassi (IRN)
312.5kg (688½lb)

1952 1 R. Chimishkian (URS)
337.5kg (744lb)
2 N. Saksonov (URS)
332.5kg (733lb)
3 R. Wilkes (TRI)
322.5kg (710½lb)

1956 1 I. Berger (USA)
352.5kg (777lb)
2 Y. Minaev (URS)
342.5kg (755lb)
3 M. Zieliński (POL)
335.0kg (738½lb)

1960 1 Y. Minaev (URS)
372.5kg (821lb)
2 I. Berger (USA)
362.5kg (799lb)
3 S. Mannironi (ITA)
352.5kg (777lb)

1964 1 Y. Miyake (JPN)
397.5kg (876½lb)
2 I. Berger (USA)
382.5kg (843½lb)
3 M. Nowak (POL)
377.5kg (832lb)

1968 1 Y. Miyake (JPN)
392.5kg (865½lb)
2 D. Zhanidze (URS)
387.5kg (854½lb)
3 Y. Miyake (JPN)
385.0kg (848½lb)

1972 1 N. Nurikyan (BUL)
402.5kg (887½lb)
2 D. Zhanidze (URS)
400.0kg (881¾lb)
3 J. Benedek (HUN)
390.0kg (859½lb)

1976 1 N. Kolesnikov (URS)
285.0kg (628lb)
2 G. Todorov (BUL)
280.0kg (617lb)
3 K. Hirai (JPN)
275.0kg (606lb)

1980 1 V. Mazin (URS)
290kg (639¼lb)
2 S. Dimitrov (BUL)
287.5kg (634lb)
3 M. Seweryn (POL)
282.5kg (622¾lb)

Lightweight
Weight limit 67.5kg (148¼lb)

1948 1 I.H. Shams (EGY)
360.0kg (793½lb)
2 A. Hamouda (EGY)
360.0kg (793½lb)
3 J. Halliday (GBR)
340.0kg (749½lb)

1952 1 T. Kono (USA)
362.5kg (799lb)
2 Y. Lopatin (URS)
350.0kg (771½lb)
3 V. Barberis (AUT)
350.0kg (771½lb)

1956 1 I. Rybak (URS)
380.0kg (837¾lb)
2 R. Khabutdinov (URS)
372.5kg (821lb)
3 C.H. Kim (KOR)
370.0kg (815½lb)

1960 1 V. Bushuev (URS)
397.5kg (876¼lb)
2 H.L. Tan (SIN)
380.0kg (837¾lb)
3 A.W. Aziz (IRQ)
380.0kg (837¾lb)

1964 1 W. Baszanowski (POL)
432.5kg (953¼lb)
2 V. Kaplunov (URS)
432.5kg (953¼lb)
3 M. Zieliński (POL)
420.0kg (925¾lb)

1968 1 W. Baszanowski (POL)
437.5kg (963½lb)
2 P. Jalayer (IRN)
422.5kg (931¼lb)
3 M. Zieliński (POL)
420.0kg (925¾lb)

1972 1 M. Kirzhinov (URS)
460.0kg (1014lb)
2 M. Kuchev (BUL)
450.0kg (992lb)
3 Z. Kaczmarek (POL)
437.5kg (964½lb)

1976 1 P. Korol (URS)
305.0kg (672¼lb)
2 D. Senet (FRA)
300.0kg (661¼lb)
3 K. Czarneck (POL)
295.0kg (650¼lb)

1980 1 Y. Rusev (BUL)
342.5kg (755¼lb)
2 J. Kunz (GDR)
335kg (738lb)
3 M. Pachov (BUL)
325kg (716½lb)

Middleweight
Weight limit 75kg (165¼lb)

1948 1 F. Spellman (USA)
390.0kg (859½lb)
2 P. George (USA)
382.5kg (843½lb)
3 S.J. Kim (KOR)
380.0kg (837¾lb)

1952 1 P. George (USA)
400.0kg (881½lb)
2 G. Gratton (CAN)
390.0kg (859¾lb)
3 S.J. Kim (KOR)
382.5kg (843¾lb)

1956 1 F. Bogdanovski (URS)
420.0kg (925¾lb)
2 P. George (USA)
412.5kg (909½lb)
3 E. Pignatti (ITA)
382.5kg (843¾lb)

1960 1 A. Kurinov (URS)
437.5kg (964½lb)
2 T. Kono (USA)
427.5kg (942½lb)
3 G. Veres (HUN)
405.0kg (892¾lb)

1964　1　H. Zdrazila (TCH)
　　　　445.0kg (981lb)
　　　2　V. Kurentsov (URS)
　　　　440.0kg (970lb)
　　　3　M. Ohuchi (JPN)
　　　　437.5kg (964¼lb)

1968　1　V. Kurentsov (URS)
　　　　475.0kg (1047lb)
　　　2　M. Ohuchi (JPN)
　　　　455.0kg (1003lb)
　　　3　K. Bakos (HUN)
　　　　440.0kg (970lb)

1972　1　Y. Bikov (BUL)
　　　　485.0kg (1069lb)
　　　2　M. Trabulsi (LIB)
　　　　472.5kg (1041½lb)
　　　3　A. Silvino (ITA)
　　　　470.0kg (1036lb)

1976　1　Y. Mitkov (BUL)
　　　　335.0kg (738½lb)
　　　2　V. Militosyan (URS)
　　　　330.0kg (729lb)
　　　3　P. Wenzel (GDR)
　　　　327.5kg (721lb)

1980　1　A. Zlatev (BUL)
　　　　360kg (793½lb)
　　　2　A. Pervy (URS)
　　　　357.5kg (788¼lb)
　　　2　N. Kolev (BUL)
　　　　345kg (760¾lb)

Light heavyweight
Weight limit 82.5kg (181¾lb)

1948　1　S. Stanczyk (USA)
　　　　417.5kg (920¼lb)
　　　2　H. Sakata (USA)
　　　　380.0kg (837¾lb)
　　　3　G. Magnusson (SWE)
　　　　375.0kg (826¾lb)

1952　1　T. Lomakhin (URS)
　　　　417.5kg (920¼lb)
　　　2　S. Stanczyk (USA)
　　　　415.0kg (914¾lb)
　　　3　A. Vorobyev (URS)
　　　　407.5kg (898¼lb)

1956　1　T. Kono (USA)
　　　　447.5kg (986½lb)
　　　2　V. Stepanov (URS)
　　　　427.5kg (942¼lb)
　　　3　J. George (USA)
　　　　417.5kg (920¼lb)

1960　1　I. Paliński (POL)
　　　　442.5kg (975½lb)
　　　2　J. George (USA)
　　　　430.0kg (947¾lb)
　　　3　J. Bochenek (POL)
　　　　420.0kg (925¾lb)

1964　1　R. Plyukfelder (URS)
　　　　475.0kg (1047lb)
　　　2　G. Tóth (HUN)
　　　　467.5kg (1030¼lb)
　　　3　G. Veres (HUN)
　　　　467.5kg (1030¼lb)

1968　1　B. Selitski (URS)
　　　　485.0kg (1069lb)
　　　2　V. Belyaev (URS)
　　　　485.0kg (1069lb)
　　　3　N. Ozimek (POL)
　　　　472.5kg (1041½lb)

1972　1　L. Jensen (NOR)
　　　　507.5kg (1118½lb)
　　　2　N. Ozimek (POL)
　　　　497.5kg (1096¾lb)
　　　3　G. Horváath (HUN)
　　　　495.0kg (1091½lb)

1976　1　V. Shary (URS)
　　　　365.0kg (804½lb)
　　　2　T. Stoichev (BUL)
　　　　360.0kg (793½lb)
　　　3　P. Baczako (HUN)
　　　　345.0kg (760½lb)

1980　1　Y. Vardanyan (URS)
　　　　400kg (882lb)
　　　2　B. Blagoyev (BUL)
　　　　372.5kg (821½lb)
　　　3　D. Poliacik (TCH)
　　　　367.5kg 810¼lb)

Middle heavyweight
Weight limit 90kg (198½lb)

1952   1   N. Schemansky (USA)
           445.0kg (981lb)
       2   G. Novak (URS)
           410.0kg (902½lb)
       3   L. Kilgour (TRI)
           402.5kg (887½lb)

1956   1   A. Vorobyev (URS)
           462.5kg (1019½lb)
       2   D. Sheppard (USA)
           442.5kg (975½lb)
       3   J. Debuf (FRA)
           425.0kg (936½lb)

1960   1   A. Vorobyev (URS)
           472.5kg (1041½lb)
       2   T. Lomakhin (URS)
           457.5kg (1008½lb)
       3   L. Martin (GBR)
           445.0kg (981lb)

1964   1   V. Golovanov (URS)
           487.5kg (1074¾lb)
       2   L. Martin (GBR)
           475.0kg (1047lb)
       3   I. Paliński (POL)
           467.5kg (1030½lb)

1968   1   K. Kangasniemi (FIN)
           517.5kg (1140½lb)
       2   Y. Talts (URS)
           507.5kg (1118¾lb)
       3   M. Golab (POL)
           495.0kg (1091¼lb)

1972   1   A. Nikolov (BUL)
           525.0kg (1157¼lb)
       2   A. Shopov (BUL)
           517.5kg (1140½lb)
       3   H. Bettembourg (SWE)
           512.5kg (1129¾lb)

1976   1   D. Rigert (URS)
           382.5kg (843lb)
       2   L. James (USA)
           362.5kg (798¾lb)
       3   A. Shopov (BUL)
           360.0kg (793½lb)

1980   1   P. Baczako (HUN)
           377.5kg (832½lb)
       2   R. Alexandrov (BUL)
           375kg (826¾lb)
       3   F. Mantek (GDR)
           375kg (826¾lb)

Heavyweight
Weight limit 110kg (242½lb)

1972   1   Y. Talts (URS)
           580.0kg (1278½lb)
       2   A. Kraichev (BUL)
           562.5kg (1240lb)
       3   S. Grützner (GDR)
           555.0kg (1223½lb)

1976   1   Y. Zaitsev (URS)
           385.0kg (848½lb)
       2   K. Semerdjiev (BUL)
           385.0kg (848½lb)
       3   T. Rutkowski (POL)
           377.5kg (832lb)

1980   1   L. Taranenko (URS)
           422.5kg (931¼lb)
       2   V. Christov (BUL)
           405kg (893lb)
       3   G. Szalai (HUN)
           390kg (860lb)

Super heavyweight
Weight limit over 110kg (242½lb)

1948   1   J. Davis (USA)
           452.5kg (997½lb)
       2   N. Schemansky (USA)
           425.0kg (936¾lb)
       3   A. Charité (HOL)
           412.5kg (909½lb)

1952   1   J. Davis (USA)
           460.0kg (1014lb)
       2   J. Bradford (USA)
           437.5kg (964½lb)
       3   H. Selvetti (ARG)
           432.5kg (953½lb)

1956	1	P. Anderson (USA) 500.0kg (1102¼lb)
	2	H. Selvetti (ARG) 500.0kg (1102¼lb)
	2	A. Pigaiani (ITA) 452.5kg (997½lb)
1960	1	Y. Vlasov (URS) 537.5kg (1184¾lb)
	2	J. Bradford (USA) 512.5kg (1129¾lb)
	3	N. Schemansky (USA) 500.0kg (1102¼lb)
1964	1	L. Zhabotinski (URS) 572.5kg (1262lb)
	2	Y. Vlasov (URS) 570.0kg (1256½lb)
	3	N. Schemansky (USA) 537.5kg (1184¾lb)
1968	1	L. Zhabotinski (URS) 572.5kg (1262lb)
	2	S. Reding (BEL) 555.0kg (1223½lb)
	3	J. Dube (USA) 555.0kg (1223½lb)
1972	1	V. Alekseev (URS) 640.0kg (1410¾lb)
	2	R. Mang (FRG) 612.0kg (1344¾lb)
	3	G. Bonk (GDR) 572.5kg (1262lb)
1976	1	V. Alekseev (URS) 440.0kg (969¾lb)
	2	G. Bonk (GDR) 405.0kg (892½lb)
	2	H. Losch (GDR) 387.5kg (854lb)
1980	1	S. Rakhmanov (URS) 440kg (970lb)
	2	J. Heuser (GDR) 410kg (904lb)
	3	T. Rutkowski (POL) 407.5kg (898½lb)

Wrestling: freestyle

Light flyweight

Weight limit 48kg (105lb 13oz)

1972	1	R. Dmitriev (URS)
	2	O. Nikolov (BUL)
	3	E. Javadpour (IRN)
1976	1	K. Issaev (BUL)
	2	R. Dmitriev (URS)
	3	A. Kudo (JPN)
1980	1	C. Pollio (ITA)
	2	S. Hong Jang (PRK)
	3	S. Kornilayev (URS)

Flyweight

Weight limit 52kg (114lb 10oz)

1948	1	L. Viitala (FIN)
	2	H. Balamir (TUR)
	3	T. Johansson (SWE)
1952	1	H. Gemici (TUR)
	2	Y. Kitano (JPN)
	3	M. Mollaghassermi (IRN)
1956	1	M. Tsalkalamanidze (URS)
	2	M. Khojastehpour (IRN)
	3	H. Akbas (TUR)
1960	1	A. Bilek (TUR)
	2	M. Matsubara (JPN)
	3	M. Saifpour Saidabadi (IRN)
1964	1	Y. Yoshida (JPN)
	2	C. S. Chang (KOR)
	3	S. Aliaakbar Haydari (IRN)
1968	1	S. Nakata (JPN)
	2	R. Sanders (USA)
	3	S. Sukhbaatar (MGL)
1972	1	K. Kato (JPN)
	2	A. Alakhverdiev (URS)
	3	H. K. Gwong (PRK)
1976	1	Y. Takada (JPN)
	2	A. Ivanov (URS)
	3	H. S. Jeon (KOR)

1980	1	A. Beloglazov (URS)
	2	W. Stecyk (POL)
	3	N. Selimov (BUL)

Bantamweight
Weight limit 57kg (125lb 10½oz)

1948	1	N. Akkar (TUN)
	2	G. Leeman (USA)
	3	C. Kouyos (FRA)
1952	1	S. Ishii (JPN)
	2	R. Mamedbekov (URS)
	3	K. S. Jadav (IND)
1956	1	M. Dagistanli (TUR)
	2	M. Yaghoubi (IRN)
	3	M. Shakhov (URS)
1960	1	T. McCann (USA)
	2	N. Zalev (BUL)
	3	T. Trojanowski (POL)
1964	1	Y. Uetake (JPN)
	2	H. Akbas (TUR)
	3	A. Ibragimov (URS)
1968	1	Y. Uetake (JPN)
	2	D. Behm (USA)
	3	A. Gorgori (IRN)
1972	1	H. Yanagida (JPN)
	2	R. Sanders (USA)
	3	L. Klinga (HUN)
1976	1	V. Umin (URS)
	2	H. D. Bruchert (GDR)
	3	M. Arai (JPN)
1980	1	S. Beloglazov (URS)
	2	H. Pyong Li (PRK)
	3	D. Ouinbold (MGL)

Featherweight
Weight limit 62kg (136lb 11oz)

1948	1	G. Bilge (TUR)
	2	I. Sjölin (SWE)
	3	A. Müller (SUI)
1952	1	B. Sit (TUR)
	2	N. Guivehtchi (IRN)
	3	J. Henson (USA)

1956	1	S. Sasahara (JPN)
	2	J. Mewis (BEL)
	3	E. Penttilä (FIN)
1960	1	M. Dagistani (TUR)
	2	S. Ivanov (BUL)
	3	V. Rubashvili (URS)
1964	1	O. Watanabe (JPN)
	2	S. Ivanov (BUL)
	3	N. Khokhashvili (URS)
1968	1	M. Kaneko (JPN)
	2	E. Todorov (BUL)
	3	S. Seyed-Abassy (IRN)
1972	1	Z. Abdulbekov (URS)
	2	V. Akdag (TUR)
	3	I. Krastev (BUL)
1976	1	J. M. Yang (KOR)
	2	Z. Oidov (MGL)
	3	G. Davis (USA)
1980	1	M. Abushev (URS)
	2	M. Doukov (BUL)
	3	G. Hadjiioannidis (GRE)

Lightweight
Weight limit 68kg (149lb 14½oz)

1948	1	C. Atik (TUR)
	2	G. Frändfors (SWE)
	3	H. Baumann (SUI)
1952	1	O. Anderberg (SWE)
	2	J. T. Evans (USA)
	3	D. Tovfighe (IRN)
1956	1	E. Habibi (IRN)
	2	S. Kasahara (JPN)
	3	A. Bestaev (URS)
1960	1	S. Wilson (USA)
	2	V. Sinyavski (URS)
	3	E. Dimov (Valchev) (BUL)
1964	1	E. Valchev (BUL)
	2	K. J. Rost (GER)
	3	I. Horiuchi (JPN)
1968	1	A. Movahed Ardabili (IRN)
	2	E. Valchev (JPN)
	3	S. Danzandarjas (MGL)

1972	1	D. Gable (USA)
	2	K. Wada (JPN)
	3	R. Ashuraliev (URS)

1976	1	D. Pinigin (URS)
	2	L. Keaser (USA)
	3	Y. Sugawara (JPN)

1980	1	S. Absaidov (URS)
	2	I. Yankov (BUL)
	3	S. Sejdi (YUG)

Welterweight
Weight limit 74kg (163lb 2¼oz)

1948	1	Y. Dogu (TUR)
	2	R. Garrard (AUS)
	3	L. Merrill (USA)

1952	1	W. Smith (USA)
	2	P. Berlin (SWE)
	3	A. Modjtabavi (IRN)

1956	1	M. Ikeda (JPN)
	2	I. Zengin (TUR)
	3	V. Balavadze (URS)

1960	1	D. Blubaugh (USA)
	2	I. Ogan (TUR)
	3	M. Bashir (PAK)

1964	1	I. Ogan (TUR)
	2	G. Sagaradze (URS)
	3	M. A. Sanatkaran (IRN)

1968	1	M. Atalay (TUR)
	2	D. Robin (FRA)
	3	D. Purev (MGL)

1972	1	W. Wells (USA)
	2	J. Karlsson (SWE)
	3	A. Seger (FRG)

1976	1	J. Date (JPN)
	2	M. Barzegar (IRN)
	3	S. Dziedzic (USA)

1980	1	V. Raitchev (BUL)
	2	J. Davaajav (MGL)
	3	D. Karabin (TCH)

Middleweight
Weight limit 82kg (180lb 12½oz)

1948	1	G. Brand (USA)
	2	A. Candemir (TUR)
	3	E. Lindën (SWE)

1952	1	D. Tsimakuridze (URS)
	2	G. R. Takhti (IRN)
	3	G. Gurics (HUN)

1956	1	N. Stanchev (BUL)
	2	D. Hodge (USA)
	3	G. Skhirtladze (URS)

1960	1	H. Güngör (TUR)
	2	G. Skhirtladze (URS)
	3	H. Y. Antonsson (SWE)

1964	1	P. Gardshev (BUL)
	2	H. Güngör (TUR)
	3	D. Brand (USA)

1968	1	B. Gurevich (URS)
	2	M. Jigjid (MGL)
	3	P. Gardshev (BUL)

1972	1	L. Tediashvili (URS)
	2	J. Peterson (USA)
	3	V. Jorga (ROM)

1976	1	J. Peterson (USA)
	2	V. Novojilov (URS)
	3	A. Seger (FRG)

1980	1	I. Abilov (BUL)
	2	M. Aratsilov (URS)
	3	I. Kovacs (HUN)

Light heavyweight
Weight limit 90kg (198lb 6¾oz)

1948	1	H. Wittenberg (USA)
	2	F. Stöckli (SUI)
	3	B. Fahlkvist (SWE)

1952	1	V. Palm (SWE)
	2	H. Wittenberg (USA)
	3	A. Atan (TUR)

1956	1	G. R. Takhti (IRN)
	2	B. Kulaev (URS)
	3	P. S. Blair (USA)

1960	1	A. Atli (TUR)
	2	G. R. Takhti (IRN)
	3	A. Albul (URS)

1964	1	A. Medved (URS)
	2	A. Ayik (TUR)
	3	S. Mustafov (BUL)

1968	1	A. Ayik (TUR)
	2	S. Lomidze (URS)
	3	J. Csatári (HUN)

1972	1	B. Peterson (USA)
	2	G. Strakhov (URS)
	3	K. Bajko (HUN)

1976	1	L. Tediashvili (URS)
	2	B. Peterson (USA)
	3	S. Morcov (ROM)

1980	1	S. Organesvan (URS)
	2	U. Neupert (GDR)
	3	A. Cichon (POL)

Heavyweight
Weight limit under 100kg (200lb 7¼oz)

1948	1	G. Bóbis (HUN)
	2	B. Antonsson (SWE)
	3	J. Armstrong (AUS)

1952	1	A. Mekokishvili (URS)
	2	B. Antonsson (SWE)
	3	K. Richmond (GBR)

1956	1	H. Kaplan (TUR)
	2	H. Mekhmedov (BUL)
	3	T. Kangasniemi (FIN)

1960	1	W. Dietrich (FRG)
	2	H. Kaplan (TUR)
	3	S. Tsarasov (URS)

1964	1	A. Ivanitsky (URS)
	2	L. Djiber (BUL)
	3	H. Kaplan (TUR)

1968	1	A. Medved (URS)
	2	O. Duralyev (BUL)
	3	W. Dietrich (FRG)

1972	1	I. Yarygin (URS)
	2	K. Baianmunkh (MGL)
	3	J. Csatári (HUN)

1976	1	I. Yarygin (URS)
	2	R. Hellickson (USA)
	3	D. Kostov (BUL)

1980	1	I. Mate (YUG)
	2	S. Tchervenkov (BUL)
	3	J. Strnisko (TCH)

Super heavyweight
Weight limit over 100kg (220lb 7¼oz)

1972	1	A. Medved (URS)
	2	O. Duralyev (BUL)
	3	C. Taylor (USA)

1976	1	S. Andiev (URS)
	2	J. Balla (HUN)
	3	L. Simon (ROM)

1980	1	S. Andiev (URS)
	2	J. Balla (HUN)
	3	A. Sandurski (POL)

Wrestling: Greco-Roman
Light flyweight
Weight limit under 48kg (105lb 13oz)

1972	1	G. Berceanu (ROM)
	2	R. Alliabadi (IRN)
	3	S. Anghelov (BUL)

1976	1	A. Shumakov (URS)
	2	C. Berceanu (ROM)
	3	S. Anghelov (BUL)

1980	1	Z. Ushkempirov (URS)
	2	C. Alexandru (ROM)
	3	F. Seres (HUN)

Flyweight
Weight limit under 52kg (114lb 10½oz)

1948	1	P. Lombardi (ITA)
	2	K. Olcay (TUR)
	3	R. Kangasmäki (FIN)

1952	1	B. Gurevich (URS)
	2	I. Fabra (ITA)
	3	L. Honkala (FIN)

1956	1	N. Solovyev (URS)
	2	I. Fabra (ITA)
	3	D.A. Egribas (TUR)

1960	1	D. Pirvulescu (ROM)
	2	O. Sayed (EGY)
	3	M. Paziraye (IRN)

1964	1	T. Hanahara (JPN)
	2	A. Kerezov (BUL)
	3	D. Pirvulescu (ROM)

1968	1	P. Kirov (BUL)
	2	V. Bakulin (URS)
	3	M. Zeman (TCH)

1972	1	P. Kirov (BUL)
	2	K. Hirayama (JPN)
	3	G. Bognanni (ITA)

1976	1	V. Konstantinov (URS)
	2	N. Ginga (ROM)
	3	K. Hirayama (JPN)

1980	1	V. Blagidze (URS)
	2	L. Racz (HUN)
	3	M. Mladenov (BUL)

Bantamweight
Weight limit under 57kg (125lb 10½oz)

1948	1	K. Pettersén (SWE)
	2	A.M. Hassan (EGY)
	3	H. Kaya (TUR)

1952	1	I. Hódos (HUN)
	2	Z. Khihab (LIB)
	3	A. Terian (URS)

1956	1	K. Vyrupaev (URS)
	2	E. Vesterby (SWE)
	3	F. Horvat (ROM)

1960	1	O. Karavaov (URS)
	2	I. Cernea (ROM)
	3	P. Dinko (BUL)

1964	1	M. Ichiguchi (JPN)
	2	V. Trostyanski (URS)
	3	I. Cernea (ROM)

1968	1	J. Varga (HUN)
	2	I. Baciu (ROM)
	3	I. Kochergin (URS)

1972	1	R. Kazakov (URS)
	2	H.J. Veil (FRG)
	3	R. Bjoerlin (FIN)

1976	1	P. Ukkola (FIN)
	2	I. Frgic (YUG)
	3	F. Mustafin (URS)

1980	1	S. Serikov (URS)
	2	J. Lipien (POL)
	3	B. Ljungbeck (SWE)

Featherweight
Weight limit 62kg (136lb 11oz)

1948	1	M. Oktav (TUR)
	2	O. Anderberg (SWE)
	3	F. Tóth (HUN)

1952	1	Y. Punkin (URS)
	2	I. Polyák (HUN)
	3	A. Rashed (EGY)

1956	1	R. Mäkinen (FIN)
	2	I. Polyák (HUN)
	3	R. Zhneladze (URS)

1960	1	M. Sille (TUR)
	2	I. Polyák (HUN)
	3	K. Vyrupaev (URS)

1964	1	I. Polyák (HUN)
	2	R. Rurua (URS)
	3	B. Martinović (YUG)

1968	1	R. Rurua (URS)
	2	H. Fujimoto (JPN)
	3	S. Popescu (ROM)

1972	1	G. Markov (BUL)
	2	H.H. Wehling (GDR)
	3	K. Lipien (POL)

1976	1	K. Lipien (POL)
	2	N. Davidyan (URS)
	3	L. Reczi (HUN)

1980	1	S. Migiakis (URS)
	2	I. Toth (HUN)
	3	B. Kramorenko (URS)

Lightweight
Weight limit 68kg (149lb 14½oz)

1948	1	G. Freij (SWE)
	2	A. Eriksen (NOR)
	3	K. Ferencz (HUN)

1952	1	S. Safin (URS)
	2	G. Freij (SWE)
	3	M. Athanasov (TCH)

1956	1	K. Lehtonen (FIN)
	2	R. Dogan (TUR)
	3	G. Tóth (HUN)

1960	1	A. Koridze (URS)
	2	B. Martinović (YUG)
	3	G. Freij (SWE)

1964	1	K. Ayvaz (TUR)
	2	V. Bularca (ROM)
	3	D. Gvantseladze (URS)

1968	1	M. Munemura (JPN)
	2	S. Horvath (YUG)
	3	P. Galaktopoulos (GRE)

1972	1	S. Khisamutdinov (URS)
	2	S. Apostolov (BUL)
	3	G.M. Ranzi (ITA)

1976	1	S. Nalbandyan (URS)
	2	S. Rusu (ROM)
	3	H.H. Wehling (GDR)

1980	1	S. Rusu (ROM)
	2	A. Supron (POL)
	3	L.E. Skiold (SWE)

Welterweight
Weight limit 74kg (163lb 2½oz)

1948	1	G. Andersson (SWE)
	2	M. Szilvási (HUN)
	3	H. Hansen (DEN)

1952	1	M. Szilvási (HUN)
	2	G. Andersson (SWE)
	3	K. Taha (LIB)

1956	1	M. Bayrak (TUR)
	2	V. Maneev (URS)
	3	P. Berlin (SWE)

1960	1	M. Bayrak (TUR)
	2	G. Maritschnigg (GER)
	3	R. Schiermeyer (FRA)

1964	1	A. Kolesov (URS)
	2	C. Todorov (BUL)
	3	B. Nyström (SWE)

1968	1	R. Vesper (GDR)
	2	D. Robin (FRA)
	3	K. Bajkó (HUN)

1972	1	V. Macha (TCH)
	2	P. Galaktopoulos (GRE)
	3	J. Karlsson (SWE)

1976	1	A. Bykov (URS)
	2	V. Macha (TCH)
	3	K.H. Helbing (FRA)

1980	1	F. Kocsis (HUN)
	2	A. Bykov (URS)
	3	M. Huhtala (FIN)

Middleweight
Weight limit 82kg (180lb 12½oz)

1948	1	A. Grönberg (SWE)
	2	M. Tayfur (TUR)
	3	E. Gallegati (ITA)

1952	1	A. Grönberg (SWE)
	2	K. Rauhala (FIN)
	3	N. Belov (URS)

1956	1	G. Kartozia (URS)
	2	D. Dobrev (BUL)
	3	R. Jansson (SWE)

1960	1	D. Dobrev (BUL)
	2	L. Metz (GDR)
	3	I. Taranu (ROM)

1964	1	B. Simić (YUG)
	2	J. Kormanik (TCH)
	3	L. Metz (GER)

1968	1	L. Metz (GDR)
	2	V. Olenik (URS)
	3	B. Simić (YUG)

1972	1	C. Hegedus (HUN)
	2	A. Nazarenko (URS)
	3	M. Nenadić (YUG)

1976	1	M. Petkovic (YUG)
	2	V. Cheboksarov (URS)
	3	L. Kolev (BUL)

1980	1	G. Korban (URS)
	2	J. Polgowicz (POL)
	3	P. Pavlov (BUL)

Light heavyweight
Weight limit 90kg (198lb 6½oz)

1948	1	K.E. Nilsson (SWE)
	2	K. Gröndahl (FIN)
	3	I. Orabi (EGY)

1952	1	K. Gröndahl (FIN)
	2	S. Shikhladze (URS)
	3	K.E. Nilsson (SWE)

1956	1	V. Nikolaev (URS)
	2	P. Sirakov (BUL)
	3	K.E. Nilsson (SWE)

1960	1	T. Kiş (TUR)
	2	K. Bimbalov (BUL)
	3	G. Kartozia (URS)

1964	1	B. Radev (BUL)
	2	P. Svensson (SWE)
	3	H. Kiehl (GER)

1968	1	B. Radev (BUL)
	2	N. Yakovenko (URS)
	3	N. Martinescu (ROM)

1972	1	V. Rezantsev (URS)
	2	J. Corak (YUG)
	3	C. Kwieciński (POL)

1976	1	V. Retzansev (URS)
	2	S. Ivanov (BUL)
	3	C. Kwieciński (POL)

1980	1	N. Nottny (HUN)
	2	I. Kanygin (URS)
	3	P. Disu (ROM)

Heavyweight
Weight limit under 100kg (220lb 7½oz)

1948	1	A. Kireççi (TUR)
	2	T. Nilsson (SWE)
	3	G. Fantoni (ITA)

1952	1	Y. Kotas (URS)
	2	J. Ruzicka (TCH)
	3	T. Kovanen (FIN)

1956	1	A. Parfenov (URS)
	2	W. Dietrich (GER)
	3	A. Bulgarelli (ITA)

1960	1	I. Bogdan (URS)
	2	W. Dietrich (GER)
	3	B. Kubat (TCH)

1964	1	I. Kozma (HUN)
	2	A. Roshchin (URS)
	3	W. Dietrich (GER)

1968	1	I. Kozma (HUN)
	2	A. Roshchin (URS)
	3	P. Kment (TCH)

1972	1	N. Martinescu (ROM)
	2	N. Iakovenko (URS)
	3	F. Kiss (HUN)

1976	1	N. Bolboshin (URS)
	2	K. Goranov (BUL)
	3	A. Skrzlewski (POL)

1980	1	G. Raikov (BUL)
	2	R. Bierla (POL)
	3	V. Andrei (ROM)

Super heavyweight
Weight over 100kg (220lb 7½oz)

1972	1	A. Roshchin (URS)
	2	A. Tomov (BUL)
	3	V. Dolipschi (ROM)

1976	1	A. Kolchinski (URS)
	2	A. Tomov (BUL)
	3	R. Codreanu (ROM)

1980	1	A. Kolchinski (URS)
	2	A. Tomov (BUL)
	3	H. Bchara (LIB)

Yachting

Finn

1948	1	P. Elvstrøm (DEN)
	2	R. Evans (USA)
	3	J.H. de Jong (HOL)

1952	1	P. Elvstrøm (DEN)
	2	C. Currey (GBR)
	3	R. Sarby (SWE)

1956	1	P. Elvstrøm (DEN)
	2	A. Nelis (BEL)
	3	J. Marvin (USA)

1960	1	P. Elvstrøm (DEN)
	2	A. Chuchelov (URS)
	3	A. Nelis (BEL)

1964	1	W. Kuhweide (GER)
	2	P. Barrett (USA)
	3	H. Wind (DEN)

1968	1	V. Mankin (URS)
	2	H. Raudaschl (AUT)
	3	F. Albarelli (ITA)

1972	1	S. Maury (FRA)
	2	I. Hatzipavlis (GRE)
	3	V. Potapov (URS)

1976	1	J. Shumann (GDR)
	2	A. Balashov (URS)
	3	J. Bertrand (AUS)

1980	1	E. Rechardt (FIN)
	2	W. Mayrhofer (AUT)
	3	A. Balashov (URS)

Tempest

	Gold	Silver	Bronze
1972	URS	GBR	USA
1976	SWE	URS	USA

Event not held in 1980

Soling

	Gold	Silver	Bronze
1972	USA	SWE	CAN
1976	DEN	USA	GDR
1980	DEN	URS	GRE

Flying Dutchman

	Gold	Silver	Bronze
1960	NOR	DEN	GER
1964	NZL	GBR	USA
1968	GBR	FRG	BRA
1972	GBR	FRA	FRG
1976	FRG	GBR	BRA
1980	ESP	IRL	HUN

Star

	Gold	Silver	Bronze
1948	USA	CUB	HOL
1952	ITA	USA	POR
1956	USA	ITA	BAH
1960	URS	POR	USA
1964	BAH	USA	SWE
1968	USA	NOR	ITA
1972	AUS	SWE	FRG
1976	Not held		
1980	URS	AUT	ITA

Tornado

	Gold	Silver	Bronze
1976	GBR	USA	FRG
1980	BRA	DEN	SWE

470

	Gold	Silver	Bronze
1976	FRG	ESP	AUS
1980	BRA	GDR	FIN

5.5 metres

	Gold	Silver	Bronze
1952	USA	NOR	SWE
1956	SWE	GBR	AUS
1960	USA	DEN	SUI
1964	AUS	SWE	USA
1968	SWE	SUI	GBR

Event not held 1972, 1976 or 1980

FINIALISTS IN ALL SPORTS IN
1980 OLYMPIC GAMES

Archery

Archery (men)

		Points
1	T. Poikolainen (FIN)	2445
2	B. Ischenko (URS)	2452
3	G. Ferrari (ITA)	2449
4	M. Blenkarne (GBR)	2446
5	B. Nagy (HUN)	2446
6	V. Yesheyev (URS)	2432
7	K. Laasonen (FIN)	2419
8	T. Reniers (HOL)	2418
9	R. Gogniaux (BEL)	2414
10	K. Wlosik (POL)	2410

Archery (women)

		Points
1	K Losaberidze (URS)	2491
2	N. Butuzova (URS	2477
3	P. Meriluoto (FIN)	2449
4	Z. Padevetova (TCH)	2405
5	O. G. Sun (PRK)	2401
6	C. Floris (HOL)	2382
7	M. Szeliga (POL)	2365
8	L. Tschanz (SUI)	2346
9	T. Donovan (AUS)	2343
10.	F. Capetta (ITA)	2342

Association Football

Quarter finals
URS 2   KUW 1
TCH 3   CUB 0
GDR 4   IRQ 0
YUG 3   ALG 0

Semi finals
URS 0   GDR 1
YUG 0   TCH 2

Final
GDR 0   TCH 1

Placings
1 TCH
2 GDR
3 URS
4 YUG

Athletics (men)

100 metres

		Time
1	A. Wells (GBR)	10.25
2	S. Leonard (CUB)	10.25
3	P. Petrov (BUL)	10.39
4	A. Aksinin (URS)	10.42
5	O. Lara (CUB)	10.43
6	V. Muravyov (URS)	10.44
7	M. Woronin (POL)	10.46
8	H. Panzo (FRA)	10.49

200 metres

		Time
1	P. Mennea (ITA)	20.19
2	A. Wells (GBR)	20.21
3	D. Quarrie (JAM)	20.29
4	S. Leonard (CUB)	20.30
5	B. Hoff (GDR)	20.50
6	L. Dunecki (POL)	20.68
7	M. Woronin (POL)	20.81
8	O. Lara (CUB)	21.19

400 metres

		Time
1	V. Markin (URS)	44.60
2	R. Mitchell (AUS)	44.84
3	F. Schaffer (GDR)	44.87
4	A. Juantorena (CUB)	45.09
5	A Brijdenbach (BEL)	45.10
6	M. Solomon (TRI)	44.55
7	D. Jenkins (GBR)	44.56
8	J. Coombs (TRI)	46.33

800 metres

		Time
1	S. Ovett (GBR)	1:45.4
2	S. Coe (GBR)	1:45.9
3	N. Kirov (URS)	1:46.0
4	A. Guimares (BRA)	1:46.2
5	A. Busse (GDR)	1:46.9
6	D. Wagenknecht (GDR)	1:47.0
7	J. Marajo (FRA)	1:47.3
8	D. Warren (GBR)	1:49.3

1500 metres

		Time
1	S. Coe (GBR)	3:38.4
2	J. Straub (GDR)	3:38.8
3	S. Ovett (GBR)	3:39.0
4	A. Busse (GDR)	3:40.2
5	V. Fontanella (ITA)	3:40.4
6	J. Plachy (TCH)	3:40.7
7	J. Marajo (FRA)	3:41.5
8	S. Cram (GBR)	3:42.0
9	D. Zdravkovic (YUG)	3:43.1

5000 metres

		Time
1	M. Yifter (ETH)	13:21.0
2	S. Nyambui (TAN)	13:21.6
3	K. Maaninka (FIN)	13:22.0
4	E. Coghlan (IRL)	13:22.8
5	M Ryffel (SUI)	13:23.1
6	D. Millonig (AUT)	13:23.3
7	J. Treacy (IRL)	13:23.7
8	A Fedotkin (URS)	13:24.1

10000 metres

		Time
1	M. Yifter (ETH)	27:42.7
2	K. Maaninka (FIN)	27:44.3
3	M. Kedir (ETH)	27:44.7
4	T. Kotu (ETH)	27:46.5
5	L. Viren (FIN)	27:50.5
6	J. Peter (GDR)	28:05.6
7	W. Schildhauer (GDR)	28:11.0
8	E. Sellik (URS)	28:13.8
9	W. Scott (AUS)	28:15.1
10	I. Floriou (ROM)	28:16.3
11	B. Foster (GBR)	28:22.6
12	M. McLeod (GBR)	28:40.8
13	M. Vainio (FIN)	28:46.3
14	G. Tebroke (HOL)	28:50.1
	A. Prieto (ESP) – failed to finish	

Marathon

		Time
1	W. Cierpinski (GDR)	2h 11:03.0
2	C. Nijboer (HOL)	2h 11:20.0
3	S. Dzhumanazarov (URS)	2h 11:35.0
4	V. Kotov (URS)	2h 12:05.0
5	L. Moseyev (URS)	2h 12:14.0
6	R. Gomez (MEX)	2h 12:39.0
7	D. Medi (ETH)	2h 12:44.0
8	M. Magnani (ITA)	2h 13:12.0
9	K. Lismont (BEL)	2h 13:27.0
10	R. De Castella (AUS)	2h 14:31.0

110 metres hurdles

		Time
1	T. Munkelt (GDR)	13.39
2	A Casanas (CUB)	13.40
3	A. Puchkov (URS)	13.44
4	A. Prokofyev (URS)	13.49
5	J. Pusty (POL)	13.68
6	A. Bryggare (FIN)	13.76
7	J. Moracho (ESP)	13.78
8	Y. Chervanev (URS)	15.80

400 metres hurdles

		Time
1	V. Beck (GDR)	48.70
2	V. Arkhipenko (URS)	48.86
3	G. Oakes (GBR)	49.11
4	N. Vassiliev (URS)	49.34
5	R. Kopitar (YUG)	49.67
6	H. Toboc (ROM)	49.84
7	F. Meier (SUI)	50.00
8	Y. Bratanov (BUL)	56.35

3000 metres steeplechase

		Time
1	B. Malinowski (POL)	8:09.7
2	F. Bayi (TAN)	8:12.5
3	E Tura (ETH)	8:13.6
4	D. Ramon (ESP)	8:15.8
5	F. Sanchez (ESP)	8:18.0
6	G. Gerbi (ITA)	8:15.5
7	B. Maminski (POL)	8:19.5
8	A. Dimov (URS)	8:19.8
9	V. Bichea (ROM)	8:23.9
10	D. Moravcik (TCH)	8:29.1
11	L. Babaci (ALG)	8:31.8
12	T. Ekblom (FIN)	8:40.9

4 × 100 metres relay

		Time
1	(URS) (V. Muravyov, N. Sidorov, A. Aksinin, A. Prokofev)	38.26
2	(POL) (K. Zwolinski, Z. Licznerski, L. Dunecki, M. Woronin)	38.33
3	(FRA) (A. Richard, P. Barre, B. Petitboirs, H. Panzo)	38.53
4	(GBR) (M. McFarlane, A. Wells, C. Sharp, A. McMaster)	38.62
5	(GDR) (S. Schlegel, E. Ray, B. Hoff, T. Munkelt)	38.73
6	(BUL) (A. Pavlov, V. Ivanov, I. Karaniotov, P. Petrov)	38.99
7	(NGR) (H. Adio, K. Elegbede, S. Oyeledun, P. Okodogbe)	39.12
8	(BRA) (M. Castro, N. Santos, K. Nakaya, F. Araujo)	39.54

4 × 400 metres relay

	Time
1 (URS) (R. Valiulis, M. Linge, N. Chernetsky, V. Markin)	3:01.1
2 (GDR) (K. Thiele, A. Knebel, F. Schaffer, V. Beck)	3:01.3
3 (ITA) (S. Malinverni, M. Zuliani, R. Tozzi, P. Mennea)	3:04.3
4 (FRA) (J. Fellice, R. Froissart, D. Dubois, F. Demarthon)	3:04.8
5 (BRA) (P. Correia, A. Ferreira, A. Guimaraes, G. Pegado)	3:05.9
6 (TRI) (J. Coombs, C. Joseph, R. Mohammed, M. Solomon)	3:06.6
7 (TCH) (J. Lomicky, D. Malovec, F. Brecka, K. Kolar)	3:07.0
GBR failed to finish	

20 kilometres walk

	Time
1 M. Damilano (ITA)	1h 23:35.5
2 P. Pochinchuk (URS)	1h 24:45.4
3 R. Wieser (GDR)	1h 25:58.2
4 Y. Yevsyukov (URS)	1h 26:28.3
5 J. Marin (ESP)	1h 26:45.6
6 R. Gonzalez (MEX)	1h 27:48.6
7 B. Bulakowski (POL)	1h 28:36.3
8 K-H. Stadtmuller (GDR)	1h 29:21.7
9 R. Salonen (FIN)	1h 31:32.0
10 R. Mills (GBR)	1h 32:37.8

50 kilometres walk

	Time
1 H. Gauder (GDR)	3h 49:24.0
2 J. Llopart (ESP)	3h 51:25.0
3 Y. Ivchenko (URS)	3h 56:32.0
4 B. Simonsen (SWE)	3h 57:08.0
5 V. Fursov (URS)	3h 58:32.0
6 J. Marin (ESP)	4h 03:08.0
7 S. Rola (POL)	4h 07:07.0
8 W. Sawall (AUS)	4h 08:25.0
9 L. Sator (HUN)	4h 10:53.0
10 P. Blazek (TCH)	4h 16:26.0

High jump

	Height (m)
1 G. Wessig (GDR)	†*2.36
2 J. Wszola (POL)	2.31
3 J. Freimuth (GDR)	2.31
4 H. Lauterbach (GDR)	2.29
5 R. Dalhauser	2.24
6 V. Komnenic (YUG)	2.24
7 A. Proteasa (ROM)	2.21
8 A. Grigoriev (URS)	2.21
9 M. Naylor (GBR)	2.21
10 G. Belkov (URS)	2.21

Long jump

	Distance (m)
1 L. Dombrowski (GDR)	8.54
2 F. Paschek (GDR)	8.21
3 V. Podluzhnyi (URS)	8.18
4 L. Szalma (HUN)	8.13
5 S. Jaskulka (POL)	8.13
6 V. Belsky (URS)	8.10
7 A. Corgos (ESP)	8.09
8 Y. Yanev (BUL)	8.02
9 R. Bernhard (SUI)	7.88
10 P. Deroche (FRA)	7.77

Triple jump

	Distance (m)
1 J. Uudmae (URS)	17.35
2 V. Saneyev (URS)	17.24
3 J. Oliveira (BRA)	17.22
4 K. Connor (GBR)	16.87
5 I. Campbell (AUS)	16.72
6 A. Tchotchev (BUL)	16.56
7 B. Bakosi (HUN)	16.47
8 K. Lorraway (AUS)	16.44
9 Y. Anikin (URS)	16.12
10 M. Spasojevic (YUG)	16.09

† = world record
* = Olympic record

Pole vault

		Height (m)
1	W. Kozakiewicz (POL)	†*5.78
2	K. Volkov (URS)	5.65
3	T. Slusarski (POL)	5.65
4	P. Houvion (FRA)	5.65
5	J-M. Bellot (FRA)	5.60
6	M. Klimczyk (POL)	5.55
7	T. Vigneron (FRA)	5.45
8	S. Kulibaba (URS)	5.45
9	T. Haapakoski (FIN)	5.45
10	M. Zalar (SWE)	5.35

Shot

		Distance (m)
1	V. Kiselyov (URS)	*21.35
2	A. Baryshnikov (URS)	21.08
3	U. Beyer (GDR)	21.06
4	R. Stahlberg (FIN)	20.82
5	G. Capes (GBR)	20.50
6	H. J. Jacobi (GDR)	20.32
7	J. Vlk (TCH)	20.24
8	V. Milic (YUG)	20.07
9	A. Yarosh (URS)	19.93
10	H. Halldorsson (ISL)	19.55

Discus

		Distance (m)
1	V. Rasshchupkin (URS)	66.64
2	I. Bugar (TCH)	66.38
3	L. Delis (CUB)	66.32
4	W. Schmidt (GDR)	65.64
5	Y. Dumchev (URS)	65.58
6	I. Douguinets (URS)	64.04
7	E. Vladimirov (BUL)	63.18
8	V. Velev (BUL)	63.04
9	M. Tuokko (FIN)	61.84
10	J. Santa Cruz (CUB)	61.52

Hammer

		Distance (m)
1	Y. Sedykh (URS)	†*81.80
2	S. Litvinov (URS)	80.64
3	Y. Tamm (URS)	78.96
4	R. Steuk (GDR)	77.54
5	D. Gerstenberg (GDR)	74.60
6	E. Dulgherov (BUL)	74.04
7	G. Urlando (ITA)	73.90
8	I. Golda (POL)	73.74
9	H. Huhtala (FIN)	71.96
10	J. Tiainen (FIN)	71.38

Javelin

		Distance (m)
1	D. Kula (URS)	91.20
2	A. Makarov (URS)	89.64
3	W. Hanisch (GDR)	86.72
4	K. Puuste (URS)	86.10
5	A. Puranen (FIN)	85.12
6	P. Sinersaari (FIN)	84.34
7	D. Fuhrmann (GDR)	83.50
8	M. Nemeth (HUN)	82.40
9	A. Aho (FIN)	80.58
10	F. Paragi (HUN)	79.52

Decathlon

		Points
1	D. Thompson (GBR)	8495
2	Y. Kutsenko (URS)	8331
3	S. Zhelanov (URS)	8135
4	G. Werthner (AUT)	8050
5	J. Zeilbauer (AUT)	8007
6	D. Ludwig (POL)	7978
7	A. Andonov (BUL)	7927
8	S. Grummt (GDR)	7892
9	E. Jokinen (FIN)	7826
10	J. Szczerkowski (POL)	7822

† = world record
* = Olympic record

Athletics (women)

100 metres

		Time
1	L. Kondratyeva (URS)	11.06
2	M. Gohr (GDR)	11.07
3	I. Auerswald (GDR)	11.14
4	L. Haglund (SWE)	11.16
5	R. Muller (GDR)	11.16
6	K. Smallwood (GBR)	11.28
7	C. Rega (FRA)	11.32
8	H. Hunte (GBR)	11.34

200 metres

		Time
1	B. Wockel (GDR)	*22.03
2	N. Bochina (URS)	22.19
3	M. Ottey (JAM)	22.20
4	R. Muller (GDR)	22.47
5	K. Smallwood (GBR)	22.61
6	B. Goddard (GBR)	22.72
7	D. Boyd (AUS)	22.76
8	S. Lannaman (GBR)	22.80

400 metres

		Time
1	M. Koch (GDR)	*48.88
2	J. Kratochvilova (TCH)	49.46
3	C. Lathan (GDR)	49.66
4	I. Nazarova (URS)	50.07
5	N. Zyuskova (URS)	50.17
6	G. Lowe (GDR)	51.33
7	P. Haggman (FIN)	51.35
8	L. Macdonald (GBR)	52.40

800 metres

		Time
1	N. Olizarenko (URS)	†*1:53.5
2	O. Mineyeva (URS)	1:54.9
3	T. Providokhina (URS)	1:55.5
4	M. Kampfert (GDR)	1:56.3
5	H. Ullrich (GDR)	1:57.2
6	J. Januchta (POL)	1:58.3
7	N. Chtereva (BUL)	1:58.8
8	G. Dorio (ITA)	1:59.2

1500 metres

		Time
1	T. Kazankina (URS)	*3:56.6
2	C. Wartenberg (GDR)	3:57.8
3	N. Olizarenko (URS)	3:59.6
4	G. Dorio (ITA)	4:00.3
5	U. Bruns (GDR)	4:00.7
6	L. Smolka (URS)	4:01.3
7	M. Puica (ROM)	4:01.3
8	I. Silai (ROM)	4:03.0
9	N. Marasescu (ROM)	4:04.8

100 metres hurdles

		Time
1	V. Komisova (URS)	*12.56
2	J. Klier (GDR)	12.63
3	L. Langer (POL)	12.65
4	K. Claus (GDR)	12.66
5	G. Rabsztyn (POL)	12.74
6	I. Litovchenko (URS)	12.84
7	B. Gartz (GDR)	12.93
8	Z. Bielczyk (POL)	13.08

† = world record
* = Olympic record

4 × 100 metres relay

		Time
1	(GDR) (R. Muller, B. Wockel, I. Auerswald, M. Gohr)	†*41.60
2	(URS) (V. Komisova, L. Maslakova, V. Anisimova, N. Bochina)	42.10
3	(GBR) (H. Hunte, K. Smallwood, B. Goddard, S. Lannaman)	42.43
4	(BUL) (S. Popova, L. Panyotova, M. Chichkova, C. Entcheva)	42.67
5	(FRA) (V. Grandrieux, C. Rega, F. Naigre, E. Sulter)	42.84
6	(JAM) (L. Hodges, J. Pusey, R. Allwood, M. Ottey)	43.19
7	(POL) (L. Langer, E. Stachurska, Z. Bielczyk, G. Rabsztyn)	43.59
	SWE failed to finish	

High jump

		Height (m)
1	S. Simeoni (ITA)	1.97
2	U. Kielan (POL)	1.94
3	J. Kirst (GDR)	1.94
4	R. Ackermann (GDR)	1.91
5	M. Sysoeva (URS)	1.91
6	A. Reichstein (GDR)	1.91
7	C. Stanton (AUS)	1.91
8	C. Popa (ROM)	1.88
9	T. Bykova (URS)	1.88
10	A. Matai (HUN)	1.85
11	L. Miller (GBR)	1.85
12	K. Soetewey (BEL)	1.80

Long jump

		Distances (m)
1	T. Kolpakova (URS)	*7.06
2	B. Wujak (GDR)	7.04
3	T. Skachko (URS)	7.01
4	A. Wlodarczyk (POL)	6.95
5	S. Siegl (GDR)	6.87
6	J. Nygrynova (TCH)	6.83
7	S. Heinman (GDR)	6.71
8	L. Alfeyeva (URS)	6.71
9	S. Hearnshaw (GBR)	6.50
10	S. Reeve (GBR)	6.46

4 × 400 metres relay

		Time
1	(URS) (T Prorochenko, T. Goistchik, N. Zyuskova, I. Nazarova)	3:20.2
2	(GDR) (G. Lowe, B. Krug, C. Lathan, M. Koch)	3:20.4
3	(GBR) (L. Macdonald, M. Probert, J. Hoyte-Smith, D. Hartley)	3:27.5
4	(ROM) (I. Korodi, N. Lazarciuc, M. Samungi, E. Tarita)	3:27.7
5	(HUN) (I. Orosz, J. Forgacs, E. Toth, I. Pal)	3:27.9
6	(POL) (G. Oliszewska, E. Katolik, J. Januchta, M. Dunecka)	3:27.9
7	(BEL) (L. Alaerts, R. Berg, A. Michel, R. Wallez)	3:31.6
	BUL failed to finish	

Shot

		Distance (m)
1	I. Slupianek (GDR)	†*22.41
2	S. Krachevskaya (URS)	21.42
3	M. Pufe (GDR)	21.20
4	N. Abashidze (URS)	21.15
5	V. Vesselinova (BUL)	20.72
6	E. Stoyanova (BUL)	20.22
7	N. Akhrimenko (URS)	19.74
8	I. Reichenbach (GDR)	19.66
9	M. Sarria (CUB)	19.37
10	Z. Bartonova (TCH)	18.40

Discus

		Distance (m)
1	E. Jahl (GDR)	*69.96
2	M. Petkova (BUL)	67.90
3	T. Lesovaya (URS)	67.40
4	G. Beyer (GDR)	67.08
5	M. Pufe (GDR)	66.12
6	F. Tacu (ROM)	64.38
7	G. Murashova (URS)	63.84
8	S. Bojkova (BUL)	63.14
9	M. Ritchie (GBR)	61.16
10	C. Romero (CUB)	60.86

† = world record   * = Olympic record

Javelin

		Distance (m)
1	M. Colon (CUB)	*68.40
2	S. Gunba (URS)	67.76
3	U. Hommola (GDR)	66.56
4	U. Richter (GDR)	66.54
5	I. Vantcheva (BUL)	65.38
6	T. Biryulina (URS)	65.08
7	Z. Raduly (ROM)	64.08
8	R. Fuchs (GDR)	63.94
9	B. Blechacz (POL)	61.46
10	A. Todorova (BUL)	60.66

Pentathlon

		Points
1	N. Tkachenko (URS)	†*5083
2	O. Rukavishnikova (URS)	4937
3	O. Kuragina (URS)	4875
4	R. Neubert (GDR)	4698
5	M. Papp (HUN)	4562
6	B. Pollak (GDR)	4553
7	V. Dimitrova (BUL)	4458
8	E. Kounova (BUL)	4431
9	F. Picaut (FRA)	4424
10	S. Barlag (HOL)	4333

Basketball

Basketball (men)

Final
YUG 86   ITA 77

Placings
1 YUG
2 ITA
3 URS
4 ESP

Basketball (women)

Final
URS 104   BUL 73

Placings
1 URS
2 BUL
3 YUG
4 HUN

Boxing

Light flyweight (48kg)

1 S. Sabyrov (URS)
2 H. Ramos (CUB)
3 I.Moustafov (BUL)
3 Byong Uk Li (PRK)

Flyweight (under 51kg)

1 P. Lessov (BUL)
2 V. Miroshnichenko (URS)
3 J. Varadi (HUN)
3 H. Russell (IRL)

Bantamweight (under 54kg)

1 J. Hernandez (CUB)
2 B. J. Pinango (VEN)
3 M. Anthony (GUY)
3 D. Cipere (ROM)

Featherweight (under 57kg)

1 R. Fink (GDR)
2 A. Horta (CUB)
3 V. Rybakov (URS)
3 K. Kosedowski (POL)

Lightweight (under 60kg)

1 A. Herrera (CUB)
2 V. Demianenko (URS)
3 R. Nowakowski (GDR)
3 K. Adach (POL)

Light welterweight (under 63.5kg)

1 P. Oliva (ITA)
2 S. Konakbaev (URS)
3 A. Willis (GBR)
3 J. Aguilar (CUB)

Welterweight (under 67kg)

1 A. Aldama (CUB)
2 J. Mugabi (UGA)
3 K-H. Kruger (GDR)
3 K. Szczerba (POL)

Light middleweight (under 71kg)

1 A. Martinez (CUB)
2 A. Koshkin (URS)
3 J. Franek (TCH)
3 D. Kastner (GDR)

Middleweight (under 75kg)

1 J. Gomez (CUB)
2 B. Savchenko (URS)
3 V. Silaghi (ROM)
3 J. Rybicki (POL)

Light Heavyweight (under 81kg)

1 S. Kacar (YUG)
2 P. Skrzecz (POL)
3 H. Bauch (GDR)
3 R. Rojas (CUB)

Heavyweight (81kg+)

1 T. Stevenson (CUB)
2 P. Zaev (URS)
3 I. Levai (HUN)
3 J. Fanghanel (GDR)

Canoeing (men)

Canadian singles, 500 metres

		Time
1	S. Postrekhin (URS)	1:53.37
2	L. Lubenov (BUL)	1:53.49
3	O. Heukrodt (GDR)	1:54.38
4	T. Wichman (HUN)	1:54.58
5	M. Lbik (POL)	1:55.90
6	T. Gronlund (FIN)	1:55.94
7	L. Varabiev (ROM)	1:56.80
8	H. Blažik (TCH)	1:56.83
9	M. Ljubek (YUG)	2:03.43

Canadian pairs, 500 metres

		Time
1	(L. Foltan, I. Vaskuti) (HUN)	1:43.39
2	(I. Potzaichin, P. Capustal) (ROM)	1:44.12
3	(B. Ananiev, N. Ilkov) (BUL)	1:44.83
4	(M. Wisla, J. Dunajski) (POL)	1:45.10
5	(J. Vrdlovec, P. Kubicek) (TCH)	1:46.48
6	(S. Petrenko, A. Vinogradov) (URS)	1:46.95
7	(N. Suarez, S. Magaz) (ESP)	1:48.18
8	(B. Lindelof, E. Zeidlitz) (SWE)	1:48.69
9	(F. Lambert, P. Langlois) (FRA)	1:50.33

Kayak singles, 500 metres

		Time
1	V. Parfenovich (URS)	1:43.43
2	J. Sumegi (AUS)	1:44.12
3	V. Diba (ROM)	1:44.90
4	M. Janic (YUG)	1:45.63
5	F-P. Bischof (GDR)	1:45.97
6	A. Andersson (SWE)	1:46.32
7	I. G. Ferguson (NZL)	1:47.36
8	F. Masar (TCH)	1:48.18
9	Z. Sztaniti (HUN)	1:48.34

Kayak pairs, 500 metres

		Time
1	(V. Parfenovich, S. Chukhrai) (URS)	1:32.38
2	(H. Menendez, G. Del Riego) (ESP)	1:33.65
3	(R. Helm, B. Olbricht) (GDR)	1:34.00
4	(F. Hervieu, A. Lebas) (FRA)	1:36.22
5	(B. Kelly, R. Lee) (AUS)	1:36.45
6	(A. Giura, I. Birlandeanu) (ROM)	1:36.96

Canadian singles, 1000 metres

		Time
1	L. Lubenov (BUL)	4:12.38
2	S. Postrekhin (URS)	4:13.53
3	E. Leue (GDR)	4:15.02
4	L. Dvorak (TCH)	4:15.25
5	L. Varabiev (ROM)	4:16.68
6	T. Gronlund (FIN)	4:17.37
7	T. Falk (SWE)	4:20.66
8	M. Ljubek (YUG)	4:22.40
9	T. Wichmann (HUN)	4:45.30

Canadian pairs, 1000 metres

		Time
1	(L. Patzaichin, T. Simionov) (ROM)	3:47.65
2	(O. Heukrodt, U. Madeja) (GDR)	3:49.93
3	(V. Yurchenko, Y. Lobanov) (URS)	3:51.28
4	(M. Ljubek, M. Nisovic) (YUG)	3:51.30
5	(J. Vrdlovec. P. Kubicek) (TCH)	3:52.50
6	(M. Dopierala, J. Pinczura) (POL)	3:53.01
7	(R. Karmadjiev, K. Koutsev) (BUL)	3:53.89
8	(T. Buday, O. Frey) (HUN)	3:54.31
9	(B. Lindelof, E. Zeidlitz) (SWE)	3:58.62

Kayak singles, 1000 metres

		Time
1	R. Helm (GDR)	3:48.77
2	A. Lebas (FRA)	3:50.20
3	I. Birladeanu (ROM)	3:50.49
4	J. Sumegi (AUS)	3:50.63
5	O. Perri (ITA)	3:51.95
6	F. Masar (TCH)	3:52.10
7	M. Janic (YUG)	3:53.50
8	I. G. Ferguson (NZL)	3:53.78
9	A. Andersson (SWE)	3:54.54

Kayak pairs, 1000 metres

		Time
1	(V. Parfenovich, S. Chukhrai) (URS)	3:26.72
2	(I. Szabo, I. Joos) (HUN)	3:28.49
3	(L. Ramos-Misione, H. Menendez) (ESP)	3:28.66
4	(A. Giura, N. Ticu) (ROM)	3:28.94
5	(P. Hempel, H. Nolte) (GDR)	3:31.02
6	(J. Marrero, R. Cunill) (CUB)	3:31.12
7	(R. Stevens, G. Jan Lebbink) (HOL)	3:33.18
8	(A. B. Thompson, G. S. Walker) (NZL)	3:33.83
9	(A. Mastrandrea, D. Merli) (ITA)	3:52.32

Kayak fours, 1000 metres

		Time
1	(R. Helm, B. Olbricht, H. Marg, B. Duvigneau) (GDR)	3:13.76
2	(M. Zafiu, V. Diba, I. Geanta, N. Esanu) (ROM)	3:15.35
3	(B. Borissov, B. Milenkov, L. Khristov, I. Manev) (BUL)	3:15.46
4	(R. Oborski, G. Koltan, D. Welna, G. Sledziewski) (POL)	3:16.33
5	(J. Deme, J. Ratkai, J. Kosztyan, Z. Sztaniti) (HUN)	3:17.27
6	(F. Barouh, P. Berard, P. Boccara, P. Lefoulon) (FRA)	3:17.60
7	(G. Makhnev, S. Nagornyi, A. Avdeyev, V. Tainikov) (URS)	3:19.83
8	(B. Kelly, R. Lee, K. Vidler, C. Baulch) (AUT)	3:19.87
9	(L-E. Moberg, P. Lundh, T. Thoresson, B. Andersson) (SWE)	3:20.74

Canoeing (women)

Kayak singles, 500 metres

		Time
1	B. Fischer (GDR)	1:57.96
2	V. Gescheva (BUL)	1:59.48
3	A. Melnikova (URS)	1:59.66
4	M. Stefan (ROM)	2:00.90
5	E. Eichler (POL)	2:01.23
6	A. Andersson (SWE)	2:01.33
7	K. Povazsan (HUN)	2:01.52
8	B. Knopf (FRA)	2:02.91
9	L. A. Perrett (GBR)	2:04.89

Kayak pairs, 500 metres

1	(C. Genauss, M. Bischof) (GDR)	1:43.88
2	(G. Alexeyeva, N. Trofimova) (URS)	1:46.91
3	(E. Rakusz, M. Zakarias) (HUN)	1:47.95
4	(E. Babeanu, A. Buhaev) (ROM)	1:48.04
5	(A. Andersson, K. Olsson) (SWE)	1:49.27
6	(A-M. Loriot, V. Leclerc) (FRA)	1:49.48
7	(E. Eichler, E. Wojtaszek) (POL)	1:51.31
8	(F. M. Wetherall, L. A. Smither) (GBR)	1:52.76
9	(V. Mintcheva, N. Yanakieva) (BUL)	1:53.12

Cycling

Sprint

1	L. Hesslich (GDR)
2	Y. Cahard (FRA)
3	S. Kopylov (URS)
4	A. Tkac (TCH)
5	H. Salee (DEN)
6	H. Isler (SUI)
7	K. Tucker (AUS)
8	O. Dazzan (ITA)

1000 metres time trial

		Time
1	L. Thoms (GDR)	†*1:02.955
2	A. Panfilov (URS)	*1:04.845
3	D. Weller (JAM)	*1:05.241
4	G. Bontempi (ITA)	*1:05.478
5	Y. Cahard (FRA)	*1:05.584
6	H. Isler (SUI)	*1:06.273
7	P. Kocek (TCH)	*1:06.368
8	B. Sorensen (DEN)	1:07.422
9	T. Tinsley (GBR)	1:07.542
10	K. Tucker (AUS)	1:07.709

4000 metres pursuit (individual)

1 R. Dill-Bundi (SUI)
2 A. Bondue (FRA)
3 H-H Orsted (DEN)
4 H. Wolf (GDR)
5 V. Osokin (URS)
6 S. Yates (GBR)
7 P. Bincoletto (ITA)
8 M. Penc (TCH)
9 K. Poole (AUS)
10 J. Smeets (BEL)

4000 metres pursuit (team)

1 (URS)
2 (GDR)
3 (TCH)
4 (ITA)
5 (FRA)
6 (AUS)
7 (GBR)
8 (SUI)
9 (POL)
10 (BEL)

Road race (individual)

		Time
1	S. Sukhoruchenkov (URS)	4h 48:28.9
2	C. Lang (POL)	4h 51:26.9
3	Y. Barinov (URS)	4h 51:26.9
4	T. Barth (GDR)	4h 56:12.9
5	T. Wojtas (POL)	4h 56:12.9
6	A. Yarkin (URS)	4h 56:54.9
7	A. Van Der Poel (HOL)	4h 56:54.9
8	C. Faure (FRA)	4h 56:54.9
9	M. Madiot (FRA)	4h 57:00.9
10	A. Petermann (GDR)	4h 57:17.9

101 kilometres team time trial

		Time
1	(Y. Kashirin, O. Logvin, S. Shelpakov, A. Yarkin) (URS)	2h 01:21.7
2	(F. Boden, B. Drogan, O. Ludwig, H-J. Hartnick) (GDR)	2h 02:53.2
3	(M. Klasa, V. Konecny, A. Kostadinov, J. Skoda) (TCH)	2h 02:53.9
4	(S. Ciekanski, J. Jankiewicz, C. Lang, W. Plutecki) (POL)	2h 04:13.8
5	(M. De Pellegrin, G. Giacomini, I. Maffei, A. Minetti) (ITA)	2h 04:36.2
6	(B. Assenov, V. Khoubenov, Y. Pentchev, N. Staikov) (BUL)	2h 05:55.2
7	(H. Hannus, K. Puisto, P. Wackstrom, S. Wackstrom) (FIN)	2h 05:58.2
8	(B. Bulic, V. Poloncic, B. Ropret, B. Udovic) (YUG)	2h 07:12.0
9	(R. Downs, D. Fretwell, S. Jones, J. Waugh) (GBR)	2h 07:30.6
10	(P. Kersgaard, M. Marcussen, J. Worre, J. Pedersen) (DEN)	2h 07:42.3

Equestrianism

Dressage (individual)

		Points
1	E. Theurer (AUT) *Mon Cherie*	1370
2	Y. Kovshov (URS) *Igrok*	1300
3	V. Ugryumov (URS) *Shkval*	1234
4	V. Misevich (URS) *Plot*	1231
5	K. Kyrklund (FIN) *Piccolo*	1121
6	A. Donescu (ROM) *Dor*	960
7	G. Gadjev (BUL) *Vnimatelen*	881
8	S. Ivanov (BUL) *Aleko*	850
9	P. Mandajiev (BUL) *Stchibor*	846
10	J. Zagor (POL) *Helios*	804

Show jumping (individual)

		Points
1	J. Kowalczyk *Artemor*	8.00
2	N. Korolkov (URS) *Espadron*	9.50
3	J. Perez Heras (MEX) *Alymony*	12.00
4	Mendez Herbruger (GUA) *Pampa*	12.00
5	V. Poganovsky (URS) *Topky*	15.50
6	W. Hartman (POL) *Norton*	16.00
7	B. Hevesi (HUN) *Bohem*	24.00
8	M. Kozicki (POL) *Bremen*	24.50
9	V. Chukanov (URS) *Gepatit*	24.75
10	B. Pavlov (BUL) *Monblan*	26.50

Dressage (team)

		Points
1	URS (Y. Kovshov *Igrok*, V. Ugryumov *Shkval*, V. Misevich *Plot*)	4383
2	BUL (P. Mandajiev *Stchibor*, S. Ivanov *Aleko*, G. Gadiev *Vnimatelen*)	3580
3	ROM (A. Donescu *Dor*, D. Veliku *Decebal*, P. Rosca *Derbist*)	3346
4	POL (J. Zagor *Helios*, E-K. Morciniec *Sum*, W. Wasowska *Damask*)	2945

Show jumping (team)

		Points
1	URS (V. Chukanov *Gepatit*, V. Poganovsky *Topky*, V. Asmaev *Reis*, N. Korolkov *Espadron*)	20.25
2	POL (M. Kozicki *Bremen*, J. Kowalczyk *Artemor*, W. Hartman *Norton*, J. Bobik *Szampan*)	56.00
3	MEX (J. Perez Heras *Alymony*, J. Gomez Portugal *Massacre*, V.G. Tazzer *Caribe*, A. Valdes Lacarra *Lady Mirka*)	59.75
4	HUN (B. Hevesi *Bohem*, F. Krucso *Vadrozsa*, A. Balogi *Artemis*, J. Varro *Gambrinusz*)	124.00
5	ROM (A. Bozan *Prejmer*, D. Popescu *Sonor*, I. Popa *Licurici*, D. Velea *Fudul*)	150.50
6	BUL (D. Ghenov *Makbet*, K. Katchov *Povod*, N. Dimitrov *Vals*, B. Pavlov *Monblan*)	159.50

Three day event (individual)

		Dressage	Endurance	Jumping	Total
1	F.E. Roman (ITA) *Rossinan*	54.40	49.20	5.0	108.60
2	A. Blinov (URS) *Galzun*	64.40	56.40	0.0	120.80
3	Y. Salnikov (URS) *Pintset*	53.00	93.6	5.0	151.60
4	V. Volkov (URS) *Tshketi*	54.00	125.6	5.0	184.60
5	T. Dontchev (BUL) *Medisson*	66.40	114.4	5.0	185.80
6	M. Szlapka (POL) *Erywan*	52.40	184.4	5.0	241.80
7	A. Casagrande (ITA) *Daleye*	61.20	190.0	15.0	266.20
8	M. Roman (ITA) *Dourakine 4*	63.40	218.0	0.0	281.40
9	M. Sciocchetti (ITA) *Rohan De Lechereo*	55.20	243.2	10.0	308.40
10	Y. Mendivil (MEX) *Remember*	53.00	264.0	2.75	319.75

Three day event (team)

		Points
1	URS (A. Blinov *Galzun*, Y. Salnikov *Pintset*, V. Volkov *Tshketi*, S. Rogozhin *Gelespont*)	457.00
2	ITA (F.E. Roman *Rossinan*, A. Casagrande *Daleye*, M. Roman *Dourakine 4*, M. Sciocchetti *Rohan De Lechereo*)	656.20
3	MEX (Y. Mendivil *Remember*, R. Barcena *Bombona*, S.J. Perez *Quelite*, L. Vazquez *Cocaleco*)	1172.85
4	HUN (L. Cseresnyes *Fapipa*, I. Grozner *Bibros*, Z. Horvath *Lamour*, M. Olah *Ados*)	1603.40

POL, BUL, IND were eliminated

Fencing (men)

Foil (individual)

		Wins
1	V. Smirnov (URS)	1 (+ 4 hits)
2	P. Jolyot (FRA)	1 (0 hits)
3	A. Romankov (URS)	1 (− 4 hits)

Foil (team)

1	FRA
2	URS
3	POL
4	GDR

Epée (individual)

		Wins
1	J. Harmenberg (SWE)	4
2	E. Kolczonay (HUN)	3
3	P. Riboud (FRA)	3
4	R. Edling (SWE)	3
5	A. Mozhaev (URS)	1
6	I. Popa (ROM)	1

Epée (team)

1	FRA
2	POL
3	URS
4	ROM

Sabre (individual)

		Wins
1	V. Krovopuskov (URS)	4
2	M. Burtsev (URS)	4
3	I. Gedovari (HUN)	3
4	V. Etropolski (BUL)	2
5	K. Etropolski (BUL)	1
6	M. Maffei (ITA)	1

Barrage for 1st and 2nd place,
Krovopuskov (URS) bt Burtsev (URS) 5-3.

Sabre (team)

1	URS
2	ITA
3	HUN
4	POL

Fencing (women)

Foil (individual)

		Wins
1	P. Trinquet (FRA)	4
2	M. Maros (HUN)	3
3	B. Wysoczanska (POL)	3
4	E. Stahl (ROM)	2
5	B. Latri-Gaudin (FRA)	2
6	D. Vaccaroni (ITA)	1

Foil (team)

1	FRA
2	URS
3	HUN
4	POL

Gymnastics (men)

Combined exercises (individual)

		Points
1	A. Dityatin (URS)	118.650
2	N. Andrianov (URS)	118.225
3	S. Deltchev (BUL	118.000
4	A. Tkachyov (URS)	117.700
5	R. Bruckner (GDR)	117.300
6	M. Nikolay (GDR)	116.750
7	L. Hoffmann (GDR)	116.025
8	J. Tabak (TCH)	115.675
9	D. Grecu (ROM)	115.225
10	Z. Magyar (HUN)	115.225

Parallel bars

		Points
1	A. Tkachyov (URS)	19.775
2	A. Dityatin (URS)	19.750
3	R. Bruckner (GDR)	19.650
4	M. Nikolay (GDR)	19.600
5	S. Deltchev (BUL)	19.575
6	R. Leon (CUB)	19.500

Horizontal bar

		Points
1	S. Deltchev (BUL)	19.825
2	A. Dityatin (URS)	19.750
3	N. Andrianov (URS)	19.675
4	R-P. Hemmann (GDR)	19.525
5	M. Nikolay (GDR)	19.525
6	S. Suarez (CUB)	19.450

Horse

		Points
1	Z. Magyar (HUN)	19.925
2	A. Dityatin (URS)	19.800
3	M. Nikolay (GDR)	19.775
4	R. Bruckner (GDR)	19.725
5	A. Tkachyov (URS)	19.475
6	F. Donath (HUN)	19.400

Vault

		Points
1	N. Andrianov (URS)	19.825
2	A. Dityatin (URS)	19.800
3	R. Bruckner (GDR)	19.775
4	R-P. Hemmann (GDR)	19.750
5	S. Deltchev (BUL)	19.700
6	J. Tabak (TCH)	19.525

Rings

		Points
1	A. Dityatin (URS)	19.875
2	A. Tkachyov (URS)	19.725
3	J. Tabak (TCH)	19.600
4	R. Bruckner (GDR)	19.575
5	S. Deltchev (BUL)	19.475
6	D. Grecu (ROM)	10.850

Floor exercises

		Points
1	R. Bruckner (GDR)	19.750
2	N. Andrianov (URS)	19.725
3	A. Dityatin (URS)	19.700
4	J. Tabak (TCH)	19.675
5	P. Kovacs (HUN)	19.425
6	L. Hoffmann (GDR)	18.725

Combined exercises (team)

		Points
1	URS N. Andrianov, E. Azarian, A. Dityatin, B. Makuts, V. Markelov, A. Tkachyov	589.60
2	GDR R.P. Hemmann, L. Hoffmann, L. Mack, M. Nikolay, A. Bronst, R. Bruckner	581.15
3	HUN F. Donath, G. Guczoghy, Z. Kelemen, P. Kovacs, Z. Magyar, I. Vamos	575.00
4	ROM R. Bucuro, S. Cepol, A. Georgescu, D. Grecu, N. Oprescu, K. Szilier	572.30
5	BUL O. Banghiev, S. Deltchev, P. Petkov, R. Petkov, Y. Radantchev, D. Yordanov	571.55
6	TCH R. Babiak, J. Konecny, M. Kucerik, J. Migdau, J. Tabak, K. Zoulik	569.80
7	CUB M. Arroyo, E. Bravo, M. Castro, R. Leon, J. Roche, S. Suarez	563.20
8	FRA H. Boerio, Y. Boquel, M. Boutard, W. Moy, J. Suty, M. Touchais	559.20
9	PRK H. Cho, G.S. Han, G. Kang, G.J. Kim, S.G. Li, S. Song	551.35

Gymnastics (women)

Combined exercises (individual)

		Points
1	E. Davydova (URS	79.150
2	M. Gnauck (GDR)	79.075
2	N. Comaneci (ROM)	79.075
4	N. Shaposhnikova (URS)	79.025
5	N. Kim (URS)	78.425
6	E. Eberle (ROM)	78.400
7	R. Dunka (ROM)	78.350
8	S. Kraker (GDR)	78.200
9	K. Rensch (GDR)	78.125
10	R. Zemanova (TCH)	77.850

Asymmetric bars

		Points
1	M. Gnauck (GDR)	19.875
2	E. Eberle (ROM)	19.850
3	S. Kraker (GDR)	19.775
3	M. Ruhn (ROM)	19.775
3	M. Filatova (URS)	19.775
6	N. Kim (URS)	19.725

Beam

		Points
1	N. Comaneci (ROM)	19.800
2	E. Davydova (URS)	19.750
3	N. Shaposhnikova (URS)	19.725
4	M. Gnauck (GDR)	19.700
5	R. Zemanova (TCH)	19.650
6	E. Eberle (ROM)	19.400

Horse vault

		Points
1	N. Shaposhnikova (URS)	19.725
2	S. Kraker (GDR)	19.675
3	M. Ruhn (ROM)	19.650
4	E. Davydova (URS)	19.575
5	N. Comaneci (ROM)	19.350
6	M. Gnauck (GDR)	19.300

Floor exercises

		Points
1	N. Kim (URS)	19.875
1	N. Comaneci (ROM)	19.875
3	N. Shaposhnikova (URS)	19.825
3	M. Gnauck (GDR)	19.825
5	E. Eberle (ROM)	19.750
6	J. Labakova (TCH)	19.725

Combined exercises (team)

			Points
1	URS	Y. Davydova, M. Filatova, N. Kim, Y. Naimoushina, N. Shaposhnikova, S. Zakharova	394.90
2	ROM	N. Comaneci, R. Dunka, E. Eberle, M. Ruhn, D. Turner, C.E. Grigoras	393.50
3	GDR	M. Gnauck, S. Hindorff, S. Kraker, K. Rensch, K. Sube, B. Suss	392.55
4	TCH	D. Brydlova, J. Labakova, E. Mareckova, K. Sarisska, A. Sauerova, R. Semanova	388.80
5	HUN	L. Almasi, E. Czanyi, M. Egervari, E. Flander, E. Hanti, E. Ovari	384.30
6	BUL	E. Eftimova, D. Filipova, G. Marinova, A. Rakhneva, K. Toneva, S. Topalova	382.10
7	POL	A. Jaroszek, A. Jokiel, M. Maiza, L. Matraszek, K. Snopko, W. Zelaskowska	376.25
8	PRK	J. Choe, M. Choe, M. Kang, C.S. Kim, O.S. Lo, M.W. Sin	364.05

Handball

Handball (men)

1	GDR
2	URS
3	ROM
4	HUN
5	ESP
6	YUG

Handball (women)

1	URS
2	YUG
3	GDR
5	HUN
5	TCH
7	CGO

Hockey

Hockey (men)

	P	W	D	L	F	A	Points
ESP	5	4	1	–	33	3	9
IND	5	3	2	–	39	6	8
URS	5	3	–	2	30	11	6
POL	5	2	1	2	19	15	5
CUB	5	1	–	4	7	42	2
TAN	5	–	–	5	3	54	–

Placings

1 IND
2 ESP
3 URS

4 POL
5 CUB
6 TAN

Hockey (women)

		P	W	D	L	F	A	Points
1	ZIM	5	3	2	–	13	4	8
2	TCH	5	3	1	1	10	5	7
3	URS	5	3	–	2	11	5	6
4	IND	5	2	1	2	9	6	5
5	AUT	5	2	–	3	6	11	4
6	POL	5	–	–	5	0	18	–

Judo

60 kilograms

1 T. Rey (FRA)
2 R. Rodriguez (POR)
3 T. Kincses (HUN)
3 A. Emizh (URS)

65 kilograms

1 N. Solodukhin (URS)
2 Z. Damdin (MGL)
3 I. Nedkov (BUL)
3 J. Pawlowski (POL)

71 kilograms

1 E. Gamba (ITA)
2 N. Adams (GBR)
3 K-H. Lehmann (GDR)
3 R. Davaadalai (MGL)

78 kilograms

1 S. Khabareli (URS)
2 J. Ferrer (CUB)
3 B. Tchoullouyan (FRA)
3 H. Heinke (GDR)

86 kilograms

1   J. Roethlisberger (SUI)
2   I. Azcuy (CUB)
3   A. Jatskevich (URS)
3   D. Ultsch (GDR)

Over 95 kilograms

1   A. Parisi (FRA)
2   D. Zaprianov (BUL)
3   V. Kocman (TCH)
3   R. Kovacevic (YUG)

95 kilograms

1   R. Van de Walle (BEL)
2   T. Khubuluri (URS)
3   D. Lorenz (GDR)
3   H. Numan (HOL)

Open

1   D. Lorenz (GDR)
2   A. Parisi (FRA)
3   A. Mapp (GBR)
3   A. Ozsvar (HUN)

Modern Pentathlon

Individual

		Riding	Fencing	Shooting	Swimming	Cross country	Total points
1	A. Starostin (URS)	1068	1000	1110	1216	1174	5568
2	T. Szombathelyi (HUN)	1100	1026	1088	1144	1144	5502
3	P. Lednev (URS)	1026	1026	1022	1104	1204	5382
4	S. Rasmuson (SWE)	936	922	1000	1332	1183	5373
5	T. Maracsko (HUN)	980	964	956	1208	1171	5279
6	J. Pyciak-Peciak (POL)	1070	844	978	1172	1204	5268
7	L. Pettersson (SWE)	1050	922	1088	1156	1027	5243
8	M. Kadlec (TCH)	1084	792	1088	1088	1177	5229
9	G. Horvath (SWE)	1036	870	1132	1152	1039	5229
10	H. Hulkkonen (FIN)	980	1000	1066	1100	1081	5227

Team

		Points
1	URS (A. Starostin, P. Lednev, E. Lipeev)	16126
2	HUN (T. Szombathelyi, T. Maracsko, L. Horvath)	15912
3	SWE (S. Rasmuson, L. Pettersson, G. Horvath)	15845
4	POL (J. Pyciak-Peciak, J. Olesinski, M. Bajan)	15634
5	FRA (P. Four, J. Bouzou, A. Cortes)	15345
6	TCH (M. Kadlec, J. Barto, B. Starnovsky)	15339
7	FIN (H. Hulkkonen, J. Pelli, P. Santanen)	15087
8	GBR (D. Nightingale, P. Whiteside, N. Clark)	15062
9	ESP (F. Galera, J. Serrano, M. Montesinos)	14699
10	BUL (S. Monev, N. Nikolov, B. Batikov)	14545

Rowing (men)

Single sculls

		Time
1	P. Karppinen (FIN)	7:09.61
2	V. Yakusha (URS)	7:11.66
3	P. Kersten (GDR)	7:14.88
4	V. Lacina (TCH)	7:17.57
5	H. Svensson (SWE)	7:19.38
6	H. Matheson (GBR)	7:20.28

Double sculls

		Time
1	J. Dreifke, K. Kroppelien (GDR)	6:24.33
2	Z. Pancic, M. Stanulov (YUG)	6:26.34
3	Z. Pecka, V. Vochoska (TCH)	6:29.07
4	J. Clark, C. Baillieu (GBR)	6:31.13
5	A. Fomchenko, Y. Duleyev (URS)	6:35.34
6	W. Kujda, P. Tobolski (POL)	6:39.66

Coxless pairs

		Time
1	B. Landvoigt, J. Landvoigt (GDR)	6:48.01
2	Y. Pimenov, N. Pimenov (URS)	6:50.50
3	C. Wiggin, M. Carmichael j(GBR)	6:51.47
4	C. Postoiu, V. Toma (ROM)	6:53.49
5	M. Vrastil, M. Knapek (TCH)	7:01.54
6	A. Larson, A. Wilgotson (SWE)	7:02.52

Coxed pairs

		Time
1	H. Jarhling, F.W. Ulrich, G. Spohr (GDR)	7:02.54
2	V. Pereverzev, G. Kryuchkin, A. Lukyanov (URS)	7:03.35
3	D. Mrdulas, Z. Celent, J. Reic (YUG)	7:04.92
4	P. Ceapura, G. Bularda, L. Lovrenski (ROM)	7:07.17
5	T. Petkov, R. Khristov, T. Kichev (BUL)	7:09.21
6	J. Plaminek, M. Skopek, O. Hejdusek (TCH)	7:09.41

Coxless Quadruple sculls

		Time
1	GDR	5:49.81
2	URS	5:51.47
3	BUL	5:52.38
4	FRA	5:53.45
5	ESP	6:01.19
6	YUG	6:10.76

Coxless fours

		Time
1	GDR	6:08.17
2	URS	6:11.81
3	GBR	6:16.58
4	TCH	6:18.63
5	ROM	6:19.45
6	SUI	6:26.46

Coxed fours

		Time
1	GDR	6:14.51
2	URS	6:19.05
3	POL	6:22.52
4	ESP	6:26.23
5	BUL	6:28.13
6	SUI	6:30.26

Eights

		Time
1	GDR	5:49.05
2	GBR	5:51.92
3	URS	5:52.66
4	TCH	5:53.73
5	AUS	5:56.74
6	BUL	6:04.05

Rowing (women)

Single sculls

		Time
1	S. Toma (ROM)	3:40.69
2	A. Makhina (URS)	3:41.65
3	M. Schroter (GDR)	3:43.54
4	R. Spassova (BUL)	3:47.22
5	B. Mitchell (GBR)	3:49.71
6	B. Dziadura (POL)	3:51.45

Double sculls

		Time
1	Y. Khloptseva, L. Popova (URS)	3:16.27
2	C. Linse, H. Westphal (GDR)	3:17.63
3	O. Homeghi, V. Racila-Rosca (ROM)	3:18.91
4	S. Otzetova, Z. Yordanova (BUL)	3:23.14
5	H. Jarkiewicz, J. Klucznik (POL)	3:27.25
6	I. Bata, M. Langhoffer (HUN)	3:35.70

Coxless pairs

		Time
1	U. Steindorft, C. Klier (GDR)	3:30.49
2	M. Dluzewska, C. Koscianska (POL)	3:30.95
3	S. Barboulova, S. Kubatova (BUL)	3:32.39
4	F. Dospinescu, E. Oprea (ROM)	3:35.14
5	L. Zavarzina, G. Stepanova (URS)	4:12.53

Coxed quadruple sculls

		Time
1	GDR	3:15.32
2	URS	3:15.73
3	BUL	3:16.10
4	ROM	3:16.82
5	POL	3:20.95
6	HOL	3:22.64

Coxed fours

		Time
1	GDR	3:19.27
2	BUL	3:20.75
3	URS	3:20.92
4	ROM	3:22.08
5	AUS	3:26.37

Shooting

Trap shooting

		Points
1	L. Giovannetti (ITA)	198
2	R. Yambulatov (URS)	196
3	J. Damme (GDR)	196
4	J. Hojny (TCH)	196
5	E. Vallduvi (ESP)	195
6	A. Asanov (URS)	195
7	S. Basagni (ITA)	194
8	B. Hoppe (GDR)	192
9	I. Putz (HUN)	191
10	R. Sancho (ESP)	190

Skeet

		Points
1	H. Rasmussen (DEN)	196
2	L. Carlsson (SWE)	196
3	R. Castrillo (CUB)	196
4	P. Pulda (TCH)	196
5	C. Giardini (ITA)	196
6	G. Torres (CUB)	195
7	F. Perez (ESP)	195
8	A. Westergard (FIN)	195
9	T. Imnaishvili (URS)	195
10	O. Justesen (DEN)	194

Running game

		Points
1	I. Sokolov (URS)	589
2	T. Pfeffer (GDR)	589
3	A. Gazon (URS)	587
4	A. Doleschall (HUN)	584
5	T. Bodnar (HUN)	584
6	J. Lievomen (FIN)	584
7	G. Mezzani (ITA)	582
8	H. Helbig (GDR)	579
9	J. Jo (PRK)	576
10	J. Greszkiewicz (POL)	576

Rapid fire pistol

		Points
1	C. Ion (ROM)	596
2	J. Wiefel (GDR)	596
3	G. Petritsch (AUT)	596
4	V. Turla (URS)	595
5	R. Ferraris (ITA)	595
6	A. Kuzmin (URS)	595
7	M. Stan (ROM)	595
8	R. Rodriguez (CUB)	594
9	G. Soh (PRK)	604
10	L. Orban (HUN)	593

Free pistol

		Points
1	A. Melentev (URS)	581
2	H. Vollmar (GDR)	568
3	L. Diakov (BUL)	565
4	G. Soh (PRK)	565
5	S. Saarenpaa (FIN)	565
6	S. Pyzhianov (URS)	564
7	R. Skanaker (SWE)	563
8	P. Palokangas (FIN)	561
9	S. Carvalho (BRA)	558
10	S. Romanowski (POL)	558

Small bore rifle (prone)

		Points
1	K. Varga (HUN)	599
2	H. Heilfort (GDR)	599
3	P. Zaprianov (BUL)	598
4	K. Stefaniak (POL)	598
5	T. Hagmaan (FIN)	597
6	A. Mastianin (URS)	597
7	N. Matova (BUL)	597
8	W. Frescura (ITA)	597
9	O. Meuter (BEL)	597
10	P. Kosmatko (POL)	596

Small bore rifle (three positions)

		Points
1	V. Vlasov (URS)	1173
2	B. Hartstein (GDR)	1166
3	S. Johansson (SWE)	1165
4	M.Roppanen (FIN)	1164
5	A. Mitrofanov (URS)	1164
6	N. Matova (BUL)	1163
7	H. Heilfort (GDR)	1162
8	E. Pedzisz (POL)	1156
9	H. Clausen (DEN)	1156
10	I. Matrai (HUN)	1155

Swimming and Diving (men)

100 metres freestyle

		Time
1	J. Woithe (GDR)	50.40
2	P. Holmertz (SWE)	50.91
3	P. Johansson (SWE)	51.29
4	S. Kopliakov (URS)	51.34
5	R. Franceschi (ITA)	51.69
6	S. Krasyuk (URS)	51.30
7	R. Ecuyer (FRA)	52.01
8	G. Brewer (AUS)	52.22

200 metres freestyle

		Time
1	S. Kopliakov (URS)	1:49.81*
2	A. Krylov (URS)	1:50.76
3	G. Brewer (AUS)	1:51.60
4	J. Woithe (GDR)	1:51.86
5	R. McKeon (AUS)	1:52.60
6	P. Revelli (ITA)	1:52.76
7	T. Lejdstrom (SWE)	1:52.94
8	F. Rampazzo (ITA)	1:53.25

400 metres freestyle

		Time
1	V. Salnikov (URS)	3:51.31*
2	A. Krylov (URS)	3:53.24
3	I. Stukolkin (URS)	3:53.95
4	D.G. Madruga (BRA)	3:54.15
5	D. Machek (TCH)	3:55.66
6	S. Nagy (HUN)	3:56.83
7	M. Metzker (AUS)	3:56.87
8	R. McKeon (AUS)	3:57.00

1500 metres freestyle

		Time
1	V. Salnikov (URS)	14:58.27*
2	A. Chaev (URS)	15:14.30
3	M. Metzker (AUS)	15:14.49
4	R. Strohbach (GDR)	15:15.29
5	B. Petric (YUG)	15:21.78
6	R. Escalas (ESP)	15:21.88
7	Z. Wladar (HUN)	15:26.70
8	E. Petrov (URS)	15:28.24

indicates Olympic record

100 metres backstroke

		Time
1	B. Baron (SWE)	56.53
2	V. Kuznetsov (URS)	56.99
3	V. Dolgov (URS)	57.63
4	M. Rolko (TCH)	57.74
5	S. Wladar (HUN)	57.84
5	F. Eefting (HOL)	57.95
7	M. Tonelli (AUS)	57.98
8	G. Abraham (GBR)	58.38

200 metres backstroke

		Time
1	S. Wladar (HUN)	2:01.93
2	Z. Verraszto (HUN)	2:02.40
3	M. Kerry (AUS)	2:03.14
4	V. Shemetov (URS)	2:03.48
5	F. Eefting (HOL)	2:03.92
6	M. Soderlund (SWE)	2:04.10
7	D. Campbell (GBR)	2.04.23
8	P. Moorfoot (AUS)	2:06.15

100 metres breaststroke

		Time
1	D. Goodhew (GBR)	1:03.34
2	A. Miskarov (URS)	1:03.82
3	P. Evans (AUS)	1:03.96
4	A. Fedoroysky (URS)	1:04.00
5	J. Dzvonyar (HUN)	1:04.67
6	L. Spencer (AUS)	1:05.04
7	P. Restrepo (COL)	1:05.91
	A. Vermes (HUN) was disqualified	

200 metres breaststroke

		Time
1	R. Zulpa (URS)	2:15.85
2	A. Vermes (HUN)	2:16.93
3	A. Miskarov (URS)	2:17.28
4	G. Utenkov (URS)	2:19.64
5	L. Spencer (AUS)	2:19.68
6	D. Goodhew (GBR)	2:20.92
7	P. Berggren (SWE)	2:21.65
8	J. Walter (GDR)	2:22.39

100 metres butterfly

		Time
1	P. Arvidsson (SWE)	54.92
2	R. Pyttel (GDR)	54.94
3	D. Lopez (ESP)	55.13
4	K. Vervoorn (HOL)	55.25
5	E. Seredin (URS)	55.35
6	G. Abraham (GBR)	55.42
7	X. Savin (FRA)	55.66
8	A. Markovsky (URS)	55.70

200 metres butterfly

		Time
1	S. Fesenko (URS)	1:59.76
2	P. Hubble (GBR)	2:01.20
3	R. Pyttel (GDR)	2:01.39
4	P. Morris (GBR)	2:02.27
5	M. Gorelik (URS)	2:02.44
6	K. Vervoorn (HOL)	2:05.52
7	P. Arvidsson (SWE)	2:02.61
8	S. Poulter (GBR)	2:02.93

400 metres individual medley

		Time
1	A. Sidorenko (URS)	4:22.89*
2	S. Fesenko (URS)	4:23.43
3	Z. Verraszto (HUN)	4:24.24
4	A. Hargitay (HUN)	4:24.48
5	D.G. Madruga (BRA)	4:26.81
6	M. Rolko (TCH)	4:26.99
7	L. Gorski (POL)	4:28.89
8	D. Machek (TCH)	4:29.86

4 x 200 metres freestyle relay

		Time
1	URS (S. Kopliakov, V. Salnikov, I. Stukolkin, A. Krylov)	7:23.50
2	GDR (F. Pfutze, T. Woithe, D. Grabs, R. Strohbach)	7:28.60
3	BRA (J. Fernandes, M. Mattioli, C. Delgado, D. Madruga)	7:29.30
4	SWE (M. Soderlund, P. Wikstrom, P.A. Magnusson, T. Lejdstrom)	7:30.10
5	ITA (P. Revelli, R. Franceschi, A. Ceccarini, F. Rampazzo)	7:30.37
6	GBR (D. Campbell, P. Hubble, M. Smith, A. Astbury)	7:30.81
7	AUS (G. Brewer, M. Tonelli, M. Kerry, R. McKeon)	7:30.82
8	FRA (F. Noel, M. Lazzaro, D. Petit, P. Laget)	7:36.08

4 x 100 metres medley relay

		Time
1	AUS (M. Kerry, P. Evans, M. Tonelli, N. Brooks)	3:45.70
2	URS (V. Kuznetsov, A. Miskarov, E. Seredin, S. Kopliakov)	3:45.92
3	GBR (G. Abraham, D. Goodhew, D. Lowe, M. Smith)	3:47.71
4	GDR (D. Gohring, J. Walter, R. Pyttel, J. Woithe)	3:48.25
5	FRA (F. Delcourt, O. Borios, X. Savin, R. Ecuyer)	3:49.19
6	HUN (S. Wlader, J. Dzvonyar, Z. Verraszto, G. Meszaros)	3:50.29
7	HOL (F. Eefting, A. Boonstra, K. Vervoorn, C. Winkel)	3:51.81
8	BRA (R.D. Arantes Jr, S. Ribeiro, C.M. Kestener, J. Fernandes)	3:53.24

Springboard

		Points
1	A. Portnov (URS)	905.025
2	C. Giron (MEX)	892.140
3	F. Cagnotto (ITA)	871.500
4	F. Hoffman (GDR)	858.510
5	A. Kosenkov (URS)	855.120
6	C. Snode (GBR)	844.470
7	V. Troshin (URS)	820.050
8	R. Camacho (ESP)	749.340

High board diving

		Points
1	F. Hoffmann (GDR)	835.650
2	V. Heynik (URS)	819.705
3	D. Ambartsumyan (URS)	817.440
4	C. Giron (MEX)	809.805
5	D. Waskow (GDR)	802.800
6	T. Knuths (GDR)	783.975
7	S. Nemtsanov (URS)	775.860
8	N. Stajkovic (AUS)	725.145

Water Polo

		P	W	D	L	F.A	Pts
1	URS	5	5	–	–	34.21	10
2	YUG	5	3	1	1	34.32	7
3	HUN	5	3	–	2	32.30	6
4	ESP	5	2	–	3	28.31	4
5	CUB	5	–	2	3	31.38	2
6	HOL	5	–	1	4	26.33	1

Swimming and Diving (women)

100 metres freestyle

		Time
1	B. Krause (GDR)	*54.79
2	C. Metschuck (GDR)	55.16
3	I. Diers (GDR)	55.65
4	O. Klevakina (URS)	57.40
5	C. Van Bentum (HOL)	57.63
6	N. Strunnikova (URS)	57.83
7	G. Berger (FRA)	57.88
8	A. Eriksson (SWE)	57.90

200 metres freestyle

		Time
1	B. Krause (GDR)	*1:58.33
2	I. Diers (GDR)	1:59.64
3	C. Schmidt (GDR)	2:01.44
4	O. Klevakina (URS)	2:02.29
5	R. de Jong (HOL)	2:02.76
6	J. Croft (GBR)	2:03.15
7	N. Strunnikova (URS)	2:03.74
8	I. Aksyonova (URS)	2:04.00

400 metres freestyle

		Time
1	I. Diers (GDR)	4:08.76
2	P. Schneider (GDR)	4:09.16
3	C. Schmidt (GDR)	4:10.86
4	M. Ford (AUS)	4:11.65
5	I. Aksyonova (URS)	4:14.40
6	A. Maas (HOL)	4:15.79
7	R. De Jong (HOL)	4:15.95
8	O. Klevakina (URS)	4:19.18

800 metres freestyle

		Time
1	M. Ford (AUS)	*8:28.90
2	I. Diers (GDR)	8:32.55
3	H. Dahne (GDR)	8:33.48
4	I. Aksyonova (URS)	8:38.05
5	O. Komissarova (URS)	8:42.04
6	P. Verbauwen (BEL)	8:44.84
7	I. Geissler (GDR)	8:45.28
8	Y. Ivanova (URS)	8:46.45

100 metres backstroke

		Time
1	R. Reinisch (GDR)	*1:00.86
2	I. Kleber (GDR)	1:02.07
3	P. Riedel (GDR)	1:02.64
4	C. Bunaciu (ROM)	1:03.81
5	C. Verbauwen (BEL)	1:03.82
6	L. Gorchakova (URS)	1:03.87
7	M. Bosga (HOL)	1:04.47
8	M. Carosi (ITA)	1:05.10

200 metres backstroke

		Time
1	R. Reinisch (GDR)	*2:11.77
2	C. Polit (GDR)	2:13.75
3	B. Treiber (GDR)	2:14.14
4	C. Bunaciu (ROM)	2:15.20
5	Y. Van Der Straeten (BEL)	2:15.58
6	C. Verbauwen (BEL)	2:16.66
7	L. Forrest (AUS)	2:16.75
8	L. Gorchakova (URS)	2:17.72

* Olympic record

100 metres breaststroke

		Time
1	U. Geweniger (GDR)	1:10.22
2	E. Vasilkova (URS)	1:10.41
3	S. Nielsson (DEN)	1:11.16
4	M. Kelly (GBR)	1:11.48
5	E. Hakansson (SWE)	1:11.72
6	S. Brownsdon (GBR)	1:12.11
7	L. Kachushite (URS)	1:12.21
8	M. Bonon (ITA)	1:12.51

200 metres breaststroke

		Time
1	L. Kachushite (URS)	*2:29.54
2	S. Varganova (URS)	2:29.61
3	Y. Bogdanova (URS)	2:32.39
4	S. Nielsson (DEN)	2:32.75
5	I. Fleissnerova (TCH)	2:33.23
6	U. Geweniger (GDR)	2:34.34
7	B. Lobel (GDR)	2:34.51
8	S. Rinka (GDR)	2:35.38

100 metres butterfly

		Time
1	C. Metschuk (GDR)	1:00.42
2	A. Pollack (GDR)	1:00.90
3	C. Knacke (GDR)	1:01.44
4	A. Osgerby (GBR)	1:02.21
5	L. Curry (AUS)	1:02.40
6	A. Martensson (SWE)	1:02.61
7	M. Paris (CRC)	1:02.89
8	J. Osgerby (GBR)	1:02.90

200 metres butterfly

		Time
1	I. Geissler (GDR)	*2:10.44
2	S. Schonrock (GDR)	2:10.45
3	M. Ford (AUS)	2:11.66
4	A. Pollack (GDR)	2:12.13
5	D. Brzozowska (POL)	2:14.12
6	A. Osgerby (GBR)	2:14.83
7	A. Martensson (SWE)	2:15.22
8	A. Grishchenkova (URS)	2:15.70

4 x 100 metres freestyle relay

		Time
1	GDR (B. Krause, C. Metschuck, I. Diers, S. Hulsenbeck)	*3:42.71
2	SWE (C. Ljungdahl, T. Gustafsson, A. Martensson, A. Eriksson)	3:48.93
3	HOL (C. Van Bentum, W. Van Velsen, R. De Jong, A. Maas)	3:49.51
4	GBR (S. Davies, K. Lovatt, J. Willmott, J. Croft)	3:51.71
5	AUS (L. Curry, L. Van de Graaf, R. Brown, M. Pearson)	3:54.16
6	MEX (I. Reuss, D. Erdman, T. Rivera, H. Plaschinski)	3:55.41
7	BUL (D. Mintcheva, R. Dobreva, A. Kostova, S. Dangalakova)	3:56.34
8	ESP (N. Mas, M. Armengol, L. Flague, G. Casado)	3:58.73

4 x 100 metres medley relay

		Time
1	GDR (R. Reinisch, U. Geweniger, A. Pollack, C. Metschuck)	*4:06.67
2	GBR (H. Jameson, M. Kelly, A. Osgerby, J. Croft)	4:12.24
3	URS (Y. Kruglova, E. Vasilkova, A. Grishchenkova, N. Strunnikova)	4:13.61
4	SWE (A. Uvehall, E-M. Hakansson, A. Martensson, T. Gustafsson)	4:16.91
5	ITA (L. Foralosso, S. Seminatore, C.S. Scarponi, M. Vallarin)	4:19.05
5	AUS (L. Forrest, L. Curry, K. Van De Graaf, R. Brown)	4:19.90
7	ROM (C. Banaciu, B. Prass, M. Paraschiv, I. Punulescu)	4:21.27
8	BUL (S. Dangalakova, T. Bogomilova, A. Moneva, D. Mintcheva)	4:22.38

Springboard

		Time
1	I. Kalinina (URS)	725.910
2	M. Proeber (GDR)	698.895
3	K. Guthke (GDR)	685.245
4	Z. Tsirulnikova (URS)	673.665
5	M. Jaschke (GDR)	668.115
6	V. McFarlane (AUS)	651.045
7	I. Sidorova (URS)	650.265
8	L. Gonzalez (CUB)	640.005

High board diving

		Time
1	M. Jaschke (GDR)	596.250
2	S. Emirzyan (URS)	576.465
3	L. Tsotadze (URS)	575.925
4	R. Wenzel (GDR)	542.070
5	Y. Matyushenko (URS)	540.180
6	E. Tenorio (MEX)	539.455
7	V. McFarlane (AUS)	499.785
8	I. Kelemen (HUN)	476.535

indicates World and Olympic Records

Volley-Ball

Volley-ball (men)
Final
URS 3 BUL 1
Placings

1	URS
2	BUL
3	ROM
4	POL
5	BRA
6	YUG
7	CUB
8	TCH
9	ITA
10	LBA

Volley-ball (women)
Final
URS 3 GDR 1
Placings

1	URS
2	GDR
3	BUL
4	HUN
5	CUB
6	PER
7	BRA
8	ROM

Weightlifting

Flyweight
Weight limit 52kg

		(kg)	1	2	Total points
1	K. Osmanoliev (URS)	51.70	107.5	137.5	*245.0
2	B.C. Ho (PRK)	51.90	110.0	135.0	245.0
3	G.S. Han (PRK)	52.00	110.0	135.0	245.0
4	B. Olah (HUN)	52.00	110.0	135.0	245.0
5	S. Leletko (POL)	51.70	105.0	135.0	240.0
6	F. Hornyak (HUN)	52.00	107.5	130.0	237.5
7	F. Casamayor (CUB)	51.45	102.5	130.0	232.5
8	A. Jugdernamji (MGL)	51.65	97.5	117.5	215.0
9	G. Tosto (ITA)	51.95	95.0	120.0	215.0
10	I. Katsaidonis (GRE)	51.70	95.0	112.5	207.5

Bantamweight
Weight limit 56kg

		(kg)	1	2	Total points
1	D. Nunez (CUB)	55.60	125.0	150.0	*275.0
2	Y. Sarkisyan (URS)	55.80	112.5	157.5	270.0
3	T. Dembonczyk (POL)	55.60	120.0	145.0	265.0
4	A. Letz (GDR)	55.60	115.0	150.0	265.0
5	E. Yang (PRK)	55.75	112.5	150.0	262.5
6	I. Stefanovics (HUN)	55.15	115.0	145.0	260.0
7	G. Maftei (ROM)	55.40	105.0	142.5	247.5
8	P. Petre (ROM)	55.40	105.0	140.0	245.0
9	J. Choe (PRK)	55.70	105.0	137.5	242.5
10	I. Sidiropoulos (GRE)	55.95	102.5	140.0	242.5

Featherweight
Weight limit 60kg

		(kg)	1	2	Total points
1	V. Mazin (URS)	59.65	130.0	160.0	*290.0
2	S. Dimitrov (BUL)	59.40	127.5	160.0	287.5
3	M. Seweryn (POL)	59.55	127.5	155.0	282.5
4	A. Pawlak (POL)	59.65	120.0	155.0	275.0
5	J. Loscos (CUB)	59.70	125.0	150.0	275.0
6	F. Nedved (TCH)	59.70	122.5	150.0	272.5
7	V. Perez (CUB)	59.40	117.5	152.5	270.0
8	G. Radu (ROM)	60.00	115.0	150.0	265.0
9	J-C. Chavigny (FRA)	59.60	115.0	140.0	255.0
10	F.M. Fat'hi (IRQ)	60.00	115.0	137.5	252.5

Lightweight
Weight limit 67.5kg

		(kg)	1	2	Total points
1	Y. Roussev (BUL)	66.90	147.5	195.0	*342.5
2	J. Kunz (GDR)	66.90	145.0	190.0	335.0
3	M. Pachov (BUL)	67.10	142.5	182.5	325.0
4	D. Senet (FRA)	67.30	147.5	175.0	322.5
5	G. Ambrass (GDR)	66.85	140.0	180.0	320.0
6	Z. Kaczmarek (POL)	67.15	140.0	177.5	317.5
7	R. Gonzalez (CUB)	67.25	145.0	172.5	317.5
8	V. Dociu (ROM)	67.10	140.0	170.0	310.0
9	D. Drska (TCH)	67.00	130.0	160.0	290.0
10	J. Salakka (FIN)	66.65	130.0	152.5	285.5

Middleweight
Weight limit 75kg

		(kg)	1	2	Total points
1	A. Zlatev (BUL)	74.65	160.0	200.0	*360.0
2	A. Pervy (URS)	74.20	157.5	200.0	357.5
3	N. Kolev (BUL)	73.90	157.5	187.5	345.0
4	J. Echenique (CUB)	73.35	145.0	182.5	327.5
5	D. Ciorolan (ROM)	74.65	140.0	182.5	322.5
6	T. Kinnunen (FIN)	74.10	142.5	177.5	320.0
7	B. Sollevi (SWE)	74.75	137.5	172.5	310.0
8	N. Burrowes (GBR)	74.85	130.0	172.5	302.5
9	W. Rogelio (MEX)	74.85	135.0	165.0	300.0
10	V. Pedicone (ITA)	73.70	130.0	165.0	295.0

Light heavyweight
Weight limit 82.5kg

		(kg)	1	2	Total points
1	Y. Vardanyan (URS)	81.70	117.5	222.5	*400.0
2	B. Blagoev (BUL)	81.60	175.0	197.5	372.50
3	O. Poliacik (TCH)	82.00	160.0	207.5	367.5
4	J. Lisowski (POL)	81.85	150.0	205.0	355.0
5	K. Drandarov (BUL)	81.95	155.0	200.0	355.0
6	P. Rabczewski (POL)	82.30	155.0	195.0	350.0
7	D. Blasche (GDR)	80.95	152.5	192.5	345.0
8	J. Avellan (FIN)	82.35	150.0	182.5	332.5
9	V. Zrnic (TCH)	82.30	142.5	187.5	330.0
10	S. Jonsson (SWE)	82.35	142.5	185.0	327.5

*indicates Olympic Record

Middle heavyweight
Weight limit 90kg

		(kg)	1	2	Total points
1	R. Baczako (HUN)	89.10	170.0	207.5	377.5
2	R. Alexandrov (BUL)	89.40	170.0	205.0	375.0
3	E. Mantek (GDR)	88.75	165.0	205.0	375.0
4	D. Rehak (TCH)	89.50	165.0	200.0	365.0
5	W. Walo (POL)	88.30	160.0	200.0	360.0
6	L. Srsen (TCH)	89.40	160.0	197.5	357.5
7	V. Groapa (ROM)	89.25	160.0	195.0	355.0
8	N. Iliadis (GRE)	88.20	150.0	195.0	345.0
9	G. Langford (GBR)	89.05	150.0	180.0	330.0
10	N. Oberburger (ITA)	89.30	147.5	167.5	315.0

Middle heavyweight
Weight limit 100kg

		(kg)	1	2	Total points
1	O. Zaremba (TCH)	99.15	180.0	215.0	*395.0
2	I. Nikitin (URS)	99.25	177.5	215.0	392.5
3	A. Blanco (CUB)	98.15	172.5	212.5	385.0
4	M. Henning (GDR)	98.35	165.0	217.5	382.5
5	J. Solyomvari (HUN)	98.25	175.0	205.0	380.0
6	M. Funke (GDR)	98.65	170.0	207.5	377.5
7	A. Baraniak (TCH)	98.90	165.0	210.0	375.0
8	L. Varga (HUN)	97.15	172.5	195.0	367.5
9	M. Persson (SWE)	97.90	160.0	200.0	360.0
10	P. Niemi (FIN)	99.35	155.0	192.5	347.5

Heavyweight
Weight limit 110kg

		(kg)	1	2	Total points
1	L. Taranenko (URS)	109.90	182.5	240.0	*422.5
2	V. Christov (BUL)	109.55	185.0	220.0	405.0
3	G. Szalai (HUN)	108.10	172.5	217.5	390.0
4	L. Nilsson (SWE)	108.70	167.5	212.5	380.0
5	V. Hortnagl (AUS)	108.60	170.0	202.5	372.5
6	S. Tasnadi (ROM)	108.45	165.0	195.0	360.0
7	D. Mitchell (AUS)	109.10	162.5	190.0	352.5
8	D. Zarzavatsidis (GRE)	109.20	155.0	192.5	347.5
9	V. Sirkia (FIN)	109.50	150.0	192.5	342.5
10	A. Drzewiecki (GBR)	107.05	140.0	180.0	320.0

*indicates Olympic Record

Super heavyweight
Weight limit over 110kg

		(kg)	1	2	Total points
1	S. Rakhmanov (URS)	145.25	195.0	245.0	440.0
2	J. Heuser (GDR)	133.95	182.5	227.5	410.0
3	J.Rutkowski (POL)	124.90	180.0	227.5	407.5
4	R. Strejcek (TCH)	133.10	182.5	220.0	402.5
5	B. Braun (TCH)	133.10	182.5	220.0	402.5
6	F. Mendez (CUB)	134.30	175.0	220.0	395.0
7	R. Skolimowski (POL)	148.50	175.0	210.0	385.0
8	T. Naijar (SYR)	133.30	157.5	205.0	362.5

Wrestling

Light flyweight
Weight limit 48kg

1 C. Pollio (ITA)
2 S. Jang (PRK)
3 S. Kornilaev (URS)

4 J. Falandys (POL)
5 S. Mahabir (IND)
6 L. Biro (HUN)
7 R. Yordanov (BUL)
8 G. Rasovan (ROM)

Flyweight
Weight limit 52kg

1 A. Beloglazov (URS)
2 W. Stecyk (POL)
3 N. Selimov (BUL)

4 L. Szabo (HUN)
5 D. Jang (PRK)
6 N. Burgedaa (MGL)
7 K. Efremov (YUG)
8 H. Reich (GDR)

Bantamweight
Weight limit 57kg

1 S. Beloglazov (URS)
2 H.P Li (PRK)
3 D. Ouinbold (MGL)

4 I. Tzotchev (BUL)
5 A. Neagu (ROM)
6 W. Konczak (POL)
7 K. Muhsin (IRQ)
8 S. Nemeth (HUN)

Featherweight
Weight limit 62kg

1 M. Abushev (URS)
2 M. Doukov (BUL)
3 G. Hadjiioannidis (GRE)

4 R. Cascaret (CUB)
5 A. Suteu (ROM)
6 U. Nasanjargal (MGL)
7 B. Aspen (GBR)
8 Z. Szalontai (HUN)

Lightweight
Weight limit 68kg

1 S. Absaidov (URS)
2 I. Yankov (BUL)
3 S. Sejdi (YUG)

4 J. Singh (IND)
5 E. Probst (GDR)
6 O. Dusa (ROM)
7 A. Faris (IRQ)
8 P. Rauhala (FIN)

Welterweight
Weight limit 74kg

1 V. Raitchev (BUL)
2 J. Davaajav (MGL)
3 D. Karabin (TCH)

4 P. Pinigin (URS)
5 R. Scigalski (POL)
6 S. Rajander (IND)
7 I. Feher (HUN)
8 R. Niccolini (ITA)

Middleweight
Weight limit 82kg

1 I. Abilov (BUL)
2 M. Aratsilov (URS)
3 I. Kovacs (HUN)

4 H. Mazur (POL)
5 A. Memedi (YUG)
6 Z. Duvchin (MGL)
7 G. Busarello (AUS)
8 M. Eloulabi (SYR)

Light heavyweight
Weight limit 90kg

1 S. Oganesyan (URS)
2 U. Neupert (GDR)
3 A. Cichon (POL)

4   I. Ghinov (BUL)
5   D. Tseretogtokh (MGL)
6   C. Andanson (FRA)
7   I. Ivanov (ROM)
8   M. Pikos (AUS)

Heavyweight
Weight limit 100kg

1   I. Mate (URS)
2   S. Tchervenkov (BUL)
3   J. Strnisko (TCH)

4   H. Buttner (GDR)
5   T. Busse (POL)
6   V. Puscasu (ROM)
7   B. Morgan (CUB)
8   K. Bayanmunk (MGL)

Super heavyweight
Weight limit over 100kg

1   S. Andiev (URS)
2   J. Balla (HUN)
3   A. Sandurski (POL)

4   R. Gehrke (GDR)
5   A. Ianko (ROM)
6   M. Sakho (SEN)
7   P. Ivanov (BUL)
8   A. Diaz (CUB)

Wrestling (Greco-Roman)
Light flyweight
Weight limit 48kg

1   Z. Ushkempirov (URS)
2   C. Alexandru (ROM)
3   F. Seres (HUN)

4   P. Khristov (BUL)
5   R. Haaparanta (FIN)
6   A. Olvera (MEX)
7   V. Maenza (ITA)
8   R. Kierpacz (POL)

Flyweight
Weight limit 52kg

1   V. Blagidze (URS)
2   L. Racz (HUN)
3   M. Mlandenov (BUL)

4   N. Ginga (ROM)
5   A. Jelinek (TCH)
6   S. Wroblewski (POL)
7   T. Halonen (FIN)
8   A. Eloulabi (SYR)

Bantamweight
Weight limit 57kg

1   S. Serikov (URS)
2   J. Lipien (HOL)
3   B. Ljungbeck (SWE)

4   M. Botila (ROM)
5   A. Caltabiano (ITA)
6   J. Krysta (TCH)
7   G. Molnar (HUN)
8   G. Donev (BUL)

Featherweight
Weight limit 62kg

1   S. Migiakis (GRE)
2   I. Toth (HUN)
3   B. Kramorenko (URS)

4   I. Frgic (YUG)
5   P. Kirov (BUL)
6   K. Lipien (POL)
7   R. Karout (SYR)
8   M. Vejsada (TCH)

Lightweight
Weight limit 68kg

1   S. Rusu (ROM)
2   A. Supron (POL)
3   L.E. Skiold (SWE)

4   S. Nalbandyan (URS)
5   B. Bold (MGL)
6   I. Atanassov (BUL)
7   R. Hartmann (AUS)
8   K. Gaal (HUN)

Welterweight
Weight limit 74kg

1   F. Kocsis (HUN)
2   A. Bykov (URS)
3   M. Huhtala (FIN)

4   Y. Chopov (BUL)
5   L. Lundell (SWE)
6   V. Macha (TCH)
7   G. Minea (ROM)
8   J. Van Lancker (BEL)

Middleweight
Weight limit 82kg

1   G. Korban (URS)
2   J. Polgowicz (POL)
3   P. Pavlov (BUL)

4   L. Andersson (SWE)
5   D. Kuhn (GDR)
6   M. Toma (HUN)
7   M. Eloulabi (SYR)
8   M. Janota (TCH)

Light heavyweight
Weight limit 90kg

1   N. Nottny (HUN)
2   I. Kanygin (URS)
3   P. Disu (ROM)

4   F. Andersson (SWE)
5   T. Horschel (GDR)
6   J. Poll (CUB)
7   C. Andanson (FRA)
8   G. Pozidis (GRE)

Heavyweight
Weight limit under 100kg

1   G. Raikov (BUL)
2   R. Bierla (POL)
3   V. Andrei (ROM)

4   R. Memisevic (YUG)
5   G. Pikilidis (GRE)
6   O. Dvorak (TCH)
7   N. Balboshin (URS)
8   S. Studsgaard (DEN)

Super heavyweight
Weight limit over 100kg

1   A. Kolchinsky (URS)
2   A. Tomov (BUL)
3   H. Bchara (LIB)

4   J. Farkas (HUN)
5   P. Ilic (YUG)
6   A. Dias (CUB)
7   R. Codrean (ROM)
8   M. Galinski (POL)

Yachting

Soling

		Race							
		1	2	3	4	5	6	7	Points
1	P. Jensen, V. Bandolowski, E. Hansen (DEN)	1	5	6	5	2	1	1	23.00
2	D. Budnikov, A. Budnikov, N. Polyakov (URS)	3	8	3	2	5	2	2	30.40
3	A. Boudouris, A. Gavrilis, A. Rapanakis (GRE)	9	3	1	6	1	4	3	31.10
4	D. Below, B. Klenke, M. Zachries (GDR)	7	1	5	1	3	6	5	37.40
5	G. Bakker, S. Bakker, D. Coster (HOL)	2	2	7	4	4	5	7	45.00
6	V. Brun, G. Brun, R. Souza (BRA)	4	7	2	3	7	3	6	47.10
7	J-F. Corminboeuf, R-C. Guignard, R. Perret (SUI)	5	4	8	9	6	7	9	71.70
8	J. Andersson, G. Andersson, B. Larsson (SWE)	6	9	9	7	8	8	4	75.70
9	J. Bartosik, J. Wujecki, Z. Kotla (POL)	8	6	4	8	9	9	8	76.70

Finn

		Race 1	2	3	4	5	6	7	Points
1	E. Rechardt (FIN)	4	1	4	DSQ	3	1	9	36.70
2	W. Mayrhofer (AUS)	1	6	7	11	2	2	10	46.70
3	A. Balashov (URS)	6	14	3	1	5	16	1	47.40
4	C. Biekarck (BRA)	9	5	1	13	9	5	2	53.00
5	J. Schumann (GDR)	3	3	2	8	7	7	16	54.40
6	K. Carlson (SWE)	2	12	15	4	4	3	DNF	63.70
7	R. Skarbinski (POL)	7	17	8	6	6	9	3	71.10
8	M. Neelman (HOL)	5	11	12	7	18	4	5	76.00
9	I. Rujak (HUN)	DSQ	8	6	5	12	12	6	83.40
10	I. Hadjipavlis (GRE)	DSQ	16	9	12	1	10	12	89.00

Flying Dutchman

		Race 1	2	3	4	5	6	7	Points
1	A. Abascal, M. Noguer (ESP)	4	1	2	4	1	1	DNC	19.00
2	D. Wilkins, J. Wilkinson (IRL)	2	11	4	5	2	2	2	30.00
3	S. Detre, Z. Detre (HUN)	1	9	5	3	11	9	1	45.70
4	W. Haase, W. Wenzel (GDR)	5	4	3	9	4	3	8	51.40
5	V. Leontyev, V. Zubanov (URS)	6	7	1	1	8	7	9	51.70
6	Jorgen Moller, Jacob Moller (DEN)	DSQ	3	6	6	6	4	3	54.50
7	J. Vollebregt, S. Vollebregt (HOL)	8	2	8	8	3	5	4	54.70
8	R. Conrad, M. Kaufmann Jr (BRA)	3	5	9	7	5	6	DNF	63.40
9	D. Mandic, Z. Kalebic (YUG)	9	8	11	2	10	10	5	74.00
10	M. Savelli, R. Gazzei (ITA)	7	6	10	DNF	7	8	6	79.40

DSQ – Disqualified
DNF – did not complete race
DNC – non-competitor
RET – retired
PMS – prematurely started

Star

		Race							
		1	2	3	4	5	6	7	Points
1	V. Mankin, A. Muzychenko (URS)	2	1	1	5	1	6	7	24.70
2	H. Raudaschl, K. Ferstl (AUS)	1	4	DSQ	3	2	1	9	31.70
3	G. Gorla, A. Peraboni (ITA)	3	3	3	4	4	2	6	36.10
4	P. Sundelin, H. Lindstrom (SWE)	6	5	5	1	5	7	2	44.70
5	J. Christensen, M. Nielsen (DEN)	4	7	12	2	6	5	1	45.70
6	B. Binkhorst, J. Vandenberg (HOL)	10	2	2	11	3	3	10	49.40
7	A. Gorostegui, J. Benavides (ESP)	7	8	7	6	7	4	12	72.70
8	W-E. Richter, O. Engelhardt (GDR)	8	13	6	13	10	9	4	83.70
9	E. Souza Ramos, P. Erzberger (BRA)	9	11	8	8	9	11	5	85.00
10	G. Holovits, T. Holovits (HUN)	5	12	9	7	12	8	11	87.00

Tornado

		Race							
		1	2	3	4	5	6	7	Points
1	A. Welter, L. Bjorkstrom (BRA)	3	1	3	6	1	1	5	21.40
2	P. Due, P. Kjergard (DEN)	7	2	2	3	2	5	3	30.40
3	G. Marstrom, J. Ragnarsson (SWE)	1	4	7	2	6	2	4	33.70
4	V. Potapov, A. Zybin (URS)	6	3	5	4	3	3	1	35.10
5	M. Van Walt, G. Brasser (HOL)	4	5	1	5	4	6	2	39.00
6	P. Narko, J. Siira (FIN)	5	6	4	1	5	4	6	47.70
7	H. Porkert, H. Kupfner (AUS)	2	7	6	RET	7	7	8	67.70
8	U. Steingross, J. Schramme (GDR)	8	8	8	7	8	DNF	7	82.00
9	B. Kramer, J. Kruger (HOL)	9	9	9	9	10	8	9	89.0
10	T. Pentzhev, K. Krastev (BUL)	11	10	10	8	9	DNF	10	94.00
		11	10	10	8	9	DNF	10	19.00

470

		Race							
		1	2	3	4	5	6	7	Points
1	M. Soares, E. Penido (BRA)	2	1	6	1	5	10	6	36.40
2	J. Borowski, E. Swensson (GDR)	5	8	1	9	6	1	2	38.70
3	J. Lindgren, G. Tallberg (FIN)	4	2	3	5	9	7	1	39.70
4	H. Van Gent, J. Van Den Hondel (HOL)	10	3	8	7	2	3	4	49.40
5	L. Wrobel, T. Stocki (POL)	1	9	7	4	1	11	12	53.00
6	G. Doreste, A. Rigau (ESP)	6	6	2	3	8	4	9	54.10
7	E. Treves, E. Necchi (ITA)	3	5	10	10	7	2	5	57.70
8	L. Bengtsson, S. Benatsson (SWE)	7	7	4	2	11	5	7	60.00
9	F. Kistler, J.L. Dreyer (SUI)	9	11	5	6	4	6	3	62.10
10	V. Ignatenko, S. Zhdanov (URS)	8	4	9	8	3	DSQ	8	70.70

CURRENT OLYMPIC RECORDS

Archery (men)

Double FITA	2571 points	D. Pace (USA)	1976

Archery (women)

Double FITA	2499 points	L. Ryon (USA)	1976

Athletics (men)

100 metres	9.95	J. Hines (USA)	1968
200 metres	19.83	T. Smith (USA)	1968
400 metres	43.86	L. Evans (USA)	1968
800 metres	1:43.50	A. Juantorena (CUB)	1976
1500 metres	3:34.91	K. Keino (KEN)	1968
5000 metres	13:20.34	B. Foster (GBR)	1976
10,000 metres	27:38.35	L. Viren (FIN)	1972
Marathon	2h 09:55	W. Cierpinski (GDR)	1976
20 kilometres walk	1h 23:36	M. Damilano (ITA)	1980
50 kilometres walk	3h 49:24	H. Gauder (GDR)	1980
110 metres hurdles	13.24	R. Milburn (USA)	1972
400 metres hurdles	47.64	E. Moses (USA)	1976
3000 m steeplechase	8:08.02	A. Garderud (SWE)	1976
4×100 metres relay	38.19	USA	1972
4×400 metres relay	2:56.16	USA	1968
High jump	2.36m	G. Wessig (GDR)	1980
Long jump	8.90m	R. Beamon (USA)	1968
Triple jump	17.39m	V. Saneyev (URS)	1968
Pole vault	5.78m	W. Kozakiewicz (POL)	1980
Shot put	21.35m	V. Kiselyev (URS)	1980
Discus	68.28m	M. Wilkins (USA)	1976
Hammer	81.80m	Y. Sedykh (URS)	1980
Javelin	94.58m	M. Nemeth (HUN)	1976
Decathlon	8617 points	B. Jenner (USA)	1976

Athletics (women)

100 metres	11.01	A. Richter (FRG)	1976
200 metres	22.03	B. Wockel (GDR)	1980
400 metres	48.88	M. Koch (GDR)	1980
800 metres	1:53.43	N. Olizarenko (URS)	1980
1500 metres	3:56.56	T. Kazankina (URS)	1980
100 metres hurdles	12.56	V. Komissova (URS)	1980
4×100 metres relay	41.60	GDR	1980
4×400 metres relay	3:19.23	GDR	1976
High jump	1.97m	S. Simeoni (ITA)	1980
Long jump	7.06m	T. Kolpakova (URS)	1980
Shot put	22.41m	I. Slupianek (GDR)	1980
Discus	69.96m	E. Jahl (GDR)	1980
Javelin	68.40m	M. Colon (CUB)	1980

Cycling

10000m time trial	1:02.955	L. Thoms (GDR)	1980
4000m individual pursuit	4:34.92	R. Dill-Bundi (SUI)	1980
4000 m team pursuit	4:14.64	USSR	1980

Rowing (men)

Single sculls	6:52.46	S. Drea (IRL)	1976
Double sculls	6:12.48	NOR	1976
Quadruple sculls	5:47.83	USSR	1976
Coxless Pairs	6:33.02	GDR	1976
Coxed Pairs	7:01.10	BUL	1976
Coxless Fours	5:53.65	GDR	1976
Coxed Fours	6:09.28	URS	1976
Eights	5:32.17	GDR	1976

Rowing (women)

Single sculls	3:40.69	S. Toma (ROM)	1980
Double sculls	3:16.27	URS	1980
Quadruple sculls	3:08.49	GDR	1976

Coxless Pairs	3:30.49	GDR	1980
Coxed Fours	3:19.27	GDR	1980
Eights	3:00.19	URS	1976

Shooting

Small-bore rifle, three positions	1173 points	V. Vlasov (URS)	1980
Small-bore rifle, prone	599	H. Jun Li (PRK)	1972
	599	K. Smieszek (FRG)	1976
	599	K. Varga (HUN)	1980
	599	H. Heilfort (GDR)	1980
Free pistol	581	A. Melentev (URS)	1980
Rapid fire pistol	597	N. Klaar (GDR)	1976
Running game	589	I. Sokolov (URS)	1980
	589	T. Pfeffer (GDR)	1980
Trap	199	A. Scalzone (ITA)	1972
Skeet	198	Y. Petrov (URS)	1968
	198	R. Garagnani (ITA)	1968
	198	K. Wirnhier (FRG)	1968
	198	J. Panacek (TCH)	1976
	198	E. Swinkels (HOL)	1976
	198	L. Giovannetti (ITA)	1980

Swimming (men)

Freestyle

100 metres	49.99	J. Montgomery (USA)	1976
200 metres	1:49.81	S. Koplikov (URS)	1980
400 metres	3:51.31	V. Salnikov (URS)	1980
1500 metres	14:58.27	V. Salnikov (URS)	1980

Backstroke

| 100 metres | 55.49 | J. Naber (USA) | 1976 |
| 200 metres | 1:59.19 | J. Naber (USA) | 1976 |

Breaststroke

| 100 metres | 1:03.11 | J. Hencken (USA) | 1976 |
| 200 metres | 2:15.11 | D. Wilkie (GBR) | 1976 |

Butterfly

| 100 metres | 54.27 | M. Spitz (USA) | 1972 |
| 200 metres | 1:59.23 | M. Bruner (USA) | 1976 |

Medley

| 200 metres | 2:07.17 | G. Larsson (SWE) | 1972 |
| 400 metres | 4:22.89 | A. Sidorenko (URS) | 1980 |

Relay

4×100 medley	3:42.22	USA	1976
4×100m freestyle	3:26.42	USA	1972
4×200m freestyle	7:23.22	USA	1976

Swimming (women)

Freestyle

100 metres	54.79	B. Krause (GDR)	1980
200 metres	1:58.33	B. Krause (GDR)	1980
400 metres	4:08.76	I. Diers (GDR)	1980
800 metres	8:28.90	M. Ford (AUS)	1980

Backstroke

| 100 metres | 1:00.86 | R. Reinisch (GDR) | 1980 |
| 200 metres | 2:11.77 | R. Reinisch (GDR) | 1980 |

Breaststroke

| 100 metres | 1:10.11 | U. Geweniger (GDR) | 1980 |
| 200 metres | 2:29.54 | L. Kachushite (URS) | 1980 |

Butterfly

| 100 metres | -1:00.13 | K. Ender (GDR) | 1976 |
| 200 metres | 2-10.44 | I. Geissler (GDR) | 1980 |

Medley

| 200 metres | 2:23.07 | S. Gould (AUS) | 1972 |
| 400 metres | 4:36.29 | P. Schneider (GDR) | 1980 |

Relay

4×100 metres medley	4:06.67	GDR		1980
4×100m freestyle	3:42.17	GDR		1980

Weightlifting

Category	Lift	kg	Name	Year
52 kilogram	Total	245	K. Osmonoliev (URS)	1980
		245	B. Chol Ho (PRK)	1980
		245	G. Si Han (PRK)	1980
		245	B. Olah (HUN)	1980
	Snatch	110	B. Chol Ho (PRK)	1980
		110	G. Si Han (PRK)	1980
		110	B. Olah (HUN)	1980
	Jerk	137.5	K. Osmonoliev (URS)	1980
50 kilogram	Total	275	D. Nunez (CUB)	1980
	Snatch	125	D. Nunez (CUB)	1980
	Jerk	157.5	Y. Sarkisian (URS)	1980
60 kilogram	Total	290	V. Mazin (URS)	1980
	Snatch	130	V. Mazin (URS)	1980
	Jerk	160	N. Kolesnikov (URS)	1976
		160	V. Mazin (URS)	1980
		160	S. Dimitrov (BUL)	1980
67.5 kilogram	Total	342.5	Y. Rusev (BUL)	1980
	Snatch	147.5	Y. Rusev (BUL)	1980
		147.5	D. Senet (FRA)	1980
	Jerk	195	Y. Rusev (BUL)	1980
75 kilogram	Total	360	A. Zlatev (BUL)	1980
	Snatch	160	A. Zlatev (BUL)	1980
	Jerk	200	A. Zlatev (BUL)	1980
		200	A. Pervy (URS)	1980
82.5 kilogram	Total	400	Y. Vardanyan (URS)	1980
	Snatch	177.5	Y. Vardanyan (URS)	1980
	Jerk	222.5	Y. Vardanyan (URS)	1980
90 kilogram	Total	382.5	D. Rigert (URS)	1976
	Snatch	170	D. Rigert (URS)	1976
		170	P. Baczako (HUN)	1980
		170	R. Alexandrov (BUL)	1980
	Jerk	212.5	D. Rigert (URS)	1976

100 kilogram	Total	395	O. Zaremba (TCH)	1980
	Snatch	180	O. Zaremba (TCH)	1980
	Jerk	217.5	M. Hennig (GDR)	1980
110 kilogram	Total	422.5	L. Taranenko (URS)	1980
	Snatch	185	V. Christov (BUL)	1980
	Jerk	240	L. Taranenko (URS)	1980
110 kilogram +	Total	440	V. Alexeyev (URS)	1976
		440	S. Rakhmanov (URS)	1980
	Snatch	195	S. Rakhmanov (URS)	1980
	Jerk	255	V. Alexeyev (URS)	1976

CURRENT WORLD RECORDS

Athletics (men)

100 metres	9.93	Calvin Smith (USA)	1983
200 metres	19.72	Pietro Mennea (ITA)	1979
400 metres	43.86	Lee Evans (USA)	1968
800 metres	1:41.73	Seb Coe (GBR)	1981
1500 metres	3:30.77	Steve Ovett (GBR)	1983
Mile	3:47.33	Seb Coe (GBR)	1981
5000 metres	13:00.41	Dave Moorcroft (GBR)	1982
10000 metres	27:22.4	Henry Rono (KEN)	1978
Marathon (world best)	2:08.13	Alberto Salazar (USA)	1981
110 metres hurdles	12.93	Ronald Neherniah (USA)	1981
400 metres hurdles	47.02	Ed Moses (USA)	1983
3000 metre steeplechase	8:05.4	Henry Rono (KEN)	1978
4 x 100 metres relay	37.86	USA	1983
4 x 400 metres relay	2:56.16	USA	1968
20 kilometre walk (world best)	1h 18:49	Daniel Bautista (MEX)	1979
50 kilometre walk (world best)	3h 37:36	Yovhon Ivchenko (USSR)	1980
High jump	2.38 metres	Zhu Jian-Hua (CHI)	1983
Long jump	8.90 metres	Bob Beamon (USA)	1968
Triple jump	17.89 metres	Joao de Oliveira (BRA)	1975
Pole vault	5.83 metres	Thierry Vigneron (FRA)	1983
Shot	22.22 metres	Udo Beyer (GDR)	1983
Discus	71.86 metres	Yuriy Dumchev (URS)	1983
Hammer	84.14 metres	Sergey Litvinov (URS)	1983
Javelin	99.72 metres	Tom Petranoff (USA)	1983
Decathlon	8779 points	Jurgen Hingsen (FRG)	1983

Athletics (women)

100 metres	10.79	Evelyn Ashford (USA)	1983
200 metres	21.71	Marita Koch (GDR)	1979
400 metres	47.99	Jarmila Kratochvilova (TCH)	1983
800 metres	1:53.28	Jarmila Kratchvilova (TCH)	1983
1500 metres	3:52.47	Tatyana Kazankina (URS)	1980
3000 metres	8:26.78	Svetlane Ulmasova (URS)	1982
Marathon (world best)	2h 22:43	Joan Benoit (USA)	1983
100 metres hurdles	12.36	Grazyna Rabsztyn (POL)	1980
400 metres hurdles	54.02	Anna Ambraziene (URS)	1983
4 x 100 metres relay	41.53	GDR	1983
4 x 400 metres relay	3:19.04	GDR	1982
High jump	2.04 metres	Tamara Bykova (URS)	1983
Long jump	7.43 metres	Anisoara Cusmir (ROM)	1983
Shot	22.45 metres	Ilena Slupianek (GDR)	1980
Discus	73.26 metres	Galina Savinkova (URS)	1983
Javelin	74.76 metres	Tiina Lillak (FIN)	1983
Heptathlon	6836 points	Ramona Neubert (GDR)	1983

Swimming (men)

Event	Mins/secs	Name	Date
100 metres freestyle	49.36	R. Gaines (USA)	1981
200 metres freestyle	1:47.87	M. Gross (FRG)	1983
400 metres freestyle	3:48.32	V. Salnikov (URS)	1983
800 metres freestyle	7:52.33	V. Salnikov (URS)	1983
1500 metres freestyle	14:54.76	V. Salnikov (URS)	1983
100 metres backstroke	55.19	R. Carey (USA)	1983
200 metres backstroke	1:58.93	R. Carey (USA)	1983
100 metres breaststroke	1:02.28	S. Lundquist (USA)	1983
200 metres breaststroke	2:14.77	V. Davis (CAN)	1982

100 metres butterfly	53.44	M. Gribble (USA)	1983
200 metres butterfly	1:57.05	M. Gross (FRG)	1983
200 metres individual medley	2:02.25	A. Baumann (CAN)	1982
400 metres individual medley	4:19.78	R. Prado (BRA)	1982
4 x 100 metres medley relay	3:40.84	USA	1982
4 x 100 metres freestyle relay	3:19.26	USA	1982
4 x 200 metres freestyle relay	7:20.40	FRG	1983

Swimming (women)

100 metres	54.79	B. Krause (GDR)	1980
200 metres freestyle	1:58.23	C. Woodhead (USA)	1979
400 metres freestyle	4:06.28	T. Wickham (AUS)	1978
800 metres freestyle	8:24.62	T. Wickman (AUS)	1978
1500 metres freestyle	16:04.49	K. Lineham (USA)	1979
100 metres backstroke	1:00.86	R. Reinisch (GDR)	1980
200 metres backstroke	2:09.91	C. Sirch (GDR)	1982
100 metres breaststroke	1:08.51	U. Geweniger (GDR)	1983
200 metres breaststroke	2:28.36	L. Kachushite (URS)	1979
100 metres butterfly	57.93	M. Meagher (USA)	1981
200 metres butterfly	2:05.96	M. Meagher (USA)	1981
200 metres individual medley	2:11.73	U. Geweniger (GDR)	1981
400 metres individual medley	4:36.10	P. Schneider (GDR)	1982
4 x 100 metres medley relay	4:05.79	GDR	1983
4 x 100 metres freestyle relay	3:42.71	GDR	1980

FORM GUIDE TO LEADING OLYMPIC SPORTS

Athletics (men)

100 metres

Time
9.93	C. Smith (USA)
9.97	C. Lewis (USA)
10.03	M. Lattany (USA)
10.06	R. Brown (USA)
10.06	E. King (USA)
10.06	L. Penalver (CUB)
10.08	D. Green (USA)
10.13	S. Floyd (USA)
10.14	J. Nunez (DOM)
10.15	A. Wells (GBR)

200 metres

Time
19.75	C. Lewis (USA)
19.99	C. Smith (USA)
20.03	L. Myricks (USA)
20.16	E. Quow (USA)
20.22	M. Lattany (USA)
20.22	P. Mennea (ITA)
20.26	B. Jackson (USA)
20.29	C. Davis (USA)
20.29	D. Williams (CAN)
20.32	J. Butler (USA)

400 metres

Time
44.50	E. Skamrahl (FRG)
44.62	B. Cameron (JAM)
44.73	J. Rolle (USA)
44.80	C. Whitlock (USA)
44.87	S. Nix (USA)
44.94	E. Carey (USA)
44.96	S. Uti (NIG)
44.96	M. Franks (USA)
44.97	W. McCoy (USA)
44.98	C. Phillips (USA)

800 metres

Time
1:43.61	S. Cram (GBR)
1:43.65	W. Wulbeck (FRG)
1:43.80	S. Coe (GBR)
1:43.98	P. Elliott (GBR)
1:44.04	J. Cruz (BRA)
1:44.20	J. Ndiwa (KEN)
1:44.20	R. Druppers (HOL)
1:44.29	D. Paige (USA)
1:44.32	J. Robinson (USA)
1:44.38	S. Aouita (MAR)

1500 metres

Time
3:30.77	S. Ovett (GBR)
3:31.24	S. Maree (USA)
3:31.66	S. Cram (GBR)
3:32.54	S. Aouita (MAR)
3:32.71	S. Scott (USA)
3:32.97	P. Deleze (SUI)
3:33.18	J. Abascal (ESP)
3:33.44	J-L. Gonzalez
3:33.84	J. Walker (NZL)
3:34.01	G. Williamson (GBR)

Mile

Time
3:49.21	S. Scott (USA)
3:49.73	J. Walker (NZL)
3:49.98	T. Wessinghage (FRG)
3:50.30	S. Maree (USA)
3:50.49	S. Ovett (GBR)
3:50.59	J. Spivey (USA)
3:50.73	W. Waigwa (KEN)
3:50.76	J-L. Gonzalez (ESP)
3:50.98	J. Marajo (FRA)
3:51.59	E. Coghlan (IRL)

5000 metres
Time

13:08.54	F. Mamede (POR)
13:14.13	A. Leitao (POR)
13:17.69	D. Padilla (USA)
13:18.53	A. Prieto (ESP)
13:18.86	T. Wessinghage (FRG)
13:19.24	J. Spivey (USA)
13:19.38	M. Ryffel (SUI)
13:19.73	J. Hill (USA)
13:20.07	M. Vainio (FIN)
13:20.94	E. Martin (GBR)

10000 metres
Time

27:23.44	C. Lopes (POR)
27:24.95	W. Schildhauer (GDR)
27:25.13	F. Mamede (POR)
27:30.69	H. Kunze (GDR)
27:31.19	N. Rose (GBR)
27:37.59	A. Cova (ITA)
27:39.14	S. Jones (GBR)
27:43.46	A. Prieto (ESP)
27:44.05	M. Shintaku (JPN)
27:46.93	G. Shahanga (TAN)

Marathon
Time

2h 08:37.0	R. de Castella (AUS)
2h 08:38.0	T. Seko (JPN)
2h 08:39.0	C. Lopes (POR)
2h 08:55.0	T. Soh (JPN)
2h 08:55.0	J. Ikangaa (TAN)
2h 08:59.0	R. Dixon (NZL)
2h 09:01.0	G. Meyer (USA)
2h 09:08.0	G. Smith (GBR)
2h 09:11.0	S. Soh (JPN)
2h 09:12.0	R. Gomez (MEX)

110 metres hurdles
Time

13.11	G. Foster (USA)
13.17	S. Turner (USA)
13.32	T. Campbell (USA)
13.44	A. Bryggare (FIN)
13.44	R. Kingdom (USA)
13.46	A. Prokofyev (URS)
13.47	W. Gault (USA)
13.48	T. Munkelt (GDR)
13.49	G. Bakos (HUN)
13.50	A. Oschkenat (GDR)

400 metres hurdles
Time

47.02	E. Moses (USA)
47.78	A. Phillips (USA)
48.05	D. Patrick (USA)
48.42	D. Lee (USA)
48.49	H. Schmid (FRG)
48.78	A. Kharlov (URS)
48.87	L. Cowling (USA)
48.88	S. Nylander (SWE)
48.99	A. Yatsevich (URS)
49.03	J. Thomas (USA)

3000 metres steeplechase
Time

8:12.37	H. Marsh (USA)
8:12.62	B. Maminski (POL)
8:15.06	P. Ilg (FRG)
8:15.16	G. Fell (GBR)
8:15.59	J. Mahmoud (FRA)
8:16.59	F. Sanchez (ESP)
8:17.42	K. Rono (KEN)
8:17.75	C. Reitz (GBR)
8:18.22	R. Tuwei (KEN)
8:19.38	R. Hackney (GBR)

20 kilometres walk
Time

1h 19:30.0	J. Pribilinec (TCH)
1h 19:41.0	E. Canto (MEX)
1h 19:43.0	A. Solomin (URS)
1h 20:00.0	J. Marin (ESP)
1h 20:10.0	M. Damilano (ITA)
1h 20:30.0	Y. Yevsukov (URS)
1h 20:40.0	D. Colin (MEX)
1h 20:51.0	D. Smith (AUS)
1h 20:55.0	R. Weigel (GDR)
1h 21:11.0	C. Mattioli (ITA)

50 kilometres walk
Time

3h 40:46.0	J. Marin (ESP)
3h 41:31.0	R. Weigel (GDR)
3h 43:23.0	H. Gauder (GDR)
3h 45:37.0	R. Gonzalez (MEX)
3h 45:49.0	A. Perlov (URS)
3h 46:12.0	D. Meisch (GDR)
3h 47:48.0	J. Llopart (ESP)
3h 48:26.0	S. Yung (URS)
3h 49:47.0	V. Dorovskiy (URS)
3h 50:43.0	M. Bermudez (MEX)

4 × 100 metres relay

Time

37.86	USA
38.30	GDR
38.37	ITA
38.41	URS
38.55	CUB
38.56	FRG
38.69	CAN
38.72	POL
38.75	JAM
38.87	HUN

4 × 400 metres relay

Time

2:59.91	USA
3:00.79	URS
3:01.83	FRG
3:02.28	GBR
3:02.62	GDR
3:02.79	BRA
3:03.15	CUB
3:03.25	ITA
3:03.25	TCH
3:03.36	SAF

High jump

Height (m)

2.38	Z. Jian-Hua (CHN)
2.35	V. Sereda (URS)
2.34	P. Frommeyer (FRG)
2.34	C. Thranhardt (FRG)
2.34	E. Annys (BEL)
2.33	I. Paklin (URS)
2.33	T. Peacock (USA)
2.33	P. Sjoberg (SWE)
2.32	G. Avdeyenko (URS)
2.32	F. Centelles (CUB)

Long jump

Distance (m)

8.79	C. Lewis (USA)
8.39	J. Grimes (USA)
8.33	S. Rodin (URS)
8.28	A. Beskrovniy (URS)
8.28	M. Conley (USA)
8.24	L. Szalma (HUN)
8.21	L. Myricks (USA)
8.21	Y. Alli (NIG)
8.19	M. McRae (USA)
8.18	R. Spry (USA)

Triple jump

Distance (m)

17.55	V. Grishchenkov (URS)
17.53	A. Beskrovniy (URS)
17.42	Z. Hoffman (POL)
17.40	L. Betancourt (CUB)
17.35	K. Lorraway (AUS)
17.33	P. Bouschen (FRG)
17.30	V. Bordukov (URS)
17.27	S. Abbyasov (URS)
17.27	G. Yemets (URS)
17.27	O. Protsenko (URS)

Pole vault

Height (m)

5.83	T. Vigneron (FRA)
5.82	P. Quinon (FRA)
5.76	J. Buckingham (USA)
5.75	B. Pursley (USA)
5.74	P. Bogatyrov (URS)
5.74	A. Krupskiy (URS)
5.72	K. Volkov (URS)
5.71	F. Bohni (SUI)
5.71	A. Chernyayev (URS)
5.71	A. Parnov (URS)

Shot

Distance (m)

22.22	U. Beyer (GDR)
21.94	D. Laut (USA)
21.68	E. Sarul (POL)
21.61	K. Akins (USA)
21.44	R. Machura (TCH)
21.43	M. Lehmann (USA)
21.40	J. Bojars (URS)
21.36	U. Timmermann (GDR)
21.22	B. Oldfield (USA)
21.20	J. Kubes (TCH)

Discus

Distance (m)

71.86	Y. Dumchev (URS)
71.32	B. Plucknett (USA)
71.18	A. Burns (USA)
71.06	L. Delis (CUB)
70.72	I. Bugar (TCH)
70.36	M. Wilkins (USA)
70.00	J. Martinez (CUB)
68.30	J. Powell (USA)
68.12	I. Nagy (ROM)
67.26	G. Valent (TCH

Hammer
Distance (m)

84.14	S. Litvinov (URS)
82.92	I. Nikulin (URS)
81.18	Y. Tarasyuk (URS)
81.12	G. Shevtsov (URS)
81.02	J. Tiainen (FIN)
80.94	Y. Sedykh (URS)
80.26	K-H. Riehm (FRG)
80.18	Z. Kwasny (POL)
80.04	K. Ploghaus (FRG)
80.00	A. Chyuzhas (URS)

Javelin
Distance (m)

99.72	T. Petranoff (USA)
96.72	D. Michel (GDR)
94.20	H. Puuste (URS)
91.88	D. Kula (URS)
91.44	K. Tafelmeier (FRG)
91.24	K. van der Merwe (SAF)
91.14	K. Eldebrink (SWE)
90.90	P. Sinersaari (FIN)
90.66	E. Vilhjalmsson (ISL)
90.58	M. O'Rourke (NZL)

Decathlon
Points

8779	J. Hingsen (FRG)
8718	S. Wentz (FRG)
8666	D. Thompson (GBR)
8538	G. Degtyarov (URS)
8501	U. Freimuth (GDR)
8457	G. Kratschmer (FRG)
8418	K. Akhapkin (URS)
8412	A. Nevskiy (URS)
8369	A. Rizzi (FRG)
8337	T. Voss (GDR)
8337	S. Niklaus (SUI)

Athletics (women)

---

100 metres
Time

10.79	E. Ashford (USA)
10.81	M. Gohr (GDR)
10.83	M. Koch (GDR)
10.94	D. Williams (USA)
11.03	S. Gladisch (GDR)
11.06	F. Griffith (USA)
11.07	M. Ottey (JAM)
11.07	A. Nuneva (BUL)
11.08	A. Brown (USA)
11.09	O. Antonova (URS)
11.09	N. Georgieva (BUL)

200 metres
Time

21.82	M. Koch (GDR)
21.88	E. Ashford (USA)
21.99	C. Cheeseborough (USA)
22.19	M. Ottey (JAM)
22.23	F. Griffith (USA)
22.26	K. Cook (GBR)
22.31	R. Givens (USA)
22.40	J. Kratochvilova (TCH)
22.41	A. Brown (USA)
22.42	N. Georgieva (BUL)
22.42	B. Wockel (GDR)

400 metres

Time

47.99	J. Kratochvilova (TCH)
48.59	T. Kocembova (TCH)
49.19	M. Pinigina (URS)
49.75	G. Bussmann (FRG)
50.06	M. Payne (CAN)
50.19	I. Baskakova (URS)
50.26	S. Busch (GDR)
50.48	O. Vladykina (URS)
50.48	D. Rubsam (GDR)
50.63	M. Ivanova (URS)

800 metres

Time

1:53.28	J. Kratochvilova (TCH)
1:55.96	Y. Podkopayeva (URS)
1:56.11	L. Gurina (URS)
1:56.21	Z. Zaitseva (URS)
1:56.81	T. Providokhina (URS)
1:56.96	Z. Moravcikova (TCH)
1:57.06	D. Melinte (ROM)
1:57.08	R. Agletdinova (URS)
1:57.28	M. Matejkovicova (TCH)
1:57.4	L. Borisova (URS)

1500 metres

Time

3:57.12	M. Decker (USA)
3:59.31	R. Agletdinova (URS)
4:00.12	F. Lovin (ROM)
4:00.3	Y. Podkopayeva (URS)
4:00.62	M. Radu (ROM)
4:00.7	T. Sorokina (URS)
4:01.19	Z. Zaitseva (URS)
4:01.23	T. Kazankina (URS)
4:01.29	C. Wartenberg (GDR)
4:01.4	I. Nikitina (URS)

3000 metres

Time

8:32.08	T. Kazankina (URS)
8:34.04	A. Yushina (URS)
8:34.60	G. Zakharova (URS)
8:34.62	M. Decker (USA)
8:35.06	S. Guskova (URS)
8:35.11	B. Kraus (FRG)
8:35.55	S. Ulmasova (URS)
8:37.06	W. Sly (GBR)
8:37.32	T. Pozdnyakova (URS)
8:37.40	O. Dvirna (URS)

Marathon

Time

2h 22:43.0	J. Benoit (USA)
2h 25:29.0	G. Waitz (NOR)
2h 26:26.0	J. Brown (USA)
2h 28:19.0	M. O'Connor (NZL)
2h 28:32.0	C. Teske (FRG)
2h 29:23.0	C. May (IRL)
2h 29:28.0	J. Gareau (CAN)
2h 30:30.0	A. Masuda (JPN)
2h 31:09.0	M. Dickerson (USA)
2h 31:12.0	R. Mota (POR)

100 metres hurdles

Time

12.42	B. Jahn (GDR)
12.49	G. Zagorcheva (BUL)
12.62	K. Knabe (GDR)
12.65	Y. Donkova (BUL)
12.72	C. Riefstahl (GDR)
12.73	L. Kalek (POL)
12.83	N. Petrova (URS)
12.84	B. Fitzgerald (USA)
12.86	S. Gusarova (URS)
12.86	C. Feuerbach (GDR)

400 metres hurdles

Time

54.02	A. Ambraziene (URS)
54.14	Y. Fesenko (URS)
54.20	E. Fiedler (GDR)
54.64	P. Pfaff (GDR)
54.72	Y. Filipishina (URS)
54.76	P. Krug (GDR)
54.80	A-L. Skoglund (SWE)
55.19	M. Wagner (FRG)
55.20	M. Navickaite (URS)
55.49	C. Fick (SAF)

4 × 100 metres relay

Time

41.53	GDR
41.61	USA
42.38	BUL
42.71	GBR
42.73	JAM
43.04	CAN
43.22	URS
43.36	FRA
43.78	TCH
43.79	FRG

4 × 400 metres relay
Time

3:19.73	GDR
3:20.32	TCH
3:21.16	URS
3:25.26	CAN
3:25.81	BUL
3:26.82	USA
3:27.13	FRG
3:27.29	GBR
3:30.08	POL
3:30.76	CUB

High jump
Height (m)

2.04	T. Bykova (URS)
2.03	U. Meyfarth (FRG)
2.01	L. Ritter (USA)
1.99	K. Brandt (GDR)
1.98	L. Kositsina (URS)
1.98	S. Costa (CUB)
1.98	V. Poluiko (URS)
1.97	N. Vasile (ROM)
1.97	A. Bienias (GDR)
1.97	S. Helm (GDR)
1.97	O. Juha (HUN)

Long jump
Distance (m)

7.43	A. Cusmir (ROM)
7.14	H. Daute (GDR)
7.04	S. Zorina (URS)
7.04	T. Proskuryakova (URS)
7.00	M. Butkiene (URS)
6.97	C. Lewis (USA)
6.92	E. Murkova (TCH)
6.90	T. Turulina (URS)
6.90	B. Kinch (GBR)
6.85	Y. Shishcherova (URS)
6.85	V. Ionescu (ROM)

Shot
Distance (m)

22.40	I. Slupianek (GDR)
21.46	H. Fibingerova (TCH)
21.05	Z. Silhava (TCH)
20.95	M. Loghin (ROM)
20.94	N. Abashidze (URS)
20.85	N. Lisovskaya (URS)
20.82	L. Schmuhl (GDR)
20.70	H. Knorscheidt (GDR)
20.58	C. Schulze (GDR)
20.54	I. Muller (GDR)

Discus
Distance (m)

73.26	G. Savinkova (URS)
70.96	G. Beyer (GDR)
70.74	M. Petkova (BUL)
70.26	M. Opitz (GDR)
70.00	Z. Silhava (TCH)
68.86	G. Murashova (URS)
68.60	N. Kugayevskikh (URS)
67.74	F. Craciunescu (ROM)
67.44	M. Ritchie (GBR)
67.32	N. Gorbachova (URS)

Javelin
Distance (m)

74.76	T. Lillak (FIN)
73.58	T. Sanderson (GBR)
72.28	S. Sakorafa (GRE)
71.00	A. Kempe (GDR)
70.90	A. Verouli (GRE)
69.54	F. Whitbread (GBR)
69.02	P. Felke (GDR)
68.76	M. Vila (CUB)
67.40	T. Laaksalo (FIN)
67.20	F. Quintavalla (ITA)

Heptathlon
Points

6836	R. Neubert (GDR)
6662	S. Paetz (GDR)
6532	A. Vater (GDR)
6526	N. Shubenkova (URS)
6493	Y. Smirnova (URS)
6485	L. Kolyadina (URS)
6457	J. Frederick (USA)
6440	V. Dimitrova (BUL)
6421	S. Thiele (GDR)
6418	V. Kurochkina (URS)

Gymnastics (men)

These were the leading results in the 1983 World Championships held in Budapest in October

Combined exercises (individual)

	Set exercises	Voluntary	Total
1 D. Belozerchev (URS)	59.10	59.60	118.70
2 F. Tong (CHN)	59.45	59.25	118.70
3 N. Li (CHN)	59.35	59.05	118.40
4 A. Akopian (URS)	58.85	59.30	118.15
5 A. Pogorelov (URS)	58.85	59.25	118.10
6 K. Gushiken (JPN)	59.15	58.90	118.05
7 Y. Lou (CHN)	58.85	59.00	117.85
8 V. Artemov (URS)	58.60	59.20	117.80
9 Z. Xu (CHN)	58.65	59.15	117.80
10 K. Sotomura (JPN)	58.65	59.05	117.70
11 G. Goczoghy (HUN)	58.50	59.15	117.65
12 X. Li (CHN)	58.55	59.00	117.55
13 Y. Korolev (URS)	58.00	59.40	117.40
14 N. Kajitani (JPN)	58.50	58.85	117.35
15 Y. Li (CHN)	58.50	58.80	117.30
16 M. Watanabe (JPN)	58.55	58.75	117.30
17 S. Kroll (GDR)	58.60	58.70	117.30
18 B. Makouts (URS)	58.30	58.95	117.25
19 J. Fischer (GDR)	58.30	58.90	117.20
20 M. Gaylord (USA)	58.40	58.75	117.15

Parallel bars

	Prelim	Final	Total
1 V. Artemov (URS)	9.950	10.000	19.950
2. Y. Lou (CHN)	9.950	10.000	19.950
3 K. Sotomura (JPN)	9.850	10.000	19.850
4 F. Tong (CHN)	9.950	9.900	19.850
5 K. Gushiken (JPN)	9.900	9.900	19.800
6 B. Conner (USA)	9.850	9.900	19.750
6 Y. Korolev (URS)	9.850	9.900	19.750
8 V. Leon (CUB)	9.825	9.900	19.725

Horizontal bar

	Prelim	Final	Total
1 D. Belozerchev (URS)	9.850	10.000	19.850
2. P. Vatuone (FRA)	9.875	9.950	19.825
2 A. Pogorelov (URS)	9.875	9.950	19.825
4 F. Tong (CHN)	9.900	9.900	19.800
4 S. Morisue (JPN)	9.950	9.850	19.800
6 Z. Xu (CHN)	9.850	9.900	19.750
7 M. Watanabe (JPN)	9.900	9.600	19.500
8 P. Vidmar (USA)	9.900	9.350	19.250

Horse

	Prelim	Final	Total
1 D. Belozerchev (URS)	10.000	10.000	20.000
2. G. Guczoghy (HUN)	9.950	10.000	19.950
2 X. Li (CHN)	9.950	10.000	19.950
4 N. Li (CHN)	9.900	10.000	19.900
5. Y. Korolev (URS)	9.900	9.950	19.850
5 S. Kroll (GDR)	9.900	9.950	19.850
7 B. Conner (USA)	9.900	9.900	19.800
8 K. Gushiken (JPN)	9.900	9.900	19.800

Vault

	Prelim	Final	Total
1 A. Akopian (URS)	9.925	9.950	19.875
2. N. Li (CHN)	9.900	9.950	19.850
3 B. Jensch (GDR)	9.850	9.975	19.825
4 Y. Lou (CHN)	9.900	9.900	19.800
4 S. Kroll (GDR)	9.900	9.900	19.800
6 D. Belozerchev (URS)	9.875	9.900	19.775
7 S. Morisue (JPN)	9.875	9.875	19.750
8 N. Hirata (JPN)	9.875	9.850	19.725

Rings

	Prelim	Final	Total
1 D. Belozerchev (URS)	9.925	10.000	19.925
1. K. Gushiken (JPN)	9.925	10.000	19.925
3 N. Li (CHN)	9.950	9.950	19.900
4 J. Fischer (GDR)	9.900	9.900	19.800
4 K. Sotomura (JPN)	9.900	9.900	19.800
6 F. Donath (HUN)	9.900	9.850	19.750
7 P. Petkov (BUL)	9.900	9.800	19.700
8 L. Molnar (ROM)	9.900	9.800	19.700

Floor exercises

	Prelim	Final	Total
1 F. Tong (CHN)	9.900	10.000	19.900
2. D. Belozerchev (URS)	9.925	9.950	19.875
3 N. Li (CHN)	9.900	9.900	19.800
4 Y. Korolev (URS)	9.850	9.900	19.750
5 B. Conner (USA)	9.825	9.900	19.725
6 C. Suarez (CUB)	9.800	9.850	19.650
7 S. Kroll (GDR)	9.800	9.800	19.600
8 K. Sotomura (JPN)	9.800	9.650	19.450

Combined exercises (individual)

	Set exercises	Voluntary	Total
1 N. Yurchenko (URS)	39.35	39.85	79.20
2 L. Agache (ROM)	39.35	39.70	79.05
3 O. Mostepanova (URS)	39.35	39.55	78.90
4 E. Szabo (ROM)	39.50	39.35	78.85
5 M. Gnauck (GDR)	39.55	39.10	78.65
6 B. Stoyanova (BUL)	39.00	39.95	78.55
7 T. Frolova (URS)	39.05	39.40	78.45
8 S. Rau (RDA)	39.30	39.05	78.35
9 O. Bitcherova (URS)	39.00	39.30	78.30
10 A. Shishova (URS)	38.85	39.35	78.20
11 L. Cutina (ROM)	38.80	39.25	78.05
12 J. McNamara (USA)	39.00	39.05	78.05
13 Z. Grancharova (BUL)	38.85	39.15	78.00
14 Y. Chen (CHN)	39.00	38.95	77.95
15 M. Stanulet (ROM)	38.70	39.15	77.85
16 N. Ilenko (URS)	39.10	38.75	77.85
17 S. Topalova (BUL)	38.80	38.95	77.75
18 K. Johnson (USA)	39.00	38.70	77.70
19 J. Labakova (TCH)	38.65	38.95	77.60
20 S. Renciu (ROM)	38.60	38.95	77.55

Combined exercises (team)

		Set exercises	Voluntary	Total
1	CHN	295.25	296.20	591.45
2	URS	294.40	296.90	591.30
3	JPN	293.75	295.10	588.85
4	USA	291.90	293.75	585.65
5	GDR	290.45	294.50	584.95
6	HUN	289.40	292.10	581.50
7	BUL	286.25	290.80	577.05
8	FRG	287.55	288.75	576.30
9	FRA	288.20	287.95	576.15
10	SUI	286.75	288.75	575.50
11	ROM	286.15	287.50	573.65
12	CUB	286.15	287.45	573.60
13	PRK	283.65	288.25	571.90
14	TCH	283.25	284.85	568.10
15	CAN	282.35	282.95	565.30
16	ITA	281.85	283.35	565.20
17	GBR	279.70	282.45	562.15
18	KOR	282.55	277.30	559.85
19	ESP	277.80	281.65	559.45
20	AUS	278.85	277.15	556.00

Gymnastics (women)

Asymmetric bars

		Prelim	Final	Total
1	M. Gnauck (GDR)	9.925	10.000	19.925
2	L. Agache (ROM)	9.900	9.900	19.800
2	E. Szabo (ROM)	9.900	9.900	19.800
4	T. Frolova (URS)	9.875	9.900	19.775
5	G. Fahnrich (GDR)	9.850	9.900	19.750
6	S. Topalova (BUL)	9.825	9.800	19.625
7	J. McNamara (USA)	9.875	9.400	19.275
8	H. Ricna (TCH)	9.850	9.350	19.200

Beam

		Prelim	Final	Total
1	O. Mostepanova (URS)	9.875	9.875	19.775
2.	H. Ricna (TCH)	9.900	9.850	19.750
3	L. Agache (ROM)	9.825	9.850	19.675
4	M. Gnauck (GDR)	9.875	9.400	19.275
5	S. Rau (GDR)	9.850	9.400	19.250
5	T. Frolova (URS)	9.750	9.500	19.250
7	I. Cervenkova (TCH)	9.850	9.300	19.150
8	A. Wilhelm (FRG)	9.725	9.400	19.125

Vault

	Prelim	Final	Total
1 B. Stoyanova (BUL)	9.900	9.925	19.825
2. L. Agache (ROM)	9.900	9.900	19.800
2 E. Szabo (ROM)	9.900	9.900	19.800
4 M. Gnauck (GDR)	9.925	9.850	19.775
5 O. Bricherova (URS)	9.875	9.775	19.650
6 S. Rau (GDR)	9.875	9.750	19.625
6 J. McNamara (USA)	9.875	9.750	19.625
8 N. Yurchenko (URS)	9.900	9.600	19.500

Floor exercises

	Prelim	Final	Total
1 E. Szabo (ROM)	9.975	10.000	19.975
2. O. Mostepanova (URS)	9.900	10.000	19.900
3 B. Stoyanova (BUL)	9.900	9.950	19.850
4 L. Agache (ROM)	9.900	9.900	19.800
5 Z. Grantcharova (BUL)	9.825	9.900	19.725
6 Y. Chen (CHN)	9.800	9.900	19.700
7 D. Morawe (GDR)	9.825	9.750	19.575
8 K. Johnson (USA)	9.775	9.400	19.175

Combined exercises (team)

	Set exercises	Voluntary	Total
1 URS	195.90	197.55	393.45
2 ROM	195.25	196.85	392.10
3 GDR	195.00	194.25	389.25
4 BUL	193.45	195.50	388.25
5 CHN	193.75	193.90	387.65
6 TCH	193.05	193.90	386.95
7 USA	192.10	192.95	385.05
8 FRG	191.15	193.65	384.80
9 HUN	190.30	191.60	381.90
10 CAN	189.15	189.05	378.20
11 PRK	187.90	190.20	378.10
12 JPN	188.75	187.25	376.00
13 ESP	186.40	187.65	374.05
14 SUI	186.85	187.10	373.95
15 ITA	184.45	186.35	370.80
16 FRA	184.30	186.40	370.70
17 GBR	183.80	186.35	370.15
18 CUB	183.75	183.35	367.10
19 KOR	181.80	183.00	364.80
20 HOL	183.55	181.25	364.80

Swimming (men)

100 Metre Freestyle

49.36	*Rowdy Gaines (USA)*
49.58	Joerg Woithe (GDR)
50.05p	Rowdy Gaines (USA)
50.13	Sergey Smiriagin (URS)
50.20	Per Johansson (SWE)
50.43	Fernando Canales (PUR)
50.47	Chris Cavanaugh (USA)
50.50	Robin Leamy (USA)
50.62	Bill Barrett (USA)
50.71	Pelle Holmertz (SWE)

200 Metre Freestyle

1:47.87	*Michael Gross (FRG)*
1:47.87	Michael Gross (FRG)
1:49.30	Sven Lodziewski (GDR)
1:49.60	Joerg Woithe (GDR)
1:49.89	Bruce Hayes (USA)
1:50.01	Thomas Fahrner (FRG)
1:50.32	Rowdy Gaines (USA)
1:50.33	Andreas Schmidt (FRG)
1:50.36	Alberto Mestre (VEN)
1:50.41	David Larson (USA)

400 Metre Freestyle

3:48.32	*Vladimir Salnikov (URS)*
3:48.32	Vladimir Salnikov (URS)
3:49.27	Sven Lodziewski (GDR)
3:51.96	Borut Petric (YUG)
3:52.25	Sviatoslav Semenov (URS)
3:52.60	Darjan Petric (YUG)
3:52.62	Matt Cetlinski (USA)
3:52.82*	Thomas Fahrner (FRG)
3:52.99	Bruce Hayes (USA)
3:53.35	Stefan Pfeiffer (FRG)

1500 Metre Freestyle

14:54.76	*Vladimir Salnikov (URS)*
14.54.76	Vladimir Salnikov (URS)
15:11.94	Sviatoslav Semenov (URS)
15:14.54	Borut Petric (YUG)
15:16.85	Stefan Pfeiffer (FRG)
15:17.67	Sven Lodziewski (GDR)
15:18.89	Rafael Escalas (ESP)
15:19.23	Jeff Kostoff (USA)
15:21.55	Darjan Petric (YUG)
15:21.60	Thomas Fahrner (FRG)

100 Metre Backstroke

55.19	*Rick Carey (USA)*
55.19	Rick Carey (USA)
56.10	Dirk Richter (GDR)
56.24	Mark Rhodenbaugh (USA)
56.25	Vladimir Shemetov (URS)
56.27	Dave Bottom (USA)
56.45	Mike West (CAN)
56.74	Viktor Kuznetsov (URS)
56.88	Sergey Zabolotnov (URS)
56.95p	Eric Ericson (USA)

200 Metre Backstroke

1:58.93	*Rick Carey (USA)*
1:58.93	Rick Carey (USA)
2:00.42	Sergei Zabolotnov (URS)
2:00.65	Vladimir Shemetov (URS)
2:01.47	Frank Baltrusch (GDR)
2:01.61	Sandor Wladar (HUN)
2:01.63	Mike West (CAN)
2:01.86	Igor Polianskiy (URS)
2:02.05	Dirk Richter (GDR)
2:02.29	Richie Hughey (USA)

100 Metre Breaststroke

1:02.28	*Steve Lundquist (USA)*
1:02.28	Steve Lundquist (USA)
1:02.36	John Moffet (USA)
1:03.08	Dmitriy Volkov (URS)
1:03.32	Robertas Zhulpa (URS)
1:03.37	Adrian Moorhouse (GBR)
1:03.42	Richard Schroeder (USA)
1:03.56	Bill Barrett (USA)
1:03.89	Pablo Restrepo (COL)
1:03.94	Bob Jackson (USA)

200 metre breaststroke

2:14.77	*Victor Davis (CAN)*
2:15.38	Steve Lundquist (USA)
2:15.93	Robertas Zhulpa (URS)
2:17.49	Adrian Moorhouse (GBR)
2:17.90	Gennadiy Utenkov (URS)
2:17.97	John Moffet (USA)
2:18.21	Doug Soltis (USA)
2:18.27	Alban Vermes (HUN)
2:18.39	Shigehiro Takahashi (JPN)
2:18.85	Richard Schroeder (USA)

100 Metre Butterfly

53.44	*Matt Gribble (USA)*
53.44	Matt Gribble (USA)
53.71	Pablo Morales (USA)
54.00	Michael Gross (FRG)
54.31	Dave Cowell (USA)
54.36	Brad Hering (USA)
54.50	Aleksey Markovskiy (URS)
54.51	Dan Thompson (CAN)
54.62	Steve Lundquist (USA)
54.72	Rafael Vidal (VEN)

200 Metre Butterfly

1:57.05	*Michael Gross (FRG)*
1:57.05	Michael Gross (FRG)
1:58.76	Craig Beardsley (USA)
1:59.00	Ricardo Prado (BRA)
1:59.17	Rafael Vidal (VEN)
1:59.22	Paolo Revelli (ITA)
1:59.64	Pablo Morales (USA)
1:59.74	Sergey Fesenko (URS)
2:00.01	Fillberto Colon (PUR)
2:00.02	Marcel Gery (TCH)

200 Metre Individual Medley

2:02.25	*Alex Baumann (CAN)*
2:02.29	Alex Baumann (CAN)
2:02.48	Giovanni Franceschi (ITA)
2:02.68	Bill Barrett (USA)
2:02.95	Jens-Peter Berndt (GDR)
2:03.24	Steve Lundquist (USA)
2:03.55	Josef Hladky (TCH)
2:03.60	Aleksandr Sidorenko (URS)
2:04.10	Ricardo Prado (BRA)
2:04.67	Pablo Morales (USA)

400 Metre Individual Medley

4:19.78	*Ricardo Prado (BRA)*
4:19.80	Alex Baumann (CAN)
4:20.41	Giovanni Franceschi (ITA)
4:20.81	Jens Peter Berndt (GDR)
4:21.26	Ricardo Prado (BRA)
4:22.38	Jeff Kostoff (USA)
4:23.52	Josef Hladky (TCH)
4:24.38	Sandor Wladar (HUN)
4:24.39	Maurizio Divano (ITA)
4:25.31	Mike O'Brien (USA)

Swimming (women)

100 Metre Freestyle

54.79	*Barbara Krause (GDR)*
55.18	Birgit Meineke (GDR)
55.49	Kristin Otto (GDR)
56.51	Conny Van Bentum (HOL)
56.52	Carrie Steinseifer (USA)
56.55r	Annemarie Verstappen (HOL)
56.57	Dara Torres (USA)
56.67	Marybeth Linzmeier (USA)
56.70	Kathy Treible (USA)
56.76	Jill Sterkel (USA)

200 Metre Freestyle

1:58.23	*Cynthia Woodhead (USA)*
1:59.45	Birgit Meineke (GDR)
1:59.63	Kristin Otto (GDR)
1:59.80	Astrid Strauss (GDR)
2:00.61	Conny Van Bentum (HOL)
2:00.99	June Croft (GBR)
2:01.03	Mary Wayte (USA)
2:01.06	Ina Beyermann (FRG)
2:01.08	Cynthia Woodhead (USA)
2:01.32	Tiffany Cohen (USA)

400 Metre Freestyle

4:06.28	*Tracey Wickham (AUS)*
4:08.05	Tiffany Cohen (USA)
4:08.07	Astrid Strauss (GDR)
4:10.37	Anke Sonnenbrodt (GDR)
4:11.83	Cynthia Woodhead (USA)
4:12.83	Michele Richardson (USA)
4:12.83	Julie Daigneault (CAN)
4:12.90	Irina Laritscheva (URS)
4:13.01	Ina Beyermann (FRG)
4:13.73	Marybeth Linzmeier (USA)

800 Metre Freestyle

8:24.62	*Tracey Wickham (AUS)*
8:29.61	Astrid Strauss (GDR)
8:30.24	Tiffany Cohen (USA)
8:31.07	Anke Sonnenbrodt (GDR)
8:36.14	Marybeth Linzmeier (USA)
8:36.52	Michele Richardson (USA)
8:37.09	Karin LaBerge (USA)
8:39.05	Manuela Gopfert (GDR)
8:39.92	Anna McVann (AUS)
8:40.31	Irina Laritscheva (URS)

100 Metre Backstroke

1:00.86	*Rica Reinisch (GDR)*
1:01.32	Ina Kleber (GDR)
1:01.48	Cornelia Sirch (GDR)
1:01.91	Kristin Otto (GDR)
1:02.08	Birte Weigang (GDR)
1:02.48	Sue Walsh (USA)
1:02.63	Kathrin Zimmerman (GDR)
1:02.84	Carmen Bunaciu (ROM)
1:02.96	Betsy Mitchell (USA)
1:02.96	Larisa Gortschakova (URS)

200 Metre Backstroke

2:09.91	*Cornelia Sirch (GDR)*
2:10.92	Cornelia Sirch (GDR)
2:11.90	Birte Weigang (GDR)
2:11.99	Kathrin Zimmerman (GDR)
2:13.86	Sue Walsh (USA)
2:14.23	Ina Kleber (GDR)
2:14.30	Kristin Otto (GDR)
2:14.41	Larisa Gortschakova (URS)
2:14.73	Aneta Patrascoiu (ROM)
2:14.91	Carmen Bunaciu (ROM)

100 Metre Breaststroke

1:08.51	*Ute Geweniger (GDR)*
1:08.51	Ute Geweniger (GDR)
1:09.62	Sylvia Gerasch (GDR)
1:10.63	Anne Ottenbrite (CAN)
1:10.77	Tania Bogomilova (BUL)
1:10.79	Petra Van Staveren (HOL)
1:10.97	Hiroko Nagasaki (JPN)
1:10.98	Sabrina Seminatore (ITA)
1:11.14	Eva-Marie Hakansson (SWE)
1:11.26	Olga Zelenkova (URS)

200 Metre Breaststroke

2:28.36	*Lina Kachushite (URS)*
2:29.91	Hiroko Nagasaki (JPN)
2:30.13	Ute Geweniger (GDR)
2:30.55	Anne Ottenbrite (CAN)
2:30.67	Sylvia Gerasch (GDR)
2:32.83	Olga Zelenkova (URS)
2:32.96	Kim Rhodenbaugh (USA)
2:33.43	Susan Rapp (USA)
2:33.80	Tania Bogomilova (BUL)
2:34.02	Larisa Belokon (URS)

100 Metre Butterfly

57.93	*Mary T. Meagher (USA)*
59.54	Laurie Lehner (USA)
1:00.19	Ines Geissler (GDR)
1:00.70	Patty King (USA)
1:00.83	Cornelia Polit (GDR)
1:00.92	Melanie Buddemeyer (USA)
1:01.01	Ute Geweniger (GDR)
1:01.08	Mary T. Meagher (USA)
1:01.10	Cinzia Savi-Scarponi (ITA)
1:01.11	Joan Pennington (USA)

200 Metre Butterfly

2:05.96	*Mary T. Meagher (USA)*
2:07.82	Cornelia Polit (GDR)
2:08.03	Ines Geissler (GDR)
2:08.63	Mary T. Meagher (USA)
2:10.90	Kathleen Nord (GDR)
2:11.33	Jacqueline Alex (GDR)
2:11.35	Tracy Caulkins (USA)
2:12.20	Petra Zindler (FRG)
2:12.45	Nancy Hogshead (USA)
2:12.87	Conny Van Bentum (HOL)

200 Metre Individual Medley

2:11.73	*Ute Geweniger (GDR)*
2:12.68	Ute Geweniger (GDR)
2:14.25	Kathleen Nord (GDR)
2:15.27	Tracy Caulkins (USA)
2:15.68	Petra Schneider (GDR)
2:16.65	Cinzia Savi-Scarponi (ITA)
2:16.72	Irina Gerassimova (URS)
2:17.34	Susan Rapp (USA)
2:17.50	Joan Pennington (USA)
2:18.00	Michele McPherson (CAN)

400 Metre Individual Medley

4:36.10	*Petra Schneider (GDR)*
4:39.54	Petra Schneider (GDR)
4:39.95	Kathleen Nord (GDR)
4:45.71	Tracy Caulkins (USA)
4:47.90	Petra Zindler (FRG)
4:48.00	Polly Winde (USA)
4:48.56	Suzanne Landells (AUS)
4:48.88	Cinzia Savi-Scarponi (ITA)
4:49.43	Elena Dendeberova (URS)
4:50.08	Sue Heon (USA)

Acknowledgements
Data compiled and researched by David Emery, Stan Greenberg and Ian Morrison.